COMMUNICATION
IN FAMILY CONTEXTS

COMMUNICATION
IN FAMILY CONTEXTS

Theories and Processes

ELIZABETH DORRANCE HALL
KRISTINA M. SCHARP

WILEY Blackwell

This edition first published 2020
© 2020 John Wiley & Sons, Inc.

All rights reserved. No part of this publication may be reproduced, stored in a retrieval system, or transmitted, in any form or by any means, electronic, mechanical, photocopying, recording or otherwise, except as permitted by law. Advice on how to obtain permission to reuse material from this title is available at http://www.wiley.com/go/permissions.

The right of Elizabeth Dorrance Hall and Kristina M. Scharp to be identified as the authors of this work has been asserted in accordance with law.

Registered Office
John Wiley & Sons, Inc., 111 River Street, Hoboken, NJ 07030, USA

Editorial Office
111 River Street, Hoboken, NJ 07030, USA

For details of our global editorial offices, customer services, and more information about Wiley products visit us at www.wiley.com.

Wiley also publishes its books in a variety of electronic formats and by print-on-demand. Some content that appears in standard print versions of this book may not be available in other formats.

Limit of Liability/Disclaimer of Warranty
While the publisher and authors have used their best efforts in preparing this work, they make no representations or warranties with respect to the accuracy or completeness of the contents of this work and specifically disclaim all warranties, including without limitation any implied warranties of merchantability or fitness for a particular purpose. No warranty may be created or extended by sales representatives, written sales materials or promotional statements for this work. The fact that an organization, website, or product is referred to in this work as a citation and/or potential source of further information does not mean that the publisher and authors endorse the information or services the organization, website, or product may provide or recommendations it may make. This work is sold with the understanding that the publisher is not engaged in rendering professional services. The advice and strategies contained herein may not be suitable for your situation. You should consult with a specialist where appropriate. Further, readers should be aware that websites listed in this work may have changed or disappeared between when this work was written and when it is read. Neither the publisher nor authors shall be liable for any loss of profit or any other commercial damages, including but not limited to special, incidental, consequential, or other damages.

Library of Congress Cataloging-in-Publication Data

Names: Hall, Elizabeth Dorrance, author. | Scharp, Kristina M., author.
Title: Communication in family contexts : theories and processes /
    Elizabeth Dorrance Hall, Michigan State University, Family Communication
    and Relationships Lab, Kristina M. Scharp, University of Washington,
    Family Communication and Relationships Lab.
Description: Hoboken, NJ : John Wiley & Sons, Inc., 2020. | Includes bibliographical
    references and index.
Identifiers: LCCN 2019019386 (print) | LCCN 2019022348 (ebook) | ISBN 9781119477341
    (paperback) | ISBN 9781119477402 (Adobe pdf) | ISBN 9781119477426 (epub)
Subjects: LCSH: Communication in families.
Classification: LCC HQ734 .H238 2020 (print) | LCC HQ734 (ebook) |
    DDC 3.06.85—dc23
LC record available at https://lccn.loc.gov/2019019386
LC ebook record available at https://lccn.loc.gov/2019022348

Cover Design: Wiley
Cover Image: © Spiritartist/Getty Images

Set in 9/12pt Ubuntu by SPi Global, Pondicherry, India
Printed and bound in Singapore by Markono Print Media Pte Ltd

10 9 8 7 6 5 4 3 2 1

Contents

Family Communication in Context 275

Case Study Index

Preface

HOW CAN I USE THIS BOOK?

Despite how often many people communicate with their families, family life is rife with both conflict and joy. Communication can create or destroy family relationships and almost always is an essential part of family maintenance. This textbook will help you understand the importance of family communication and provide you with tools to help improve your family lives.

This book is unique, and it was designed with you, the reader, in mind.

Your textbook authors have both been teaching about family communication for many years and we recognize that our students prefer information in short, concise bursts as opposed to long comprehensive summaries. That is exactly why we wrote this textbook. This book includes 33 short chapters that can be paired together to build a unique and tailored family communication course. The chapters are on classic theories like family communication patterns theory and cutting-edge research topics like difficult family conversations (Chapter 13), family distancing (Chapter 15), and in-law relationships (Chapter 24). Each chapter includes **Background Information** followed by the **Key Concepts** needed to understand the research in a given area. Next, we chose exemplary research studies to highlight in a section called **Interesting Research Findings**. **Practical Implications and Things to Consider** comes next. This section provides a little more information on the topic, connecting communication research with the "real world," often asking the reader to think about these connections. **Key Terms** highlights the most important terms and concepts in the chapter. Finally, many of the chapters include in-class activities, discussion questions, a case study, or a podcast episode to supplement the content of the chapter.

In addition, some chapters include a case study written by other family communication scholars with particular expertise on the chapter's topic. These case studies, available in 13 of the chapters, could be helpful to spark class discussion or be something you respond to before class. In our classes, we like to ask students to read the case study before coming to class. We then assign a worksheet that consists of a series of questions to get our students thinking about how the case study relates to the reading and the information taught in class that week and/or that semester/quarter. Once in class, we ask our students to discuss the case with their classmates. We find that sitting in a circle works best for this discussion. Throughout the semester/quarter we make sure each student has a chance to lead discussion with their small group. After the discussion, we ask students to use the back of their worksheet to reflect on how their opinion of what

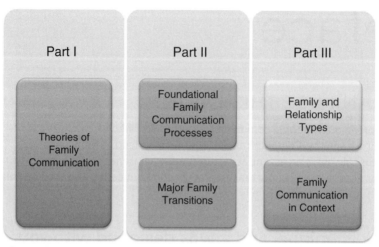

Figure 0.1 Textbook Parts

happened in the case changed based on the class discussion, if at all, and what points their classmates made changed their minds. Overall, we hope that these case studies help you see how what you learn in class has implications and uses outside of it.

Because the chapters are designed to mix and match, they are listed in alphabetical order within each section rather than grouped by topic or in any prescribed order. We encourage instructors to choose chapters that work well together for their students, and supplement these chapters with scholarly articles or popular press readings, videos, or podcasts (e.g., news stories, TED talks, or a podcast like *Relationship Matters*, https://journals.sagepub.com/page/spr/podcasts/relationship-matters).

WHAT CAN I FIND IN THIS BOOK?

Part I of this textbook contains seven chapters focused on the most commonly used family communication theories. These theories range from well-established grand theories such as family systems theory to newer theories like affection exchange theory. Nevertheless, we chose the theories that are most often used by family communication researchers to inform their work. Although many other theories appear throughout the textbook, these are the only chapters dedicated to one specific theory. We encourage you to keep a look out for other important communication theories like relational turbulence theory that you can find in the chapter about uncertainty management (Chapter 18), or attachment theory which you can find in the chapter on parent–child relationships (Chapter 27).

Part II contains two sections: foundational processes and major family transitions. Foundational processes include process-based topics relevant to family communication such as caretaking, conflict, coping and resilience, distancing, support, and uncertainty management. The chapters included in the major family transitions section represent "normative" progression through the family life cycle: cohabitation and marriage, the transition to parenthood, divorce, and remarriage. The transition to parenthood chapter is a good example of how this textbook is capturing cutting-edge research by including research on delaying or forgoing the transition to parenthood (e.g., childfree couples).

Part III covers family and relationship types such as adoptive families, in-laws, intergenerational relationships, LGBTQ families, and sibling relationships, among others. Part III also contains a section on family communication in the context of other communication research areas including health communication, organizational communication, and new technology.

HOW FAMILY COMMUNICATION INSTRUCTORS USE THIS BOOK

Dr. Amanda Holmstrom: "I used the textbook in my Fall 2018 upper-division family communication class at Michigan State University. I used it as a supplement to another textbook that I had used in the past. However, Dorrance Hall and Scharp's book would work well as a stand-alone text, particularly if instructors bundled related chapters each week – which I did on multiple occasions. I highly recommend this text as an up-to-date, focused introduction to pertinent topics and theories in the field. Students found it very accessible."

Dr. Kaitlin Phillips: "I use this family communication textbook to serve as an overview of the content we are covering that week. I set up my class as a once a week discussion-based class, and I assign a textbook chapter or two that provides the students with an overview of the topic and theory they will read about in the journal articles. In addition, I really appreciate the activities and case studies included in the book, I use them to help supplement our class discussions and prompt additional discussion about the readings for the week."

Dr. Tiffany Wang: "*Communication in Family Contexts: Theories and Processes* provides a clear and straightforward introduction to family communication that is an excellent fit for the undergraduate classroom. I especially like how each chapter is concise enough that the instructor has the flexibility to add additional readings and activities that complement each chapter."

Meet the Authors

Elizabeth and her family in Northern Michigan

Elizabeth Dorrance Hall (PhD, Purdue University) is an Assistant Professor of Communication at Michigan State University and a Director of the Family Communication and Relationships Lab (www.familycommlab.com). Elizabeth's research focuses on communication processes in close relationships, especially in the context of family. She is interested in difficult family conversations and relationships including the "black sheep" of the family. She is also interested in the power of family support and how childhood patterns of family communication influence people long after they have grown into adults. Elizabeth's research has appeared in *Communication Research*, *Communication Monographs*, *Health Communication*, the *Journal of Family Communication*, and the *Journal of Social and Personal Relationships*. She writes articles about family and interpersonal communication for *Psychology Today* (https://www.psychologytoday.com/us/blog/conscious-communication). You can find her on Twitter @edorrancehall and at www.dorrancehall.com. Elizabeth is the youngest of four children and has her parents and many siblings to thank for her interest in family communication. Elizabeth lives with her husband and their fur family of two rescue pups and a miniature black cat named Luna.

Kristina and Holly

Kristina M. Scharp (PhD, University of Iowa) is an Assistant Professor of Communication at the University of Washington (Seattle) and a Director of the Family Communication and Relationships Lab (www.familycommlab.com). She researches difficult family transitions such as parent–child estrangement, adoption, and disability diagnoses as well as the processes by which family members cope with their distress. Featured in journals such as *Communication Research*, *Human Communication Research*, *Family Relations*, and the *Journal of Family Communication*, she is particularly interested in ways people navigate entering and exiting the family. Her research has won top papers at both the International and National Communication Associations and has garnered attention from outlets such as *The New York Times*, *PBS*, *NPR*, the *Wall Street Journal*, and the *Washington Post*. Kristina and her younger brother were both internationally adopted to two loving and hilarious parents who frequently show up as examples when she teaches about family communication. Kristina also is the adoptive mom of her fur baby Holly, a black lab mix rescue with a big personality!

Meet the Case Study Contributors

Jenny L. Crowley (PhD, University of Iowa) is an Assistant Professor in the School of Communication Studies at the University of Tennessee Knoxville. Jenny's research focuses on stigma and its impact on relational and family communication processes, including information management and supportive communication. Her research also examines how alternative families communicate in ways that manage or resist stigma. Jenny is a first-generation American and fondly remembers traveling overseas as a child to visit "the family." Jenny and her husband live with their two cats, Archimedes and Spaghetti.

Patricia E. Gettings' (PhD, Purdue University) research explores how individuals communicatively negotiate the intersections of their personal and professional lives, and how these negotiations are associated with individual, relational, familial, and/or organizational outcomes. A specific area of focus is how couples transition into retirement. As mother to Greta and Elisabeth, wife of Ryan, and Assistant Professor of Communication Studies at Indiana University Southeast, Patricia regularly finds herself navigating intersections of the personal and professional areas of her own life.

Lisa M. Guntzviller (PhD, Purdue University 2013) is an Assistant Professor of Communication at the University of Illinois at Urbana-Champaign. Lisa has broad interests in interpersonal, family, and health communication, such as how parents give their adult children advice or how bilingual adolescents interpret for their Spanish-speaking parents. Lisa is biologically an only child, but has two fictive kin siblings, Jonah and Alexa. Lisa is extremely grateful to her parents for all their love and support.

Sylvia L. Mikucki-Enyart (PhD, University of Illinois at Urbana-Champaign) is an Assistant Professor in the Department of Communication Studies at the University of Iowa. Sylvia's research examines family communication during periods of anticipated (e.g., transition to extended family) and unanticipated change (e.g., late life parental divorce and remarriage). Sylvia enjoys eating copious amounts of nachos and spending time with her family, which includes her husband, son, and two dogs, Sophie "McSopherson" Enyart and Rudy "Rudy Gumdrop" Enyart. Rudy prefers her nachos with extra sour cream. Sophie is lactose intolerant.

Leslie R. Nelson (PhD, University of Missouri) is an Assistant Professor of Communication Studies at California Polytechnic State University, San Luis Obispo. Leslie's research examines how communication affects and reflects identity, sense-making, and well-being in diverse family forms. Currently, much of her research focuses on the role of communication in constructing, maintaining, negotiating, and deconstructing foster and adoptive family relationships. Leslie is lucky to be a member of a rather large (okay, very large) family that is reminiscent of the contexts she loves to focus on in her studies: adoptive, foster, transracial, and interfaith families. Leslie's "little family" consists of her partner and their Great Pyrenees, Piper.

Kelly G. Odenweller (PhD, West Virginia University) is an assistant teaching professor in the Communication Studies program at Iowa State University. Kelly's research focuses on family and gender communication. She is interested in how communication within and about families can socialize its members' gendered attitudes, values, and behaviors. Kelly appreciates her husband and two children for giving her many opportunities to use communication to teach (and be taught) about social change for men and women.

Joshua R. Pederson (PhD, University of Iowa) is an Assistant Professor of Communication Studies at the University of Alabama. Josh's research focuses on relational repair, supportive communication, and coping with challenging life experiences. He has studied how parents and adolescent children talk about responding to experiences of bullying. Josh is grateful for having a loving and supportive family environment growing up and he plans to continue that legacy with his spouse and two smart, strong, and courageous daughters.

Kaitlin E. Phillips (PhD, University of Nebraska-Lincoln) is an Assistant Professor of Communication Studies in the Languages, Philosophy, and Communication Studies Department at Utah State University. She received her PhD in Interpersonal, Family, and Intergroup Communication. She teaches courses in interpersonal communication, family communication, and communication theory. Kaitlin researches the interplay between family and personal identity focusing on how people create family identity and solidarity, and the perceptions of difference in relational quality across family members. Kaitlin is the oldest of four children, and became interested in studying siblings based on her own sibling relationships and those of her parents.

Leah M. Seurer (PhD, University of Denver) is an Assistant Professor in the Department of Communication Studies at the University of South Dakota. Her work takes a critical approach to intersections of family and health communication by examining how relational and cultural discourses circulating within the family construct meanings for familial relationships and illness within the family. Her work has been published in journals such as *Communication Monographs* and *Journal of Family Communication*.

Samuel Hardman Taylor (PhD, Cornell University) is an Assistant Professor in the Department of Communication at the University of Illinois at Chicago. Sam's research sits at the intersection of digital media and interpersonal communication. He studies how mobile phones and social media affect personal relationships and psychological well-being. Sam is the second to youngest in a big Mormon family of 11 children, and he has nearly 30 nieces and nephews. Sam currently lives with his partner, Kory, and their cat, Kiki.

Lindsey J. Thomas (PhD, University of Iowa) is an Assistant Professor of Communication at Illinois State University. Lindsey's research primarily focuses on discursive processes of family (de)construction and (de)legitimation and the ways that talk privileges some relationships while undermining others. In particular, her work has focused on the experiences of formerly fostered youth, communication surrounding pregnancy and motherhood, family estrangement, and companion animals as family members. Coincidentally, Lindsey grew up on a farm in the rural Midwest, where she developed a deep appreciation and love for nonhuman animals, and she currently shares her life in Normal with three weird cats.

Lisa Van Raalte (PhD, Arizona State University) is an Assistant Professor in the Communication Studies Department at Sam Houston State University. Lisa is interested in how communication in close relationships influences psychological, physiological, and relational health. She is specifically interested in how affection is communicated in romantic and family relationships. Lisa hopes to continue her program of research investigating specific forms of nonverbal affection such as cuddling, hugging, hand-holding, and kissing. Lisa's family lives in New Zealand and, to her benefit, were always very affectionate with each other.

Acknowledgments

The authors would first like to thank all of the family communication scholars who contributed to this textbook. We appreciate the time you took writing case studies, providing feedback, and recording podcasts. Your words and voices bring family communication scholarship to life! Thanks to our mentors who taught us about the power of family communication and encouraged our development as scholars and teachers, especially Leslie A. Baxter and Steven R. Wilson. Thanks to the team at Wiley for supporting our project from the beginning and allowing our vision for a different kind of family communication textbook to become a reality, and to John Seiter for encouraging us to pursue this project. We would like to recognize Amanda Holmstrom, Kaitlin Phillips, and Tiffany Wang for piloting our book in their Family Communication courses. We would also like to thank our family and friends who supported us as we engaged in this new endeavor. Last, but not least, we would like to thank our students over the years who shared our interest in and enthusiasm about family communication. This textbook is for you!

About the Companion Website

This book is accompanied by a companion website:

www.wiley.com/go/dorrance_hall/communication-in-family-contexts

The website includes:

- Sample Syllabus
- In-class activities

Chapter 1

An Introduction to Communication in Family Contexts

Family relationships are some of the most important and long-lasting ones we will have in our entire lives. Although many other disciplines study family relationships, we focus on the power of communication in family contexts. Indeed, how we create a family, maintain family relationships, and even distance ourselves from family members requires communication. In this chapter, we answer three questions to orient you, the reader, to this book and to the study of family communication. First, we answer "what is a family" followed by "what is family communication." Last, we describe "how to use this book."

WHAT IS A FAMILY?

Traditionally, family communication scholars define the family in one of three ways: (1) **structurally** based on form, (2) **functionally** based on task, or (3) **transactionally** based on interaction. Structural definitions rely on specific criteria (e.g., blood ties, law) to determine family membership. For example, the U.S. Census (2010) claims a family "consists of two or more people [one of whom is the householder] related by birth, marriage, or adoption, residing in the same housing unit," and scholars argue that the dominant North American ideology identifies a "real" family as the nuclear family, comprised of a heterosexual couple and their

Communication in Family Contexts: Theories and Processes, First Edition.
Elizabeth Dorrance Hall and Kristina M. Scharp.
© 2020 John Wiley & Sons, Inc. Published 2020 by John Wiley & Sons, Inc.
Companion website: www.wiley.com/go/dorrance_hall/communication-in-family-contexts

biological children. If you think of the show *Modern Family*, the family that most clearly fits the structural definition of family consists of Phil, Claire, Haley, Alex, and Luke. Phil and Claire are a mixed-sex couple with three biological children. Communication researchers have found that many people privilege blood ties when thinking about family, especially those that unite parents and children (Baxter et al., 2009).

Although structural definitions of family dominate research literature and policy, functional and transactional definitions are sometimes used to illuminate different facets of familial relationships. For example, functional definitions rely heavily on the tasks members perform. Segrin and Flora (2011) contend that functional definitions "view family as at least one adult and one or more other persons who perform certain tasks of the family life such as socialization, nurturance, development, and financial and emotional support" (p. 6). Leslie Baxter and her colleagues (2009) suggest that functional definitions afford more flexibility than structural definitions but still tend to highlight reproduction and child-rearing: what others have called a biological or genetic focus. On *Modern Family*, Cameron, Mitchell, and Lily represent a family based on function since Cameron and Mitchell, a same-sex couple, provide support for one another and are actively helping Lily, their adopted daughter, develop through socializing and nurturing her.

In addition to structure and function, family communication scholars use the criteria of "transaction" to define what it means to be a family. A transactional definition emphasizes the communication among family members and the subjective feelings, typically positive, generated by interaction. Baxter et al. (2009) argue that transactional definitions emphasize the role communication plays in constituting what it means to be a family. They explain, "Relationships are familial, according to this approach, to the extent that members feel and act like a family" (p. 172). Thus, biology and law hold little relevance when thinking about a family using a transactional definition. The whole extended family on the show *Modern Family* can be seen through a transactional lens if we examine how they feel about each other and how they communicate about being a family. The characters clearly feel and act like a family, and this alone makes them a family, no matter how they are connected through law or blood.

In brief: there are three ways to answer the question "what is a family" and each definition draws different lines around who is "in" and who is "out" with structural definitions of family being the most black and white and also limited. The transactional definition is the most flexible of the three ways.

Although many researchers have privileged structural definitions and view family as a nonvoluntary relationship, some scholars across multiple disciplines are beginning to question and challenge the structural definition of family. For example, Judith Stacey (1996) argues that "No longer is there a single culturally dominant family pattern, like the 'modern' one, to which a majority of citizens conform and most of the rest aspire" (p. 7). Instead, Stacey contends that the postmodern family, or today's family, is characterized by a variety of arrangements, which are constantly changing across the lifespan. Thus, a postmodern family is one that exemplifies the contentious, ambivalent, fluid nature of contemporary family culture and invites the possibility of different family formations. Throughout this textbook we invite you to learn about many different types of families and family relationships.

WHAT IS FAMILY COMMUNICATION?

Defining Family Communication

Family communication has been defined in many ways. To accomplish the task of defining family communication, we should first define communication. **Communication is a process, based in interaction with others, where people create, share, and regulate meaning** (Segrin & Flora, 2011). Defining communication as a process means that it is ongoing and always changing. It has no beginning or end and is influenced by its surroundings. For example, how you communicate with your sister in a restaurant will be influenced by your past conversations, what your relationship is like, how your family as a whole communicates, and quite literally, the restaurant itself (Is it noisy? Is it formal? Are you there for a specific event?). Family communication, then, is **communicating to construct and regulate shared meaning with people who are considered family**. As you read above, we take a broad definition of who "counts" as family.

Families are constituted in communication. This means that communication *creates* families. Without communication, we would not be able to socially group people by their relationships. The way I talk about and talk to my brother, in part, makes him my brother. It is also true, then, that families that do not fit a traditional narrative, such as families who are not related by blood or law, must communicate more to explain to others (and themselves) that they are a family (see Chapter 14). Many of those types of families are covered in this book including adoptive families (Chapter 23), LGBTQ families (Chapter 26), and voluntary kin (Chapter 30), among others. With this being said, we still consider all families to be discourse dependent. In other words, all families rely on communication to construct their identity to both themselves and the outside world.

This book is primarily focused on communication **within** the family, but we also cover communication **about** the family.

Intersections of Family Identity

Throughout the textbook we will present distinct family roles and relationships such as parent, child, and sibling. Yet, people perform multiple roles with multiple identities that can overlap and/or sit at the intersection of different locations in the family and contexts. For example, your textbook authors are both sisters and daughters. When we are with our families, we are performing both roles at the same time. We encourage you to think about not only the relationships individually but also to remember the ways in which they overlap and the opportunities and challenges when they do.

Levels of Family Communication

Family communication occurs at multiple levels (Figure 1.1). In this book, you will read about research and theorizing that considers family communication as a phenomenon that happens at each of these levels.

Figure 1.1 Levels of family communication.

Research that takes an **individual** look at family communication asks the individual to report about their communication with the rest of their family. They might ask one member about their family environment growing up (Was your family environment generally warm and accepting? Did you communicate often?). Other researchers focus on how individual differences such as personality or strength of identity influence communication with the rest of the family (for example, see Chapter 25).

Family communication can also be examined at the **dyadic** or **triadic** levels. This type of examination involves thinking about family communication in a more sophisticated way, recognizing that one person's communication influences and is influenced by other people in a dyad (two people) or triad (three people). Dyadic and triadic conversations are typically relaxed and without specific goals. For example, in the in-law communication chapter (Chapter 24), you will read about studies that collected information about communication patterns from an adult child, their spouse (the child in-law), and their mother (the spouse's mother in-law).

Ultimately, the family is a **small group**, and when families are together, they engage in small group communication. Within that small group, families often communicate in smaller clusters like the dyads and triads mentioned above. Small group communication is more challenging than dyadic or triadic communication because there are many voices to be heard and to consider when crafting a message. Small group communication is sometimes more structured than dyadic or triadic communication. For example, imagine planning a funeral with your brothers, sisters, and parents, or discussing with your entire family where to go on vacation next year. These conversations may benefit from some structure and guidance. Usually someone has to take on a leadership role in these situations.

Finally, researchers and theorists think of the family as an **organization** with hierarchies, power structures, and specific roles such as the decision maker, the advice giver, and the kinkeeper (see Chapter 25 for more on kinkeepers). Chapter 6 details family systems theory, a theory that considers the family a living organism that is constantly in flux and adapting to its members and its environment. Complex organizations like businesses can be thought of in the same way.

INTRODUCTION TO FAMILY COMMUNICATION ACTIVITIES*

What's in a Name?

This activity is a great way to begin class. It allows the professor to learn about the students and the students to get to know one another. Our names inherently link us to our families.

Tell the class as much as you know about the history of your full name. You may not know much about your name, but share what you do know. Why did your parents pick it? Does your last name have a meaning? What country does your last name come from? Do you share the same last name as your parents? Did you choose to change parts of your name? Do you prefer a nickname (and why)? Does your name include "Jr." or "III"?

This activity pushes you to think about some of your family stories. Family stories tell us who we are and help us form our identities. You will learn much more about family stories in Chapter 7.

Six-Word Story

Create a six-word story that describes your family. Your story can be only six words, but you can describe and explain your story in a paragraph below. You can visit the Six-Word Memoirs website for more examples (http://www.sixwordmemoirs.com/). Other examples appear below.

- Rearing well gives roots and wings.
- Kids get bigger, house gets smaller.
- Saw my mom in my reflection.
- They failed me, loved them anyway.
- Their deepest secrets were never revealed.

*Both activities were taught at the Hope Conference for Faculty Development at a session led by Lynn Turner. They have since been adapted. Thanks to Turner and the other participants for sharing.

REFERENCES

Baxter, L. A., Henauw, C., Huisman, D., Livesay, C., Norwood, K., Su, H., ... Young, B. (2009). Lay conceptions of "family": A replication and extension. *Journal of Family Communication, 9*, 170–189. doi:10.1080/15267430902963342

Segrin, C., & Flora, J. (2011). *Family communication* (2nd ed.). New York, NY: Routledge.

Stacey, J. (1996). *In the name of family: Rethinking family values in the postmodern age*. Boston, MA: Beacon Press.

U.S. Census Bureau. (2010). Current population survey: Definitions and explanations. Retrieved from http://www.census.gov/cps/about/cpsdef.html

Chapter 2

Research Paradigms and Methods that Inform Family Communication Research

Throughout this textbook, you will be reading about a variety of research studies by many different family communication scholars. Not all family communication research is the same, has the same goals, studies family communication the same way, or is evaluated by the same standards. Because of these differences, we begin this chapter with an overview of the different philosophies or approaches family communication scholars might take to completing a research study and then discuss the different types of research methods they use. We hope that you can use this chapter as a reference as you learn about research studies in different chapters.

Communication in Family Contexts: Theories and Processes, First Edition.
Elizabeth Dorrance Hall and Kristina M. Scharp.
© 2020 John Wiley & Sons, Inc. Published 2020 by John Wiley & Sons, Inc.
Companion website: www.wiley.com/go/dorrance_hall/communication-in-family-contexts

KEY CONCEPTS

The Paradigms of Research

A **paradigm** is a way of viewing the world; a way of understanding reality, building knowledge, and collecting information. Some people might call a paradigm an ideology, or even a perspective that comes with a set of beliefs. Although there are different perspectives and frameworks to understanding research, we'd like to introduce you to four that are common in family communication research (see Deetz, 2001). These four perspectives are categorized by the extent to which they promote consensus/dissensus and a priori/emergent ways of thinking. Researchers who value **consensus** are interested in patterns that apply to particular groups of people whereas those who value **dissensus** are more interested in people who do not fit those patterns. Researchers who come in with ideas about how things are related to one another (e.g., hypotheses) or what is the cause of something (e.g., power) take an **a priori** stance whereas researchers who do not come in with an idea about their findings take an **emergent** one.

Post-Positive

Researchers adopting a post-positive (or logical-empirical) perspective take a scientific approach to research that can be accomplished through quantitative methodologies. Post-positivist researchers are interested in capturing patterns in human behavior. These scholars contend that there is an objective reality and their goal is to "advance predictions and to offer generalized, law-like cause and effect explanations or functional explanations about how variables or structure are interdependent with one another" (Braithwaite & Baxter, 2008, p. 7). Researchers using this paradigm typically begin by selecting a theory relevant to the phenomenon they seek to explain or predict. This a priori process is part of protocol that helps to control or neutralize researcher subjectivity (i.e., the biases of the researcher). Ultimately, a post-positivist seeks to create and test hypotheses from a theory. Criteria for post-positive research include: (1) generalizability, (2) parsimony, (3) falsifiability, and (4) reproducibility. Controlling for extraneous variables (i.e., variables they are not interested in but might change their results), reliability, and validity are also imperative to the post-positive researcher's project. Generalizability means they are interested in an explanation that could be applied to a large population (i.e., consensus). Parsimony means that something should be simple or easy to explain. Falsifiable means the research should be testable. Finally, reproducibility means that other researchers should be able to get the same findings if they conduct the study under the same conditions. Theories that were developed from a post-positive perspective include family communication patterns theory (see Chapter 5) and relational turbulence theory (see Chapter 18).

Interpretive

Researchers adopting an interpretive perspective believe in multiple realities according to the relative positioning of an individual or group. Braithwaite and

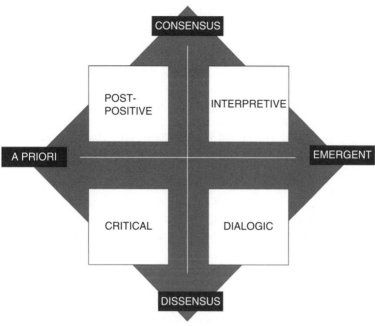

Figure 2.1 Research paradigms.

Baxter (2008) explain, "Interpretive researchers are committed to a detailed understanding of how particular social realities are produced and maintained through the everyday practices of individuals" (p. 5). Researchers using this paradigm seek to put emergent observations and interpretations in conversation with theory. Unlike the post-positive perspective, interpretive scholars would not test hypotheses or believe they were able to separate themselves from their research. In some instances, an interpretive scholar might operate completely inductively, or develop a **grounded theory**. They often use qualitative methods, gathering data through participant observation, interviews, and/or focus groups. Criteria for interpretive research include: (1) transferability, (2) heurism, (3) parsimony, and (4) intelligibility. Interpretive researchers ultimately seek to provide such an evocative account that others can recognize the experience they are researching as similar (or different) to their own. Similar to post-positivists, interpretive scholars value consensus; just not in the same way. Whereas a post-positive scholar wants to generalize to the whole population, an interpretive scholar just wants to represent a very particular group of people. Theories that correspond to the interpretive paradigm include an interpretive narrative approach (see Chapter 7) and the discourse dependence framework (see Chapter 14).

Critical

Researchers adopting a critical perspective are inherently interested in power struggles that give people more or less status or give them more or less voice.

Researchers doing critical work take into account social and historical contexts and focus on the institutionalized power structures that particularly hurt groups such as women, people of color, and non-elite social groups such as people with disabilities or the LGBTQ community (Braithwaite, Suter, & Floyd, 2018). Because they assume institutional power structures are at work, they fall into the a priori category. The goal of this research is emancipation or enlightenment and the critical researcher accomplishes this through facilitating social change. Scholars engaging in critical work often employ similar qualitative methods as interpretive scholars. Yet, unlike their interpretive peers, critical researchers are looking for contradiction and inequity as opposed to the consensus of a particular group of people or speech community (i.e., dissensus). Criteria for critical research include its ability to: (1) shed light on the voices of people who are often ignored or silenced, (2) foster social justice through emancipation, enlightenment, and empowerment, (3) facilitate change, and (4) create moments of reflexivity. Narrative performance theory is a good example of a critical theory (see Chapter 7).

Dialogic

Sometimes referred to as postmodern or poststructural, researchers adopting a dialogic perspective value dissensus and emergence. Their goal is to create a space for marginalized and silenced voices by exposing the one-sidedness and incompleteness of the world around us. Similar to the interpretive scholar, dialogic researchers focus on language and its construction of the social world. Instead of focusing on institutionalized power structures (e.g., sex, race), dialogic scholars examine local taken-for-granteds (e.g., families cannot break up, mothers should immediately love their children) and how the things we take for granted create marginalizing experiences. The goal of dialogic work, then, is not to "get it right" (like post-positive scholars) but rather to challenge fixed meanings. Creating a space for people to see something in a new light is the project of the dialogic scholar. Just like interpretive and critical scholars, dialogic researchers tend to approach their studies using a qualitative approach. Criteria for dialogic research include: (1) heurism, (2) disrupt taken-for-granteds, and (3) highlight power of language to (de)construct. Relational dialectics theory (see Chapter 9) is a good example of a dialogic theory.

For example, let's take the topic of family estrangement. Below are hypotheses and research questions that reflect how a researcher must study this topic from each paradigm:

- **Post-positive hypothesis**: Adult children with positive relationships with their parents will report less stress than adult children who have distanced themselves from their parents.
- **Interpretive research question**: What information about their estrangement do parents keep private from members of their social network?
- **Critical research question**: How does socio-economic status constrain people's ability to gain distance from their families?
- **Dialogic research question**: How do cultural ideologies compete to make the meaning of parent–child estrangement?

Qualitative Methods and Terms

Qualitative researchers draw upon a collection of methods designed to acquire, analyze, and interpret data (e.g., interviews, participant observation/field notes, document data) to understand and describe meanings, patterns, and relationships. These methods privilege the participants' experiences and words as opposed to researcher observation.

Codes: Words or short phrases that represent a meaningful (e.g., salient, descriptive, representative) response to the research question.

Discourse analysis: Discourse analysis references a variety of methodological approaches and practices. Often researchers use this to explore the ways in which people create, convey, share, acquire, and/or (mis)understand the meaning(s) of moments, events/experiences, lives, and (sub)cultures. These meaning-laden processes reflect and reify multi-level structures, and thus, discourse analysis can be used to examine multifaceted forms, patterns, organizations, orders, and/or systems of, in, and absent from communication (inter)actions.

- **Thematic analysis**: An iterative process of organizing data into patterns. For more information, we recommend reading about the six-step process outlined by Virginia Braun and Victoria Clarke (2006).

- **Thematic narrative analysis**: Narrative analysis also falls under the umbrella of discourse analysis. When researchers engage in thematic narrative analysis (TNA), they keep whole stories intact rather than pulling out themes to explain a data set; the unit of analysis for coding is a story, which can be read holistically and provide a single code (e.g., identity) that best reflects its overall type (Riessman, 2008).

- **Critical discourse analysis**: Critical discourse analyses (CDA) focus on power structures. One of the most common types of critical discourse analyses used by family communication scholars is a method called contrapuntal analysis. Contrapuntal analysis is the corresponding method of relational dialectics theory (see Chapter 9). This method focuses on how meaning is made when dominant ideologies compete with marginal ideologies (Baxter, 2011).

Ethnography: Research that emerges from long-term immersion in a culture; includes participant observation and taking field notes. Ethnographers are interested in language use, rituals, relationships, and cultural artifacts. Primarily, ethnographers of family communication typically focus on one of the three following objects of study: (1) ways of speaking or patterns of talk, (2) speech communities, or (3) native terms of talk (i.e., group-specific labels that are indicative of symbolic importance or specific meaning; Hymes, 1972).

- **Autoethnography**: The systematic study, analysis, and description of one's own experiences, interactions, culture, and identity (Tracy, 2013). We recommend Patrick Dillon's (2012) autoethnography about fatherhood.

- **Participant observation**: A method of collecting data where researchers watch, interact with, ask questions, collect documents, and/or make audio/

video recordings of participants for the purposes of understanding and generating knowledge.

Exemplar: An evocative example of a theme/category that often best represents that theme/category.

Interview types: Interviews might be conducted face-to-face, online, or in a larger group. Below are some common types of interviews.

- **Focus group**: A group of 3–12 interview participants; includes guided group discussion, question and answer, interaction, and other activity.

- **Structured**: An interview protocol that is scripted and hardly deviates from one participant to the next.

- **Semi-structured**: An interview protocol with a script but is also open to emergent questions based on participant answers.

- **Unstructured**: An interview protocol that is flexible and varies from one participant to the next. An unstructured interview might also include narrative interviews which ask participants to share their story. In a narrative interview, the question might be the same (i.e., share your story) but provides participants with maximum flexibility.

In brief: there are many ways researchers who use qualitative methods go about understanding phenomena by privileging participants' experiences and words. Sometimes they focus on emergent experiences and other times they also focus on issues of power. Researchers who use quantitative methods, on the other hand, take a fundamentally different approach to research and how they create and contribute to knowledge. Both types of researchers follow specific rules and have complex systems in place to ensure their research is rigorous and valid. Below, quantitative methods are defined.

Quantitative Methods and Terms

Actor–partner interdependence model: Put simply, this model shows how people influence each other's outcomes. In statistical language it is a model that simultaneously estimates the effect of a person's own independent variable and the effect of the same independent variable from another person on a dependent variable. The person's own independent variable is called an actor effect. The other person's independent variable is called a partner effect (see Cook & Kenny, 2005). The spillover–crossover model discussed in Chapter 32 is an example of an actor–partner interdependence model.

Content analysis: A systematic way to describe written, spoken, or visual communication. Information is broken down into categories and then summarized. For example, researchers could categorize the content of relationship talk between husbands and wives and then code marital conversations for those categories.

Correlation: Relationship between two variables that indicates that as one variable increases, the other also increases or decreases. For example, in marriages, as communication quality increases, relationship satisfaction also increases. It is important to remember that correlation is not causation, in other words, just because two variables increase or decrease together it does not mean that one causes the other. There are often other variables at play that may cause one or both of the other variables. Longitudinal studies, or data captured over time, are necessary to understand causality between variables.

Mediation: Explains the mechanism or process that underlies an observed relationship between an independent and dependent variable via inclusion of a third variable. This third variable is called a mediator. Mediators tell us how or why something works. For example, family support mediates the relationship between conversation orientation (see family communication patterns theory in Chapter 5) and student adjustment. This means that conversation orientation affects student adjustment because it affects family support first, which then has an influence on adjustment. Mediation is also known as an indirect effect.

Meta-analysis: Combines the results of multiple statistical studies to determine the effect of a variable across many samples; it is a synthesis of research. For example, a team of researchers have conducted a meta-analysis on family communication patterns which showed that high conversation orientation has consistent positive associations with psychosocial outcomes and well-being (Schrodt, Witt, & Messersmith, 2008).

Moderation: Occurs when the relationship between two variables depends on a third variable. The third variable is called a moderator. The moderator affects the strength and/or direction of the relationship.

Regression: Estimates the relationship among variables. Specifically, regression helps you understand how a dependent variable changes when you change an independent variable, holding all of the other independent variables constant.

Structural equation model (SEM): SEM is a combination of multiple regression analysis and factor analysis. SEM can test multiple regression equations at once, allowing researchers to test larger models with multiple independent and dependent variables along with mediators and moderators.

Variable: Something you are trying to measure. Researchers sometimes manipulate independent variables to see if the dependent variable changes.

- **Dependent variable**: A variable whose value depends on another value. This is the variable that is being studied and is often considered an outcome variable. For example, if researchers wanted to see how the use of meditation affected communication quality, the dependent variable would be communication quality since communication quality may depend on meditation.

- **Independent variable**: A variable whose value does not depend on another variable. Researchers usually propose that the independent variable will affect the dependent variable. In the example above, use of meditation is the independent variable.

- **Latent variable**: A variable that is not directly observed but rather inferred from other variables like "intelligence." Intelligence may be understood by measuring grades and standardized test scores.

- **Observed variable**: A variable that is directly measured like number of speaking turns in a conversation. Grades and standardized test scores are also observed variables and may be combined to create the latent variable of "intelligence."

Common Terms in Research Studies

Regardless of what type of study (i.e., qualitative or quantitative) a researcher conducts, there is certain information that is common, even if it might appear in different places in a manuscript. Here are some of those terms.

Institutional review board: Administrative body that protects the rights and welfare of human research subjects. Institutional review boards review research plans to make sure new studies do not harm human subjects.

Mean: A mean is an average. Mean might show up in a qualitative study as the mean length of participant interviews or in a quantitative study as the average response on a surveyed variable like relationship quality.

Median: Value lying at the midpoint of a set of numbers; the middle number.

N: N refers to the sample size or the total number of people in a study.

Participants: Focal individuals in the study; they participate in research with the researchers by taking a survey, answering questions in an interview, or participating in a laboratory experiment.

Sampling techniques: There are many different ways to recruit a sample of participants. Below are just some of the common ways researchers select participants for their studies.

- **Convenience sampling**: A technique that targets populations that are easy to access and inexpensive to recruit.

- **Purposeful sampling**: A technique which requires the researcher to meaningfully choose participants based on the project's research questions, hypotheses, and/or goals.

- **Random sampling**: A technique in which every member of a group has an equal chance to be selected for participation.

- **Snowball sampling**: A technique where participants help identify friends, colleagues, and/or family members who also fit the study criteria.

KEY TERMS

A priori	Falsifiable	Mediation
Consensus	Generalizability	Moderation
Correlation	Grounded theory	Observed variable
Critical	Heurism	Paradigm
Dependent variable	Independent variable	Parsimony
Dialogic	Intelligibility	Post-positive
Dissensus	Interpretive	Reproducibility
Discourse analysis	Interview types	Sampling techniques
Emergent	Latent variable	Transferability
Ethnography	Mean	
Extraneous variable	Median	

REFERENCES

Baxter, L. A. (2011). *Voicing relationships.* Thousand Oaks, CA: Sage.

Braithwaite, D. O., & Baxter, L. A. (2008). Introduction: Meta-theory and theory in interpersonal communication research. In L. A. Baxter & D. O. Braithwaite (Eds.), *Engaging theories in interpersonal communication: Multiple perspectives* (pp. 1–18). Los Angeles, CA: Sage.

Braithwaite, D. O., Suter, E. A., & Floyd, K. (2018). The landscape of meta-theory and theory in family communication research. In D. O. Braithwaite, E. A. Suter, & K. Floyd (Eds.), *Engaging theories in family communication* (2nd ed, pp. 1–16). New York, NY: Routledge.

Braun, V., & Clarke, V. (2006). Using thematic analysis in psychology. *Qualitative Research in Psychology, 3,* 77–101. doi:10.1191/1478088706qp063oa

Cook, W. L., & Kenny, D. A. (2005). The actor-partner interdependence model: A model of bidirectional effects in developmental studies. *International Journal of Behavior Development, 29,* 101–109. doi:10.1080/01650250444000405

Deetz, S. (2001). Conceptual foundations. In F. M. Jablin & L. L. Putnam (Eds.), *The new handbook of organizational communication* (pp. 3–46). Thousand Oaks, CA: Sage.

Dillon, P. J. (2012). Unbalanced: An autoethnography about fatherhood in academe. *Journal of Family Communication, 12,* 284–299. doi:10.1080/15267431.2012.686945

Hymes, D. (1972). On communicative competence. In D. Hymes & J. Gumperz (Eds.), *Directions in sociolinguistics: The ethnography of communication.* New York, NY: Holt, Rinehart & Winston.

Riessman, C. K. (2008). *Narrative methods for the human sciences.* Los Angeles, CA: Sage.

Schrodt, P., Witt, P. L., & Messersmith, A. S. (2008). A meta-analytical review of family communication patterns and their associations with information processing, behavioral, and psychosocial outcomes. *Communication Monographs, 75,* 248–269. doi:10.1080/03637750802256318

Tracy, S. J. (2013). *Qualitative research methods: Collecting evidence, crafting analysis, communicating impact.* Hoboken, NJ: Wiley-Blackwell.

RELATED READINGS

Droser, V. (2017). (Re)conceptualizing family communication: Applying Deetz's conceptual frameworks within the field of family communication. *Journal of Family Communication, 17,* 89–104. doi:10.1080/15267431.2017.1282750

Hayes, A. F. (2013). *Introduction to mediation, moderation, and conditional process analysis: A regression-based approach.* New York, NY: Guilford.

Macho, S., & Ledermann, T. (2011). Estimating, testing, and comparing specific effects in structural equation models: The phantom model approach. *Psychological Methods, 16,* 34–43. doi:10.1037/a0021763

PART I

Theories of Family Communication

Chapter 3

Affection Exchange Theory

All people need to experience affection from others. Our ability to receive and give affection is inborn, meaning all humans are equipped with these abilities. Exchanges of affection build and maintain healthy relationships and, according to Kory Floyd, aid in survival and procreation of the human species.

Affection exchange is a key form of support family members often provide to one another. When parents are affectionate toward their children, their children tend to have higher self-esteem and lower stress. This makes sense, considering affection is one of the big three interpersonal needs along with inclusion and control.

Parents display affection to their children by hugging or holding them and telling them they are loved. Affectionate communication looks similar in other family relationships. Siblings might exchange hugs or express their unconditional love for one another. Grandparents might hug or kiss their grandchildren. Affection can be displayed nonverbally through touch and verbally through written or spoken statements of warmth and positive regard. Affection can also be displayed indirectly through providing one of the many types of social support we discuss in Chapter 17 Supportive Communication in Families. What counts as affection depends on the norms of each culture. The examples provided here are based on North American culture. Affection exchange occurs when displays of affection are returned to the affection giver, for example, a daughter returning her mother's hug.

Communication in Family Contexts: Theories and Processes, First Edition.
Elizabeth Dorrance Hall and Kristina M. Scharp.
© 2020 John Wiley & Sons, Inc. Published 2020 by John Wiley & Sons, Inc.
Companion website: www.wiley.com/go/dorrance_hall/communication-in-family-contexts

BACKGROUND

Floyd (2015a) developed a theory to explain how affection exchange evolved over time as a means for human survival. Because of this human survival focus, affection exchange theory (AET) is a scientific bio-evolutionary theory. AET explains why humans communicate affection to each other, and with what consequences.

The theory claims that affectionate messages are important because they make relationships, and the humans involved in those relationships, better in many ways. Exchange of affection can bring people closer, make them feel more satisfied with their relationships, and improve their individual mental health. Evolutionarily, affection serves to pair people together which would allow them more access to resources like food, shelter, and support, and therefore, better chances of survival. Showing a partner affection also signals that the affection giver would be a viable mate and fit parent, increasing their chances of procreation.

The theory proposes that affectionate communication often occurs as an exchange, where both people in a partnership (romantic or otherwise) show each other affection. The theory also states that people can feel affection for another without expressing it, making the exchange of affection unique from simply feeling affection for another person. In the family context, it is easy to imagine a parent feeling affection for a child or a child for a parent, but unable or unwilling to express that affection in particular situations. People can also show others affection without really feeling affection. For example, a mother-in-law might give her daughter-in-law a hug every time she sees her, even if she does not feel warmth for her daughter-in-law.

KEY CONCEPTS

Affection is liking another being and feeling warmth or fondness toward him/her.

Affectionate communication is verbal and nonverbal messages that convey feelings of fondness, support, and love for another person. Affectionate communication looks like hugging, kissing, holding hands, or saying "I love you." One important thing to remember about affectionate communication is that it is the presentation (whether accurate or not) of an affectionate emotion that qualifies as the expression of affection.

Propositions of AET: Scholars often rely on the AET's propositions to form hypotheses to conduct their research. These propositions are the foundation of the theory.

- **Proposition 1**: The need and capacity for affection are inborn. This means that people do not need to think about their desire for affection. It is biological.

- **Proposition 2**: Affectionate feelings and affection expressions are distinct experiences that often, but need not, covary. Even though people often express when they feel affectionate, they do not always do so.

- **Proposition 3**: Affectionate communication is adaptive with respect to human viability and fertility. In other words, people adapt their affectionate communication to both survive and reproduce.

- **Proposition 4**: Humans vary in their optimal tolerances for affection and affectionate behavior. Some people both need and want more or less affection than others.

- **Proposition 5**: Affectionate behaviors that violate the range of optimal tolerance for affection are physiologically averse. This means that receiving not enough or even too much affection can be detrimental to a person's physical well-being.

In brief: AET's propositions state that people have a biological need for affection but some people need more affection than others. Affection helps the human species survive and reproduce. The expression and feeling of affection do not necessarily match up. That is, people can feel affection for another and not show it and vice versa. Finally, affection is not always a good thing – too much affection can be damaging, as can too little affection.

BENEFITS OF AFFECTIONATE COMMUNICATION

Research shows that simply being an affectionate person, no matter how much affection you receive from others, can be beneficial. People who are affectionate have better mental health, experience more happiness, and are more comfortable with being close to others.

Affection is not just about feeling good. The theory asserts that because affection is natural and necessary for humans to survive, the lack of affection has negative consequences for people. Research studies have shown this to be true. Lack of affection is linked to physical pain and poor sleep quality (Floyd, 2016).

According to Merril Silverstein and his team of researchers (2002), affection exchange has long-lasting effects. He found that the affection parents show their young children contributes to the amount of social support adult children provide their parents later in life.

INTERESTING RESEARCH FINDINGS

Sean Horan (2012) did a research study looking at how affection exchange was related to perceptions of relational transgressions. Horan asked college students about transgressions they experienced with their partner in the past three months. He defined transgressions as "an unfavorable behavior from a relational partner that is perceived as a violation of relational rules" (p. 116) and gave examples like broken promises, deception, neglect, a lack of sensitivity, betrayal, verbal aggression, flirting with someone else, and infidelity. Horan found that the more affection that was received in the relationship, the less severe the transgressions seemed to be. His participants reported that they ruminated, or thought about the transgression repeatedly, thus the more affection they received, the less hurt they felt. This means that if a transgression happens in a relationship where a lot of affection is received, it is likely less damaging to the relationship. Another interesting finding in this study was that *expressed* affection was not related to rumination or hurt. In other words, if you commit a transgression, you would be smart to also give affection to the person you hurt. In his study, Horan found that women reported expressing slightly more affection than men, but rates of received affection were very similar between men and women.

How Do Men Show Affection to Their Sons?

Floyd (2001), who developed AET, did a study to understand how men show affection to their sons. He recruited 50 men who reported they had at least one son. Half of those men were heterosexual and the other half reported they were bisexual or homosexual. Floyd found that the men in his study showed affection to their sons through direct verbal messages and through nonverbal gestures, but communicated affection more through supportive activities like helping out with a house project or attending a sporting event together than through verbal or nonverbal messages. Men might prefer to show affection through activities because this type of communication hides or encodes affection, allowing men to show affection without direct, verbal expression.

Floyd also explored whether his participants expressed more or less affection to their own sons than they received from their fathers. Interestingly, heterosexual men tended to show the same amount of nonverbal affection to their sons as they received from their fathers but tended to communicate more supportive affection than they had received. LGBTQ men tended to show more of all types of affection (verbal, nonverbal, and supportive) to their sons than they had received.

mohamed_hassan/pixabay

Did You Know?

- Trait affection has physiological benefits such that people who are highly trait affectionate have lower resting heart rates, lower blood pressure, and lower glucose. These people are also able to recover from stressful events more quickly.

- Our desire for affection and tendency to express affection is driven by both nature and nurture. That is to say, the desire to survive and reproduce only explains some of our affectionate behaviors. Communication and socialization also are important factors in understanding affectionate communication and its exchange process.

PRACTICAL IMPLICATIONS AND THINGS TO CONSIDER

Affection exchange is also related to the loneliness we experience. If you are feeling like you could use more affection and connection in your life, consider the following ways of increasing the affection you experience.

1. Be open to receiving affection from others. We know affection is reciprocal, so give affection more often and be open to receiving it when it comes from others.

2. Ask for the affection you need. Open communication is key to getting more affection from others when they simply do not know you need it.

3. Recognize that affection comes in many shapes and sizes. Sometimes we feel we are not getting any affection, but the truth is, we are just getting it in a form we do not recognize. Once you recognize the various forms of affection your partner (or friend, or family member) gives, work to acknowledge and appreciate those behaviors more.

Want to learn more about affection and how it relates to loneliness? Check out Kory Floyd's book, *The Loneliness Cure: Six Strategies for Finding Real Connections in Your Life* (2015b). This popular press book discusses the concept of affection hunger, helps you assess your needs, and offers six strategies for attracting more intimacy into your relational life.

KEY TERMS

Affection

Affectionate communication

Affection exchange

Inborn human needs

IN-CLASS ACTIVITY

Think about and write down a time you felt a keen sense of affection from someone else. Answer the following questions about that experience.

1. How did they show affection to you?
2. How did you respond?
3. Why does that particular memory stick out in your brain?
4. Was the affection verbal or nonverbal or both?

Now, answer the following questions to analyze and identify which relationships in your life could benefit from additional affection exchange.

1. Which relationships in your life provide you enough affection?
2. Are there relationships in your life from which you wish you experienced more affection? If yes, which ones? Why do you think those relationships do not provide enough affection exchange?
3. How could you improve the amount of affection exchange in that relationship?\

OUT-OF-CLASS ACTIVITY/HOMEWORK

1. Brainstorm a list of ways you could show affection to a close friend today. Choose one and go express it. Report back to the class on what happened next.
2. Head out to a local coffee shop or bar and observe the relationships around you. Do you notice anyone exchanging affection? How can you tell? What do their verbal and nonverbal behaviors look like?

Everyone Has Affectionate Needs

CASE STUDY BY LISA VAN RAALTE

Stephanie had a long week at work. As a companion worker at a seniors' retirement home for two years, she has developed close relationships with many of the seniors. Stephanie spends a lot of her time holding hands with the elderly and keeping their mind active with dancing and games. She enjoys spending time with her clients and knows that her presence and warm touch are helpful to the seniors' well-being and happiness. However, by the end of the work week, Stephanie feels a little overwhelmed with the amount of affection she has provided to others.

Her husband, Carlos, is a stay-at-home dad and is looking forward to having a date night with Stephanie. They hired a babysitter for the night so they can focus on their date. When Stephanie gets home, Carlos gives her their routine kiss hello but notices that Stephanie does not linger for long.

"Is everything okay, Steph?" Carlos asks.

"Yeah, I'm just really tired. I feel like I've done nothing but be of service to others all week and I am ready to relax."

Carlos, wanting to make Stephanie feel better, moves toward her to hug her. Stephanie puts a hand out and says, "Not right now" and walks upstairs to get ready for their date. Feeling a little rejected, Carlos goes to the kitchen to prepare dinner for the babysitter and the children.

After a short while, Stephanie returns and the babysitter arrives. In the car, Carlos and Stephanie share the details of their day and begin to get excited for the new restaurant they are going to. When they arrive, the waiter asks them if they would like a booth or a table – Stephanie quickly says "Booth!" with a smile. In their booth, Stephanie and Carlos hold hands while their food is being prepared. Stephanie moves closer so that the side of her leg is touching Carlos during dinner.

After dinner, Carlos remarks, "You know, I thought you were grumpy at me when you pushed my hug away."

Stephanie replies, "I'm sorry, hon, I had such a long week of touching others that I needed a little bit of space. But being here with you makes me feel so loved and safe, I want to be able to spend this time together while we don't have the kids."

Feeling valued, Carlos takes Stephanie's hand and leads her outside of the restaurant for a walk around the park. They stop to sit at a bench and Carlos puts his arm around Stephanie while she rests her head on his shoulder.

"Ahhhhhhhh," Stephanie sighs, and Carlos can feel her shoulders drop as she relaxes. They each take turns talking about their future goals and desires, and encouraging each other to be themselves.

"I'm so glad I'm able to tell you my fears, thank you for being my special pumpkin pie," Carlos says to Stephanie.

"My pleasure, pudding," Stephanie replies.

CASE STUDY DISCUSSION QUESTIONS

1. Affection can be communicated in several different ways. What type of affectionate messages did you observe between Stephanie and Carlos?
2. In what ways does the interaction between Carlos and Stephanie represent several different propositions of Affection Exchange Theory?
3. During what times in your life have you felt like you do NOT want to receive affection from others? Why do you think this is?
4. What type of communicative strategies do you think would be best for requesting more affection from a partner?

REFERENCES

Floyd, K. (2001). Human affection exchange: I. Reproductive probability as a pre-dictor of men's affection with their sons. *Journal of Men's Studies, 10*, 39–50. doi:10.3149/jms.1001.39

Floyd, K. (2015a). *Affection exchange theory*. New York, NY: John Wiley & Sons, Inc.

Floyd, K. (2015b). *The loneliness cure: Six strategies for finding real connections in your life*. Avon, MA: Adams Media.

Floyd, K. (2016). Affection deprivation is associated with physical pain and poor sleep quality. *Communication Studies, 67*, 379–398. doi:10.1080/10510974.2016.1205641

Horan, S. M. (2012). Affection exchange theory and perceptions of relational trans-gressions. *Western Journal of Communication, 76*, 109–126. doi:10.1080/1057031 4.2011.651548

Silverstein, M., Conroy, S. J., Wang, H., Giarrusso, R., & Bengtson, V. L. (2002). Reciprocity in parent–child relations over the adult life course. *Journals of Gerontology Series B: Psychological Sciences and Social Sciences, 57*, S3–S13. doi:10.1093/geronb/57.1.s3

RELATED READINGS

Denes, A., Bennett, M., & Winkler, K. L. (2017). Exploring the benefits of affec-tionate communication: Implications for interpersonal acceptance-rejection theory. *Journal of Family Theory and Review, 9*, 491–506. doi:10.1111.jftr.12218

Floyd, K., Hesse, C., & Generous, M. A. (2018). Affection exchange theory: A bio-evolutionary look at affectionate communication. In D. O. Braithwaite, E. A. Suter, & K. Floyd (Eds.), *Engaging theories in family communication* (2nd ed). New York, NY: Routledge.

Hesse, C., & Mikkelson, A. (2017). Affection deprivation in romantic relationships. *Communication Quarterly, 65*, 20–38. doi:10.1080/01463373.2016.1176942

Hesse, C., Mikkelson, A., & Saracco, S. (2018). Parent-child affection and helicopter parenting: Exploring the concept of excessive affection. *Western Journal of Communication, 82*, 457–474. doi:10.1080/10570314.2017.1362705

Chapter 4

Communication Privacy Management Theory

Sometimes, family members want to protect private information about themselves and other members of their family. Communication privacy management theory (CPM) explains this phenomenon using three primary tenets. Formalized by Sandra Petronio (2002, 2013), this theory illuminates how people manage their private information and what happens when private information (unexpectedly) becomes public.

BACKGROUND

CPM began as a homegrown theory about self-disclosure. Homegrown theories are developed by communication scholars and largely focus on communication antecedents, processes, and outcomes. In other words, they are centrally focused on communication (as opposed to theories created in psychology but adapted to communication). Based on dialectical thinking (i.e., there is a contradiction, or push and pull, between privacy and disclosure), Petronio uses the metaphor of the

Communication in Family Contexts: Theories and Processes, First Edition.
Elizabeth Dorrance Hall and Kristina M. Scharp.
© 2020 John Wiley & Sons, Inc. Published 2020 by John Wiley & Sons, Inc.
Companion website: www.wiley.com/go/dorrance_hall/communication-in-family-contexts

boundary to illustrate how private information might be managed at two levels: personal and collective boundaries.

Personal boundaries are those that house information belonging to one individual. **Collective boundaries** house information shared with at least one other person. For example, if a woman takes a test and finds out she is pregnant and she is the only one who knows, that information is within her personal boundary. As soon as she shares this information with someone else, like her partner, they co-own that information and it is within their collective boundary. As CPM matured both within the field of Communication Studies and beyond, it is now more commonly used as a way to understand how people manage information they consider to be private.

Privacy management in families is an important maintenance process. At different times, different family members will require more and less privacy. For example, as children become emerging adults, they often seek to keep more information private from their parents. Parents might also want to closely manage some information they believe is inappropriate for their children to learn. Ultimately, privacy management can yield positive outcomes for its members (e.g., bonding over shared private information) or can become problematic for the whole family when information is mismanaged. Below are some important key concepts about CPM.

KEY TENETS AND CONCEPTS OF THE THEORY

Main Tenets

CPM focuses on three main elements that explain the way individuals manage their private information: (1) privacy ownership, (2) privacy control, and (3) privacy turbulence. These elements illustrate the ways information owners draw boundaries around private information and work to control those boundaries.

Privacy Ownership

There are two primary principles that predict the way people think about the ownership of private information and their regulation of that information (Petronio, 2013). As Petronio explains, "privacy ownership defines the boundaries surrounding the information, marking it private" (p. 9). The first CPM principle explains that individuals believe they solely own their private information and thus have the right to protect or share it. The second principle predicts that when these **original owners** grant others access to their private information, these recipients become **authorized co-owners**. Original owners perceive that the authorized co-owner has a responsibility to keep the trust of the original owner. Thus, co-owners take on a role in keeping the original owner's information private. The connection between the original owners and co-owner(s) is what Petronio (2002) terms a **boundary linkage**.

In brief: private information is information people believe they own that is not available to the general public; it is personal. When they share that information with others, they invite others to become authorized co-owners.

Information co-ownership comes with the responsibility to help keep the information private. When co-owners share information they have agreed not to, it can jeopardize the relationship as this is often seen as a violation of trust.

Privacy Control

In addition to the first two ownership principles, privacy control is constituted by four additional principles. The third CPM principle states that, because individuals believe they own their private information, they also feel they have the right to control it. Individuals control information by creating **privacy rules** (i.e., principle four) which develop based on their motivations, cultural values, and situational needs (Petronio, 2013). For example, an explicit privacy rule might be, "Don't tell mom that I went out last night even though she told me I wasn't allowed." The fifth principle suggests that successful and continued control post-disclosure is achieved through coordinating and negotiating privacy rules with "authorized co-owners" about who else can know the information. Finally, principle six details the way co-ownership leads to collective boundaries that are jointly held and operated by multiple people. Research about privacy control suggests that controlling information might work especially well when owners and recipients discuss their preferences for information sharing and receiving (Scharp & Steuber, 2014).

Privacy Turbulence

Despite attempts at privacy control, privacy regulation does not always run smoothly. Principle eight posits that regulation is often unpredictable and can fall on a continuum that ranges from a minor disruption to a complete privacy breakdown. For example, a minor disruption might occur around information that people might not want to be public but also that does not carry consequences. For example, people might not want others to know they recently got in a fight with their sibling, but it is not particularly damaging information. A more serious example might be when a person does not want to share that their parent was fired from a job or that a family member has been diagnosed with a serious illness.

Key Concepts

Disclosure Criteria

There are two types of criteria people use to decide whether or not they are going to disclose private information: core and catalyst.

Core: These criteria produce stable and routine rules. They often run in the background and influence rule choices based on factors like socialization, cultural norms/expectations, and ideologies about topics such as gender and race. For example, in some families it may be a taken-for-granted rule that no members discuss family finances with people outside the family. This money-taboo may be based on what is culturally appropriate for people to discuss with others.

Catalyst: These criteria trigger a change in privacy rules. Unlike core criteria, catalyst criteria might come about due to unexpected situations, changes of motivation, amendments to privacy regulations, and reconsiderations of the cost–benefit ratio. A cost–benefit ratio explains the idea that sometimes there are costs to disclosing information (e.g., other people might share that information) as well as potential benefits (e.g., ability to get advice about a problem). For example, people might have to weigh the costs and benefits of asking for dating advice from an older sibling; on the one hand, advice would be helpful and on the other hand, the sibling might tease them about their romantic interest in the future.

Family Privacy Orientations

The consistent use of certain privacy rules over a long period of time creates family privacy orientations. These orientations reference the extent to which information is shared with people outside of the family.

Families with **high permeable orientations** freely share information with people inside and outside of the family. Families with high permeable orientations would feel comfortable sharing any kind of information with others outside the family.

A **moderate permeable orientation** means that family members are making more judicious choices about what to share and what to keep private. For example a family member might feel free to share certain types of news like when something good happens to a family member, but might not be willing to share negative news about the family.

Families with **low permeable orientations** highly restrict information inside and outside of the family. These families likely keep secrets (see Chapter 16 on Information Management and Disclosure in Families) and there would likely be consequences for members who share too much.

Private Information

Private information is information that is personal. Having private information can put owners in tough situations because they are potentially vulnerable to others learning that information.

Recalibration

After privacy turbulence happens, or information is shared that they did not want to be shared, people often change their privacy rules to cope with the breakdown, ultimately realigning their privacy management system so that it works better in the future. For example, if a brother shared the good news about his sister's new job with others, only to find out later that she was not ready for people outside of the family to know, the siblings may agree that in the future they will explicitly tell each other when information should not be shared outside the family.

Reluctant Confidant

A reluctant confidant is one who is privy to unwanted private information that is often considered a burden. Not only do reluctant confidants not want the information, they also must negotiate the implicit expectation and obligation to keep that information private or reciprocate sharing their own secret. For example, a person could become a reluctant confidant if a friend disclosed he was having an affair with a shared co-worker.

Stakeholder

Stakeholders are confidants who are perceived as being worthy of some sort of access because they serve a functional role in providing the original information owner with a needed outcome. Parents, for example, may be stakeholders in information regarding their teenager's activities and whereabouts so that they can keep them safe and transport them when needed.

INTERESTING RESEARCH FINDINGS

Let's Be Facebook Friends: Communication Privacy Management Online

With David Westermann, Associate Director of the Communication Privacy Management Center, Jeffrey Child, conducted a study about how Facebook users respond to parental Facebook friend requests (Child & Westermann, 2013). Overall, a sample of 235 young adult Facebook users tend to accept their parents' requests. Results suggest, however, that when mothers request access, Facebook users tend to restrict information access by adjusting what content was available for their mothers to see. When users do accept their mothers' requests without restriction it is more likely that they come from high permeable oriented families as well as have a higher relational quality. Alternatively, privacy restrictions were not imposed when fathers requested access and there were no differences between relational quality or trust for those who accepted the request from fathers with or without restrictions.

QUESTIONS TO CONSIDER

Would you accept your parent's Facebook friend request? Would you add them on Instagram? Snapchat? Why or why not? What content would you not want them to be able to access?

DO PEOPLE EVER FEEL THEY HAVE THE RIGHT TO KNOW OTHER PEOPLE'S INFORMATION?

Communication scholars use CPM to explore a myriad of phenomena and processes including those in health, interpersonal, and family contexts. One of your textbook author's research on adoption reunions is featured on the official CPM Center's website as an example of how CPM research can inform how people act in real-life situations (https://cpmcenter.iupui.edu/index.php/practice)

Specifically, Kristina Scharp and Keli Steuber (2014) collected stories from 60 adopted adult children who never reunited with their birth mothers. Adoptees discussed what information they would and would not want to know if they ever reunited with their birth family. Based on a thematic analysis, findings revealed six major types of information adoptees both wanted and felt they had the right to know: (1) health information, (2) birth parent information (e.g., location of the birth family), (3) extended family information (e.g., whether they had siblings), (4) adoptee identity (e.g., nationality), (5) birth mother circumstances at the time of birth, and (6) adoption circumstances such as the process of the adoption.

Furthermore, adoptees had four information management preferences for privacy ownership and control. They are: (1) a preference for full disclosure, (2) a preference for conditional disclosure, (3) protection privacy rules that illustrated that some adoptees did not know what information they wanted, and (4) a preference for nondisclosure. Of note, when adoptees considered conditional disclosure, they discussed contingencies based on specific content of the information (i.e., some topics were more or less desirable), a need to avoid hurtful information, and the disclosure preferences of the birth mother.

Theoretically, this research calls into question what happens when someone believes they have a right to information they do not already know. The findings suggest that people not only have to control their own desires and management preferences but also consider the well-being and preferences of the original information owner. Practically, this study also provides evidence that it could be beneficial for parties to discuss information preferences when boundaries are unclear. By having an explicit discussion about what people want and do not want to know, original owners might be able to be more sensitive to making another person a reluctant confidant. Overall, when adoptees and birth mothers consider these potentials for boundary turbulence, they might ultimately reduce the chances of having a negative reconnection.

PRACTICAL APPLICATIONS AND THINGS TO CONSIDER

CPM is an extremely practical theory considering family information is often personal. Did you know that approximately less than half of a sample of 273 people reported creating explicit privacy rules with people with whom they shared private information? A study by Keli Steuber and Rachel McLaren (2015) found that after someone shares private information that should not have been shared, original owners do not share similar information in the future, but if they do, less than half create privacy rules. Those who choose to recalibrate, however, are more likely to forgive, more likely to improve their relationship, and are less likely to report relational damage than people who do not make new rules and discuss how private information should be handled in the future. Based on this research, creating privacy rules could be an important tool to maintain your close relationships.

HOLIDAY PARTY TEST

Would you take your parents to a holiday party that your friends and co-workers would be attending? If you did, what kinds of privacy rules might you create? What kinds of rules would you want your parents to follow? What kinds of rules would you want your friends to follow? What kinds of rules would you want your co-workers to follow? How are those rules similar or different for the various groups of people?

KEY TERMS

Catalyst
Collective boundary
Core
Information ownership
(original and co-owners)

Permeability
Personal boundary
Privacy
Privacy control
Privacy rules

Privacy turbulence
Recalibration

Podcast with Sandra Petronio, Indiana University–Purdue University Indianapolis: www.familycommlab.com/podcast

Dr. Sandra Petronio shares her journey from grade school to professor. She discusses how Communication Privacy Management research has evolved over time and tells us about the exciting cross-cultural work being done today.

SANDRA PETRONIO PODCAST REFLECTION QUESTIONS

1. Who inspired Dr. Petronio to start researching families? How has your family inspired the interests you have?
2. What topic did Dr. Petronio first study? Why did she choose it?
3. Dr. Petronio shared some personal information about her life and, by doing so, made you a co-owner. Do you feel the need to keep this information private? Why or why not?
4. How does everyday life inform family communication theorizing?
5. What do you observe in everyday life that inspires your own questions about family communication?
6. Why does Dr. Petronio argue it is important to have agreed-on definitions of terms?
7. How can we contribute to advancing CPM according to Dr. Petronio?
8. What is a memorable lesson you can take away from Dr. Petronio's podcast?

REFERENCES

Child, J. T., & Westermann, D. A. (2013). Let's be Facebook friends: Exploring parental Facebook friend requests from a communication privacy management (CPM) perspective. *Journal of Family Communication, 13*, 46–59. doi:10.1080/152 67431.2012.742089

Petronio, S. (2002). *The boundaries of privacy: Dialectics of disclosure.* Albany, NY: State University of New York Press.

Petronio, S. (2013). Brief status report on communication privacy management theory. *Journal of Family Communication, 13*, 6–14. doi:10.1080/15267431 .2013.743426

Scharp, K. M., & Steuber, K. R. (2014). Perceived information ownership and control: Negotiating communication preferences in potential adoption reunions. *Personal Relationships, 21*, 515–529. doi:10.1111/pere.12046

Steuber, K. R., & McLaren, R. M. (2015). Privacy recalibration in personal relationships: Rule usage before and after an incident of privacy turbulence. *Communication Quarterly, 63*, 345–364. doi:10.1989/01463373.2015.1039717

RELATED READINGS

Bute, J. J., Petronio, S., & Torke, A. M. (2015). Surrogate decision makers and proxy ownership: Challenges of privacy in health care decision making. *Health Communication, 30*, 799–809. doi:10.1080/10410236.2014.900528

Kennedy-Lightsey, C. D., & Frisby, B. N. (2016). Parental privacy invasion, family communication patterns, and perceived ownership of private information. *Communication Reports, 29*, 75–86. doi:10.1080/08934215.2015.1048477

Kranstuber Horstman, H., Butaski, M., Johnson, L. J., & Colaner, C. W. (2017). The communication privacy management of adopted individuals in their social networks: Disclosure decisions in light of the discourse of biological normativity. *Communication Studies, 68*, 296–313. doi:10.1080/10510974.2017.1324890

Petronio, S., & Reierson, J. (2009). Regulating the privacy of confidentiality: Grasping the complexities through communication privacy management theory. In T. D. Afifi & W. A. Afifi (Eds.), *Uncertainty, information management, and disclosure decisions: Theories and applications* (pp. 365–383). New York, NY: Routledge.

Chapter 5
Family Communication Patterns Theory

The way we communicate with our families while growing up shapes the way we communicate for the rest of our lives. No communication theory explains how and why this works more clearly than family communication patterns (FCP) theory. Developed by Mary Anne Fitzpatrick, L. David Ritchie, and Ascan Koerner in its present form, this theory explains how families communicate to share a common view of reality. The theory allows researchers to predict how individual family members will respond to certain events and how the family as a whole will cope with and work through problems together.

BACKGROUND

The FCP framework is based on the idea that families are defined as transactional, meaning they share a history, a future, hold bonds of loyalty, and share a common identity and sense of commitment. This is a broad definition that includes blood ties as well as legal adoption, extended family members, and unrelated close others like friends and neighbors.

The history of family communication patterns research dates back to the 1970s when mass communication professors developed the theory to under-stand the influence of the media on socialization in the family. In the early 1970s,

Communication in Family Contexts: Theories and Processes, First Edition.
Elizabeth Dorrance Hall and Kristina M. Scharp.
© 2020 John Wiley & Sons, Inc. Published 2020 by John Wiley & Sons, Inc.
Companion website: www.wiley.com/go/dorrance_hall/communication-in-family-contexts

Jack McLeod and Steven Chaffee developed two dimensions they thought families varied on in terms of family norms and behaviors (McLeod & Chaffee, 1972). The first is about parental power and was called socio-orientation. The second was about how much a child was encouraged to develop an individual view of the world and was called concept-orientation. This original version of the theory assumed that family members all agree on the norms and behaviors that shape their communication patterns, an assumption we will learn later is not usually true. The names of these two orientations have evolved over the years to focus more on communication behaviors in the family. The current version of the theory is explained next.

KEY CONCEPTS

Fitzpatrick and Ritchie reinterpreted the two orientations developed by McLeod and Chaffee in the early 1990s to focus on *perceptions* of family norms concerning *communication* (Ritchie, 1991; Ritchie & Fitzpatrick, 1990).

The first dimension is called **conversation orientation**. This orientation captures how open a family is to talking about a wide variety of topics on a relatively frequent basis. These families encourage open participation in a lot of different types of interactions.

The second dimension is called **conformity orientation**. This orientation captures how strictly the parents expect their children to share their values, beliefs, and attitudes. Families high on conformity orientation do not highly value independent thinking in their children; instead they expect their children to share in their religious and political views, and follow their rules. They expect their children to be more similar than different and, as a result, expect that they get along with one another because they should not need to argue about different beliefs.

Where a family falls on the two orientations explains how they reach a shared sense of reality. Family patterns emerge from the processes by which family members create a sense of reality through conversation. This is illustrated by the construct of "coorientation," which is an awareness of shared focus on something in the social and material world between family members. When social reality is shared, agreement, accuracy and congruence in coorientation, occurs amongst family members. Families high on conformity are likely to reach coorientation because controversy is constrained. All families must achieve some level of coorientation to function.

Four Family Types

Family behavior can be placed along the two orientations described earlier (conversation and conformity), which cross to create four family types (see Table 5.1). To illustrate the difference between family types, imagine with us how each family would handle discussing the issue of a child receiving and using their first cell phone.

- **Consensual**: Families who rate high on both conformity and conversation orientations are classified as consensual. Consensual families value open and frequent communication between family members while believing that parents alone are the ones who should make decisions that affect the family. This type of family would openly discuss the possibility of using cell phones but the decision would ultimately be made by the parents. The parents would make sure to communicate to the children why and how the decision was made. **In brief: Consensual families have open and frequent communication but believe parents alone are the decision makers.**

- **Pluralistic**: Families who rate high on conversation orientation and low on conformity orientation fall into the classification of pluralistic family type. These families again value open and frequent conversation but also allow decisions to be made together, or by each individual member. Children's ideas and opinions are valued and carry as much weight as the parents'. A family discussion about cell phones would involve the entire family coming to a decision together on whether or not the children should be allowed to have them. Children would be able to argue their case and so would the parents. The arguments would be judged based on merit, not on the source of the message. **In brief: Pluralistic families have open and frequent communication and decisions are made together as a family.**

- **Protective**: Protective families rate low on conversation orientation and high on conformity orientation. In this type of family children are expected to follow parents' rules without questioning their authority. The parents in this family would make a decision about cell phone use and tell their children what they had decided without family discussion or explanation. Explaining how they came to the decision to their children is not valued in this family type. **In brief: Protective families expect children to follow the parents' rules without questioning their authority.**

- **Laissez-faire**: Families who rate low on both conversation and conformity orientation are classified as laissez-faire. Laissez-faire families do not value frequent and open conversations, nor do they value authority and hierarchy in the family. These families do communicate but not as often and not as openly as other family types. Children are allowed to make decisions but parents are not as interested in their opinions and choices. Family members of this family type have been described as "emotionally divorced" by Koerner and Fitzpatrick (1997, 2002a, 2002b, 2004). If children wanted cell phones in this family they could have them. Parents would not take the time to discuss with their children the pros, cons, or potential dangers of cell phone ownership and use.

Table 5.1 Family Types

	Low Conversation	High Conversation
High Conformity	**Protective**	**Consensual**
Low Conformity	**Laissez-Faire**	**Pluralistic**

In brief: Laissez-faire families don't value open frequent communication, parental authority, or hierarchy. Kids can make decisions without much parental involvement.

Most families exhibit behaviors that fit into more than one family type. In fact, only families who score extremely high or low on each dimension would fit into just one family type. When data are collected from multiple family members (a rare occurrence), a mixed-family type is likely.

INTERESTING RESEARCH FINDINGS

How Do Family Communication Patterns Relate to Helicopter Parenting?

Many studies have been done to understand how family communication patterns function for undergraduate college students. Entering college is a time marked by change in college students' relationships with parents and other family members as they form independent identities. First, students who come from high conversation orientation families tend to report low conformity orientation and vice versa. This means that for most students, high conformity expectations in their family indicates infrequent or limited communication. Family communication patterns likely influence how students adjust to college because a family's communication environment will dictate whether and how parents talk to their children about higher education and the challenges they will face in adjusting and thriving in school.

In a study on helicopter parenting, which occurs when parents are over-involved in a child's life through supervision, making decisions, solving problems for their emerging adult children when it is no longer developmentally appropriate to do so, Kelly Odenweller and her colleagues (2014) found that undergraduate college students who reported their parents were helicopter parents also tended to be from high conformity orientation families. Conversation orientation was not associated with reports of helicopter parenting, likely because helicopter parents do not necessarily encourage their children to participate in family decision making or be open about their inner thoughts and feelings the way that high conversation parents do. They also explain that it makes sense for conformity orientation to be related to helicopter parenting because both high conformity and helicopter parents are strict and controlling and hold high expectations for obedience from their children.

How Do Family Communication Patterns Vary Across Culture?

One of your textbook author's research has explored cultural differences in how family communication patterns influence college student adjustment and perceptions of family support. Along with a team of researchers Dorrance Hall (2017) surveyed over 900 first year undergraduates in the United States and Belgium about their family communication and how they were adjusting to life in college.

The research team chose Belgium as a comparison culture because of a few key differences between the Flemish (Flemish = Dutch/Flemish speaking Belgians) and US cultures. First, Flemish university students live on campus during the week but spend every weekend home with their parents. This increased face time with parents stands in stark contrast to how often most US university students see their parents. Second, Belgium as a country is much smaller than the United States, meaning most Belgian students are closer to home even when they are away at college. Third, Belgian enrollment fees and tuition are much lower than in the US, perhaps lessening the pressure they feel to succeed because the financial consequences of not finishing school are less severe.

In both cultures, being from a high conversation orientation family meant healthier adjustment to college in regard to making friends, participating in class, completing schoolwork, and experiencing less loneliness. Students from a high conversation orientation family also experienced more family support and perceived their parents gave them higher-quality advice about college. Findings about conformity orientation on the other hand were culture specific. For US students, conformity orientation was related to better adjustment and less loneliness but for Belgian students, conformity orientation was related to higher stress about college. This may be because conformity orientation is considered less "normal" in Belgian culture. For example, if conformity behaviors are not socially accepted as normal in Belgian culture, then those who have parents who stress conformity might suffer in unique ways. Research is underway now to understand how family communication patterns differ in the Chinese culture where "tiger parenting" is considered both normative and good parenting.

KEY TERMS

Coorientation	Conformity orientation	Family types: consensual,
Conversation orientation	Family norms	protective, pluralistic,
		laissez-faire

IN-CLASS ACTIVITY

Want to know your own family type? Fill out the survey below and tally up your scores to find out.

FAMILY COMMUNICATION PATTERNS (Ritchie & Fitzpatrick, 1990)

Let's learn more about how your family communicates. Rate the following statements from 1 to 5.

Disagree Strongly	Disagree	Neutral	Agree	Agree Strongly

1 ----------- 2 ----------- 3 ----------- 4 ------------- 5

1. In our home, my parents often have the last word.
2. My parents encourage me to challenge their ideas and beliefs.
3. My parents sometimes become irritated with my views if they are different from theirs.
4. In our family we often talk about plans and hopes for the future.
5. My parents often say something like "You'll know better when you grow up."
6. In our family we often talk about topics like politics and religion where some persons disagree with others.
7. My parents often say something like "My ideas are right and you should not question them."
8. My parents often ask my opinion when the family is talking about something.
9. My parents often say something like "A child should not argue with adults."
10. I can tell my parents almost anything.
11. My parents often say something like "There are some things that just shouldn't be talked about."
12. I usually tell my parents what I am thinking about things.
13. My parents often say something like "You should give in on arguments rather than risk making people mad."
14. I really enjoy talking with my parents, even when we disagree.
15. When anything really important is involved, my parents expect me to obey without question.
16. In our family we talk about our feelings and emotions.
17. My parents feel that it is important to be the boss.
18. My parents tend to be very open about their emotions.
19. If my parents don't approve of it, they don't want to know about it.
20. We often talk as a family about things we have done during the day.
21. When I am at home, I am expected to obey my parents' rules.
22. My parents encourage me to express my feelings.

Total of even numbered items _____ (Conversation Orientation)
Total of odd numbered items _____ (Conformity Orientation)

High conversation orientation = scores 33 and above, low = 32 and below
High conformity orientation = 33 and above, low = 32 and below.

High Conversation Orientation

Pluralistic   *Consensual*

Low Conformity   High Conformity
Orientation   Orientation

Laissez-Faire   *Protective*

Low Conversation Orientation

Circle your family type below.

Consensual family – high conversation, high conformity
Pluralistic family – high conversation, low conformity
Protective family – low conversation, high conformity
Laissez-faire – low conversation, low conformity

Extra credit: Ask a few of your family members to take the survey as well. Did their scores reflect the same family type as yours did? If not, don't be alarmed. This is actually quite common in research on multiple people from the same family. Why do you think that might be? Why would a brother and sister in the same family feel their parents communicate differently with them?

OUT-OF-CLASS ACTIVITY/HOMEWORK

Observe 1 hour of parent–child interaction in your own family, on TV, in a movie. Good options include *Parenthood*, *Modern Family*, *Blackish*, *This is Where I Leave You*. Type up a one-page reflection analyzing the interaction based on what you learned today about family communication patterns; conversation and conformity orientation.

REFERENCES

Dorrance Hall, E., McNallie, J., Custers, K., Timmermans, E., Wilson, S., & Van den Bulck, J. (2017). A cross-cultural examination of the mediating role of family support and parental advice quality on the relationship between family communication patterns and first-year college student adjustment in the United States and Belgium. *Communication Research, 44*, 638–667. doi:10.1177/0093650216657755

Koerner, A. F., & Fitzpatrick, M. (1997). Family type and conflict: The impact of conversation orientation and conformity orientation on conflict in the family. *Communication Studies, 48*, 59–75. doi:10.1080/10510979709368491

Koerner, A. F., & Fitzpatrick, M. (2002a). Toward a theory of family communication. *Communication Theory, 12*, 70–91. doi:10.1111/j.468-2885.2002.tb00260.x

Koerner, A. F., & Fitzpatrick, M. A. (2002b). Understanding family communication patterns and family functioning: The roles of conversation orientation and conformity orientation. *Communication Yearbook, 26*, 37–69. doi:10.1080/23808985

Koerner, A. F., & Fitzpatrick, M. (2004). Communication in intact families. In A. L. Vangelisti (Ed.), *Handbook of family communication* (pp. 177–195). Mahwah, NJ: Lawrence Erlbaum Associates.

McLeod, J. M., & Chaffee, S. H. (1972). The construction of social reality. In J. T. Tedeschi (Ed.), *The social influence processes*. Chicago, IL: Aldine Atherton.

Odenweller, K. G., Booth-Butterfield, M., & Weber, K. (2014). Investigating helicopter parenting, family environments, and relational outcomes for millennials. *Communication Studies, 65*, 407–425. doi:10.1080/10510974.2013.811434

Ritchie, L. D. (1991). Family communication patterns: An epistemic analysis and conceptual reinterpretation. *Communication Research, 18*, 548–565. doi:10.1177/009365091018004005

Ritchie, L. D., & Fitzpatrick, M. A. (1990). Family communication patterns: Measuring intrapersonal perceptions of interpersonal relationships. *Communication Research, 17*, 523–544. doi:10.1177/009365090017004007

RELATED READINGS

Phillips, K. E., Ledbetter, A. M., Soliz, J., & Bergquist, G. (2018). Investigating the interplay between identity and communication patterns in predicting relational intentions in families in the United States. *Journal of Communication, 68*, 590–611. doi:10.1093/joc/jqy016

Scharp, K. M., & Dorrance Hall, E. (2018). Testing a mediational model of the family communication patterns on student perceptions of the impact of the college transition through social communication apprehension. *Journal of Applied Communication Research, 46*, 429–446. doi:10.1080/00909882.2018.1502461

Schrodt, P., & Phillips, K. E. (2016). Self-disclosure and relational uncertainty and mediators of family communication and relational outcomes in sibling relationships. *Communication Monographs, 83*, 486–504. doi:1080/03637751.2016.1146406

Schrodt, P., Witt, P. L., & Messersmith, A. S. (2008). A meta-analytical review of family communication patterns and their associations with information processing, behavioral, and psychosocial outcomes. *Communication Monographs, 75*, 248–269. doi:10.1080/03637750802256318

Chapter 6

Family Systems Theory

Family systems theory is one of the most ubiquitous theories for explaining how families work together and are more than the sum of their parts (Yoshimura & Galvin, 2018). This theory describes the family like an organism which adapts to its surroundings and has interdependent parts. This means that when a change happens for one member of the family, it tends to affect all other interdependent family members.

BACKGROUND

Systems theory has a long history, dating back to the 1940s (Wiener, 1948). Originally, it was used to describe phenomena in the natural sciences and was called general systems theory (Von Bertalanffy, 1975).

Wholeness, or holism, refers to looking at the family system as a whole instead of the sum of its parts. Just like you would not want to eat the ingredients of a cupcake one by one, starting with a couple cups of flour and ending with two raw eggs, it is useful to think of the family as a whole rather than individual members added together. There is something more to the family as a whole unit that is not represented when you examine each member separately. Wholeness also captures the idea that systems are made up of two or more interrelated sub-systems. Family **sub-systems** are smaller systems within the system. Common family sub-systems are the partner sub-system, parent–child sub-system, and sibling–sibling sub-system. A family system, then, might be made up of a parent–child sub-system and a partner–partner sub-system.

Communication in Family Contexts: Theories and Processes, First Edition.
Elizabeth Dorrance Hall and Kristina M. Scharp.
© 2020 John Wiley & Sons, Inc. Published 2020 by John Wiley & Sons, Inc.
Companion website: www.wiley.com/go/dorrance_hall/communication-in-family-contexts

The concept of wholeness is important when thinking about the way we study families. More often than not family counselors speak to one family member or researchers survey or interview just one family member about the whole family experience. This is useful, but limited. Researchers are currently exploring ways of capturing the entire family dynamic through newer techniques like social network analysis, or the study of an entire network, and multi-level modeling which allows researchers to examine different levels of the family like the grandparents, parents, and children, and the ways those levels are nested within one another.

Family systems are also **ongoing**, meaning they have a past, present, and a future. Families are unique among social groups in that they provide people with a sense of place in time because families typically have a history of generations going backward in time, and often offer people a sense that generations will span into the future.

Openness is another important concept when thinking of the family as a system. Family systems take in information from the environment and provide feedback into the environment. In other words, families do not exist in isolation. They are affected by what is going on in the world around them, globally, nationally, and locally. They also affect the world around them through the work they do, the way they communicate with others, and what they produce.

Families vary in how open they are, and most families draw some sort of **boundary** around themselves. Boundaries might look like what family rituals friends are allowed to attend. For example, friends might be invited to birthday parties, but not to family holiday celebrations. Families with open boundaries allow members to come and go, whereas families with more closed boundaries would be stricter about who is considered "in" and who is considered "out" of the family.

Feedback refers to how society outside the system responds to the family and how the system responds to others. Feedback might include comments others make about the status of certain family members. For example, in Chapter 17, you will read about an adopted child who heard messages from others like "That is your dad? He doesn't look like you." These kinds of messages can impact the whole family system.

The fact that families can take in feedback and change based on that feedback is related to how **dynamic** families are. Families are ever-changing, and just like a river, they are different from one point in time to the next. Members are added through birth, marriage, adoption, among others, and taken away by death or distance. Communication among the family system is also dynamic. Open, productive communication can easily become conflict-ridden and unproductive. Families come together in times of crisis and drift apart during certain life stages such as middle adulthood. Family members also interact differently over time. Expectations for family members change as members develop and age. The way a mother disciplines her children when they are young is typically very different from her ability to discipline them later on in life.

Families are also like a system in that there is typically a **hierarchy** based on age and gender. Patterns of interaction like decision making, rule enforcement, and support can be organized by the hierarchy of its members. For example, if one sibling is in need of support, the family might look to the head of the family for guidance on who will do what and when to support that member.

Finally, family systems are **self-reflexive**, meaning they are able to examine their own behavior and change. They develop their own goals and can recognize whether or not they are working to meet them. For example, a family whose goal is to improve the quality of the earth for future generations (which they are keenly aware will likely include members of their own family system someday – due to the "ongoing" nature of the family system) might agree to recycle, plant a garden in the yard, and encourage others to reduce the amount of plastic they use. What are some examples of goals your family has as a system?

FAMILY SYSTEM PROCESSES

- **Mutual influence**: Perhaps the most useful insight we can gain from systems theory is that members of a family are **interdependent**. This means that when something happens to one member of the family, it affects the other members. For example, if a teenager broke her leg playing softball, her brother might be affected by having to switch bedrooms so she would not have to go upstairs to bed, her parents might have to plan extra time to take her to school, and the whole family would have to move more slowly when they go out. The communication patterns of certain members affect others in the family. For example, the way parents engage in conflict influences how their children will relate to others as adults.

- **Stability and regularity**: Family systems create patterns, routines, rituals, and rules that members can depend on. Humans like to strike a balance between predictability and novelty, meaning they like to depend on a "normal" schedule or set of traditions, yet also like to shake things up from time to time. If your holiday celebrations are more or less the same every year, you go to your aunt's house on a certain day and eat a meal at your grandparents another day, then your family has developed stability over the holiday ritual.

- **Change**: Families experience healthy reorganization over time whereby members are added, removed, or undergo status changes. Decision-making power in the family, for example, might be handed down through the generations as senior members of the family age or circumstances change like health issues.

- **Equifinality**: The same end state may be reached in many ways. All families work differently and there are many ways to be a family. The goal of creating a supportive, loving, caring family environment can be accomplished in many ways. We see this with regard to the fact that there are all different types of families: adoptive, blended, step, and voluntary kin just to name a few. No one way is right or wrong, just different ways to create a shared vision of reality.

INTERESTING RESEARCH FINDINGS

How Does Having Children Affect the Family System, Especially the Partner Sub-System?

Martina Zemp and her colleagues (2017) surveyed 118 couples with children in Switzerland. She found that the stress of raising children can cause issues for communication among parents and their relationship satisfaction. This study is an excellent illustration of how systems theory works. Adding a child to the system is sure to impact other parts of the system, such as the parental relationship. In fact, she found that one partner's stress about raising the child was linked to the other parent's views about the communication in the relationship. Again, this illustrates how each part of the system influences other parts.

How Does Getting Married Affect the Family System?

Sylvia Mikucki-Enyart along with her team (2015) examined the impact the transition to marriage has on the family system, including how a person's feelings about their new in-laws might impact their freshly committed relationship. In her study, she asked 154 adults about the uncertainty they felt about their in-laws. They were uncertain in three ways. They were uncertain about: their relationship with their partner, the family system, and themselves. She then surveyed 204 more children-in-law and found that their uncertainty was related to their satisfaction with their partner and their in-laws. Learn more about Mikucki-Enyart's research and in-law communication in Chapter 24.

https://pixabay.com/en/background-big-concept-expectation-2410669/

PRACTICAL IMPLICATIONS AND THINGS TO CONSIDER

Think of a time your family has had to come together to deal with an issue or challenge presented by something outside of your family system. For example, your family may have had to deal with a natural disaster, fire, or break-in at your home. Another example might be a family member losing their job or getting in a car accident caused by someone outside of the system.

- How did the family work together in the face of this issue?
- Were any members completely unaffected by the issue?
- Were your family routines and rituals interrupted by this issue? How did the family overcome these interruptions?

KEY TERMS

Boundary
Feedback
Hierarchy
Interdependence

Ongoing
Openness
Self-reflexivity

Social network
Sub-systems
Wholeness

IN-CLASS ACTIVITY

Ask students to draw their family. Leave the instructions vague so that you get different types of drawings to represent family.

Next, ask students what their family drawing looks like. Common shapes include a wheel, a genealogy chart, stick figure drawings, or a chain. Then ask them to compare their drawings with the students sitting near them to identify what is similar or different about the way they represent their families.

Ask what their picture implies about their definition of family. This is a great way to start talking about who gets included in their family system and who does not.

After discussing systems theory, ask students whether their drawing includes any of the concepts they learned, for example, did they draw a boundary around the family? Can they identify how the family is "ongoing" and has a past, present, and future, based on their picture? If they did not include this, how might they add these elements in?

REFERENCES

Mikucki-Enyart, S. L., Caughlin, J. P., & Rittenour, C. E. (2015). Content and relational implications of children-in-law's relational uncertainty within the in-law dyad during the transition to extended family. *Communication Quarterly*, *63*, 286–309. doi:10.1080/01463373.2015.1039714

Von Bertalanffy, L. (1975). *Perspectives on general system theory: Scientific-philosophical studies*. New York, NY: Braziller.

Wiener, N. (1948). Cybernetics. *Scientific American*, *179*, 14–19. doi:10.1038/scientificamerican1148-14

Yoshimura, C. G., & Galvin, K. M. (2018). General systems theory: A compelling view of family life. In D. O. Braithwaite, E. A. Suter, & K. Floyd (Eds.), *Engaging theories in family communication* (2nd ed.). New York, NY: Routledge.

Zemp, M., Nussbeck, F. W., Cummings, E. M., & Bodenmann, G. (2017). The spillover of child-related stress into parents' relationship mediated by couple communication. *Family Relations*, *66*, 317–330. doi:10.1111/fare.12244

RELATED READINGS

Colaner, C. W., & Scharp, K. M. (2016). Maintaining open adoption relationships: Practitioner insights on adoptive parents' regulation of adoption kinship networks. *Communication Studies*, *67*, 359–378. doi:10.1080/10510974.2016.1164208

Weir, K. N., Lee, S., Canosa, P., Rodrigues, N., McWilliams, M., & Parker, L. (2013). Whole family theraplay: Integrating family systems theory and theraplay to treat adoptive families. *Adoption Quarterly*, *16*, 175–200. doi:10.1080/10926755.2013.844216

Whitchurch, G. G., & Constantine, L. C. (1993). Systems theory. In P. G. Boss, W. J. Doherty, R. LaRossa, W. R. Schumm, & S. K. Steinmetz (Eds.), *Sourcebook of family theories and methods: A contextual approach* (pp. 325–352). New York, NY: Plenum Press.

White, J. M., & Klein, D. M. (2008). *Family theories* (3rd ed.). Thousand Oaks, CA: Sage.

Chapter 7
Narrative Theories

Telling stories helps individuals make sense of their lives and develop reasons or justifications for complex events. The terms **narrative** and **story** are often used interchangeably and are communicative performances that share some sort of event with oneself or with others. Many stories include a beginning, middle, and end. Family stories serve a variety of functions including but not limited to social learning (see Chapter 8), identity creation (see Chapter 14), and meaning-making (see Chapter 9). Furthermore, the stories family members tell both reflect and construct what is happening in the family including family and individual well-being. In many ways, telling stories is a way of *doing* family. A common interview question, "Tell me about yourself," can elicit a story. That story often reveals a lot about a person's identity and invokes reflection on family and other forces that have shaped a person into who they are today. There is no single narrative theory that guides our understanding of how narratives work. Therefore, we present three theoretical perspectives that inform many of the questions family communication scholars and students ask.

INTERPRETIVE NARRATIVE APPROACHES

Traditionally, narrative theorizing has largely coincided or been used with **interpretive approaches**. These approaches emphasize the ways language constitutes reality, the experiences of particular communities, and the rich detail that characterizes everyday life. Those interested in interpretive narrative approaches see stories as a way of being in the world and often are interested in relationship processes or identities. For example, Lindsey Thomas (2014) conducted a study using an interpretive narrative approach that illuminated the identities of former foster children. She found that former foster children told stories

Communication in Family Contexts: Theories and Processes, First Edition.
Elizabeth Dorrance Hall and Kristina M. Scharp.
© 2020 John Wiley & Sons, Inc. Published 2020 by John Wiley & Sons, Inc.
Companion website: www.wiley.com/go/dorrance_hall/communication-in-family-contexts

that constructed one of three different identities, (1) victim, (2) survivor, and (3) victor. In concert with taking an interpretive narrative approach, Thomas examined her data using a **thematic narrative analysis** (TNA; Riessman, 2008). TNA is often the corresponding method when using interpretive narrative approaches. This method helps identify either the types of stories people tell and/or the identities people construct in their narratives. By doing so, scholars keep a whole story intact without attending too specifically to the components of each story. In this regard, TNA is a useful method for creating story and identity typologies.

COMMUNICATED NARRATIVE SENSE-MAKING THEORY

Communicated narrative sense-making (CNSM) theory is the newest of narrative theories presented in this chapter and is based on well-established research about storytelling and health. Unlike many of the more interpretive approaches to studying narrative, CNSM is based in the **post-positive tradition** (review Chapter 2 for more about interpretive and post-positive approaches). This means CNSM is about linking components of narratives and the narratives themselves with outcomes like markers of health. According to theorist Jody Koenig Kellas (2018) the main goal of CNSM is to illuminate the communicated content, process, and function of storytelling to explain individual and relational health and well-being. Thus, three assumptions lay the foundation of this theory: (1) narratives are communicated, (2) there is a connection between storytelling and health, and (3) the link between storytelling and health is grounded in the function of narratives which include identity construction, socialization of beliefs and values, sense-making of life disruptions, and relationship connection.

In addition to the three assumptions, there are also three heuristics that guide CNSM theory. The first is **retrospective storytelling**, which suggests that the stories we both hear and tell influence our beliefs, values, behavior, and health in lasting ways. When using retrospective storytelling as a heuristic, scholars often focus on the content of the stories. Even though CNSM is mostly grounded in the post-positive paradigm, sometimes the content of stories is best understood through qualitative methods such as narrative interviews. Koenig Kellas argues that these qualitative examinations might best illuminate her first proposition:

Proposition 1: Retrospective storytelling content conveys individual, relational, and intergenerational meaning-making, values, and beliefs.

Another way scholars have explored the content of the stories has been to look at a narrative's coherence. Coherence has been linked to well-being in many ways and focuses on the extent to which a story is chronological, descriptive, emotionally congruent, shows cause and effect, and has some overall moral or sense-making. In other words, if people are able to tell a fairly coherent story, they might be better off in terms of their well-being. For example, this test of coherence can be applied to stories of family disruption or other trauma. Another avenue might be to explore the connection between redemption and health. For narrative scholars, redemptive stories are marked by the narrator's ability to overcome a negative event, often through hard work or as a result of a higher power. Based on this past research, Koenig Kellas laid out her second proposition:

Proposition 2: When framed positively (e.g., redemptively, prosocially, coherently), the content of retrospective storytelling will be related to better relationship health and well-being.

The second heuristic that guides CNSM is **interactional storytelling**. Interactional storytelling focuses on the ways stories are told in collaboration, or jointly by family members. To capture this type of storytelling, the story must be told by more than one family member. According to Koenig Kellas, there are four verbal and non-verbal behaviors that characterize different levels of sense-making when families tell stories collaboratively: engagement, turn-taking, perspective-taking, and family unit sense-making. These four levels coalesce into interactional sense-making (ISM) where higher levels are marked by warmth and involvement (i.e., engagement), dynamism and distribution of turns (i.e., turn-taking), attentiveness and confirmation (i.e., perspective-taking) as well as organization and integration (i.e., coherence). Based on this, Koenig Kellas proposed the next three propositions:

Proposition 3: Higher levels of interactional sense-making predict higher levels of narrative sense-making.

Proposition 4: Higher levels of interactional sense-making predict higher levels of health and well-being for both individuals and relationships.

Proposition 5: Higher levels of communicated perspective-taking predict higher levels of health and well-being for both individuals and relationships.

The last heuristic is **translational storytelling**. Translational storytelling emphasizes the possibilities of narrative methods, results, and theorizing to inform interventions. Interventions are programs designed to assess, improve, maintain, or modify health or well-being. An intervention could take many forms, such as a documentary, social media campaign, or health campaign. These interventions are designed to help change people's attitudes, beliefs, and/or behaviors with the ultimate goal of facilitating positive outcomes for people's health. For example, scholars have translated their work via plays, school-based interventions, school curriculum, and documentaries, all of which acted as interventions to attempt to change the behavior of others. Translational storytelling interventions often include teaching people how to reframe their narratives more positively and encourage people to make sense of their stories together (with loved ones or with coaches). Given this potential, Koenig Kellas proposed her last two propositions:

Proposition 6: Interventions that promote narrative reflection and sense-making benefit narrators in the context of difficulty, trauma, illness, and/or stress.

Proposition 7: Interventions that incorporate (a) positive narrative (re)framing techniques and/or (b) high levels of interactional sense-making will result in benefits for individuals and families in the context of difficulty, trauma, illness, and/or stress.

Taken together, these seven propositions illustrate the connection between storytelling and well-being/health. Families might be able to support their members in a variety of ways through the stories they tell to and about their family.

NARRATIVE PERFORMANCE THEORY

Narrative performance theory (NPT) was developed in 2004 by Langellier and Peterson. The theory stresses both the performance of stories (i.e., behavior and identity) and the stories' performativity (i.e., the meaning of the performance). Fundamental to NPT are the three orderings: (1) content ordering, (2) task ordering, and (3) group/identity ordering. These orderings exist in a strategic hierarchy which implies that to attend to one necessitates attending to the remaining levels. These orderings coalesce into a **critical theory** that emphasizes that family is simultaneous about the stories that are told as well as the cultural ideologies that influence the tellings (Langellier & Peterson, 2006). For example, a researcher using NPT as a framework may be interested in the stories family members tell about their geographical heritage but simultaneously focus on how culture influences who gets to share that history with the family. Thus, this third perspective focuses on power and performativity instead of experience (i.e., interpretivism) and/or outcomes (i.e., post-positivism).

Content Ordering

Content ordering refers to what makes a particular story memorable and emphasizes the genre which generates and perpetuates the family canon (i.e., set of family stories). In NPT, stories of family (mis)fortune, childhood, romance, births, deaths, and divorce might be sorted at the content level. This sorting draws attention to the function a story plays and the extent to which it can be spoken versus those stories that cannot be spoken. Furthermore, just as certain genres serve different functions, certain ideologies facilitate content ordering and restrict others.

Task Ordering

The second level of the hierarchy is task ordering. Indeed, someone must be the narrator of the story. For example, stories might be performed by a single teller or jointly told with others. Simply, task ordering is the possibility of communication among members in which some serve largely as narrators while others primarily listen.

Group/Identity Ordering

The final, and arguably the most complicated, level is group/identity ordering. In this ordering, family members perform identities that are in constant flux but also embedded in a larger cultural conversation. In this regard, performing family stories allows people to build agency and identity as well as resist major narratives of family. Indeed, it is both in the performance and with focus on performativity that the identities and their meanings take on agentic force.

INTERESTING RESEARCH FINDINGS

Communicated Sense-Making After Miscarriage

Being able to take the perspective of your relational partner is a taxing endeavor, especially when we are in conflict or trying to cope with a major family disruption. In their study, Haley Kranstuber Horstman and Amanda Holman (2017) explored the relationship between communicated perspective-taking (i.e., when conversational partners attend to and confirm each other's views) and couples' individual and relational well-being after miscarriage with 183 married couples. Grounded in communicated narrative sense-making theory, the researchers wanted to see how couples were making sense of their miscarriage. To do this, they engaged in something called actor–partner interdependence modeling. This means they were interested in how wives influenced their husbands and how husbands influenced their wives.

Their analysis found that husbands' perceptions of their wives' communicated perspective-taking (CPT) were positively related to both partners' relational satisfaction and husbands' positive affect about the miscarriage but negatively associated with wives' positive affect. This means that when husbands feel like their wives confirm their views, they are more likely to feel positively about both the marriage and the miscarriage. Alternatively, when wives attend to their husbands, they feel less positively about the miscarriage.

Wives' perceptions of husbands' perspective-taking were also related positively to their own relational satisfaction but negatively to husbands' negative emotion. Again, this means that when wives felt attended to and confirmed they were happier in their marriage, but their husbands felt less positively about the miscarriage.

This research illustrates that although communicated perspective-taking is often good for couples, engaging in this narrative process does not always yield solely positive outcomes. It is possible that women feel undue pressure to provide social support or that couples might internalize their spouses' negative emotions. Scholars and students interested in narrative performance theory might find this a particularly productive site to explore issues of power and performativity.

PRACTICAL APPLICATIONS AND THINGS TO CONSIDER

Stories are a fundamental way family members communicate to each other and to people about their families. It is important to realize that the stories we tell matter for who we think we are and for our own health. Thus, storytelling is an important mechanism by which we might be able to change our own well-being. Indeed, psychologists and other clinicians sometimes use narrative therapy which empowers people to separate themselves from their problems. By doing so, clients of narrative therapy can rewrite their stories and make changes to their thought patterns. Thus, stories can serve as a tool to help people heal from disruption and make sense of their lives.

Research shows that narrative theory, methods, and results also can influence health through intervention. Check out the work of family communication scholars Michelle Miller-Day and Michael Hecht, who developed an international drug prevention intervention called keepin' it REAL. You can view this intervention here: https://real-prevention.com

IN-CLASS ACTIVITY

Think about the stories you tell to and about your family ... and write one down. What types of questions could you answer based on the three perspectives described above? Would you need any other information? What function does this story serve in your family?

Consider: Is there anything that you could and would want to change in your story? Who has power in your stories and who has the power to tell stories about you? What do the stories you tell say about your family members and your relationships? Would other members of your family tell the story in the same way?

KEY TERMS

Coherence
Communicated narrative sense-making
Content ordering
Group/identity ordering
Interactional storytelling

Interpretive narrative approach
Narrative
Narrative performance theory
Retrospective storytelling

Task ordering
Thematic narrative analysis
Translational storytelling

REFERENCES

Koenig Kellas, J. (2018). Communicated narrative sense-making theory: Linking storytelling and well-being. In D. O. Braithwaite, E. A. Suter, & K. Floyd (Eds.), *Engaging theories in family communication* (pp. 62–74). New York, NY: Routledge.

Kranstuber Horstman, H., & Holman, A. (2017). Communicated sense-making after miscarriage: A dyadic analysis of spousal communicated perspective-taking, well-being, and parenting role salience. *Health Communication, 33*, 1317–1326. doi:10.1080/10410236.2017.1351852

Langellier, K., & Peterson, E. E. (2004). Performing narrative in daily life. In K. Langellier & E. E. Peterson (Eds.), *Storytelling in everyday life*. Philadelphia, PA: Temple University Press.

Langellier, K. M., & Peterson, E. E. (2006). "Somebody's got to pick eggs": Family storytelling about work. *Communication Monographs, 73*, 468–473. doi:10.1080/03637750601061190

Riessman, C. K. (2008). *Narrative methods for the human sciences.* Thousand Oaks, CA: Sage.

Thomas, L. J. (2014). "Once a foster child …": Identity construction in former foster children's narratives. *Qualitative Research Reports in Communication, 15*, 84–91. doi:10.1080/17459435.2014.955596

RELATED READINGS

Baxter, L. A., Norwood, K. M, Asbury, B., Jannusch, A., & Scharp, K. M. (2012). Narrative coherence in online stories told by members of the adoption triad. *Journal of Family Communication, 12*, 265–283. doi:10.1080/15267431.2012.686944

Holmberg, D., Orbuch, T. L., & Veroff, J. (2004). *Thrice told tales: Married couples tell their stories.* Mahwah, NJ: Lawrence Erlbaum Associates.

Flood-Grady, E., & Koenig Kellas, J. (2019). Sense-making, socialization, and stigma: Exploring narratives told in families about mental illness. *Health Communication.* Advanced Online Publication. doi:10.1080/10410236.2018.1431016

Kranstuber Horstman, H. (2019). Young adult women's narrative resilience in relation to mother–daughter communicated narrative sense-making and well-being. *Journal of Social and Personal Relationships.* Advanced Online Publication. doi:10.1177/0265407518756543

Langellier, K. M., & Peterson, E. E. (2018). Narrative performance theory: Making stories, doing family. In D. O. Braithwaite, E. A. Suter, & K. Floyd (Eds.), *Engaging theories in family communication* (pp. 210–220). New York, NY: Routledge.

McAdams, D. P. (1993). *The stories we live by: Personal myths and the making of the self.* New York, NY: Guilford.

McAdams, D. P. (2006). *The redemptive self: Stories Americans live by.* New York, NY: Oxford University Press.

Scharp, K. M., Barker, B. A., Rucker, S. N., & Jones, H. (2018). Exploring the identities of hearing parents who chose cochlear implantation for their children with hearing loss. *Journal of Deaf Studies and Deaf Education, 23*, 131–139. doi:10.1093/deafed/enx060

Chapter 8
Social Cognitive Theory

Social cognitive theory, sometimes referred to as social learning theory, explains how we learn from others and represents a key way children learn from their families. Although children can learn positive behaviors such as coping and resilience (Chapter 12) or how to support one another (Chapter 17), they might also learn problematic behaviors such as interpersonal violence (see Chapter 11) or substance abuse (see Chapter 13).

BACKGROUND

Social cognitive theory (SCT), developed in the 1980s by Albert Bandura, describes how socialization works in the family through behavioral modeling. The theory is based on social learning theory and proposes that gaining knowledge can be done through personal experience as well as observation of others (parents, older siblings) and media (Bandura, 1989, 2001). Basically, people learn by interacting with and observing their environment. They also learn from how others react and continue to react to their behavior and communication. In other words, learning in families is reciprocal, ever-changing, and interactive.

KEY CONCEPTS

The following concepts play an important role in how we learn from others and how we ultimately behave and communicate with others.

Communication in Family Contexts: Theories and Processes, First Edition.
Elizabeth Dorrance Hall and Kristina M. Scharp.
© 2020 John Wiley & Sons, Inc. Published 2020 by John Wiley & Sons, Inc.
Companion website: www.wiley.com/go/dorrance_hall/communication-in-family-contexts

Observational Learning

SCT describes how people can learn indirectly from their family members (and others) by seeing how their behavior is either punished or rewarded. For example, we learn just how far we can push our parents by observing our older siblings asking for more freedom as they get older. Rather than having to rediscover exactly how far we can push them when we reach a certain age, we can gather that information by watching older siblings and how their behavior is rewarded or punished by our parents. Children tend to learn manners, values, beliefs, and how the world works from observing their parents, siblings, and other family members. Beyond this, we also learn how to parent, how to love, and how to be a partner by observing our parents and older siblings' relationships.

mohamed_hassan/pixabay

A good example of observational learning focuses on money. How did you learn what was worth spending money on? How about how money should be talked about in public or how to handle financial hardship? Chances are you learned some of this through observing your parents and their relationship with money. You might have also learned from direct conversations with your parents or through taking classes or reading books on money management. These types of learning combine to inform our knowledge base.

Children are not the only ones who learn through modeling; parents learn from their children as well. Parents might observe the benefits of being connected through social media and subsequently model their children's social media behaviors. A major takeaway from this theory is that learning happens *through* communication.

Reinforcements

Reinforcements are communicative reactions to a person's behavior that either work to encourage them to keep doing what they are doing, or discourage them from continuing their behavior. For example, if you take the lead on a group project and your efforts are appreciated and you end up receiving a good grade (grade and appreciation = reinforcement), you are likely to volunteer to take the lead on a future project. If your leadership is met with conflict from other group members or no one listens to you when you try to make suggestions, you likely will not volunteer to take the lead on future projects. Reinforcements over the course of many years shape the way we act today.

Expectations

We can also predict how others will react to us. This alone might get us to do something or stop us from doing something. For example, if a person knows her sister is not likely to agree to split cleaning their shared bathroom, she might not ever ask her to do it. However, if they both really hate the chore, one sister might ask anyway because of the value she places on not having to clean alone. Expectations are based on our previous experiences, so in this case, a lifetime of knowing to what a person is likely to agree.

Self-Efficacy

To do a certain behavior, like parent for the first time, we often have to have the confidence that we can do it. Self-efficacy is our confidence in our ability to successfully perform a behavior or communication act. Our level of self-efficacy is influenced by what others have told us about ourselves, for example, whether our social network has told us we would be good parents. Self-efficacy is also influenced by our past experiences, or whether we have ever completed something like the behavior in the past. In this case, we might have been a nanny, taken care of a niece/nephew, or even taken care of a companion animal. Self-efficacy is influenced by individual factors and barriers to our success that exist in the environment. In this case, we might have financial constraints or other important responsibilities that take our time.

INTERESTING RESEARCH FINDINGS

Social cognitive theory is used to frame a large number of studies because it provides one explanation of how we learn. Whether or not this theory is explicitly referenced in a study, the philosophy behind it informs entire fields of thinking and assumptions we make about how children learn from parents, and how people in general learn.

How Do Siblings Learn About Emotions From One Another?

Laurie Kramer (2014) set out to understand how emotional understanding and regulation can be learned through sibling interaction. She found that children's relationships with their brothers and sisters provide them with ample learning opportunities. Sibling relationships are especially unique because they are long-lasting and, most of the time, involuntary (see Chapter 29 for more on how sibling relationships are unique). This often means that even when siblings fight, as children and as adults, the relationship is less likely to dissolve or "break up." This unique context makes the relationship ideal for learning about challenging communication behavior like emotions. Kramer claims sibling relationships are good contexts for developing words to talk about emotions people experience, figuring out how to identify other people's emotions, and anticipating emotional reactions of others. Sibling relationships also allow us to practice identifying and displaying complex or blended emotions (when we experience more than one emotion at once: happiness and surprise, fear and disgust).

Kramer uses social learning theory, an offshoot of social cognitive theory, to further explain why the sibling relationship is such an important context for learning about emotion. Because emotions are learned the same ways other behaviors are, the claims of social cognitive theory apply to learning how to communicate about emotion, that is, we can learn how to talk about emotions by observing how others express and describe their feelings. We can also learn how people will react to our emotional expressions by observing how others react to our siblings' emotions.

How is Concern for the Environment Passed Down Through Families?

Cecil Meeusen (2014) wanted to understand how concern about the environment, including people's values and beliefs about the environment and nature, were transmitted through generations, in this case, from parents to their children. Specifically, she was interested in how concerns about the environment were transmitted using communication patterns in the family. Using data from 3,426 Belgian adolescents and their parents, she found, perhaps unsurprisingly, that families who communicate regularly about the environment more effectively transmit environmental attitudes to their children. According to social cognitive theory, this might be because children in families who communicate about the environment feel more self-efficacy when it comes to knowing what they can do to help the environment. They also likely see how concern about the environment is rewarded within the family, by engaging in more conversations or parents expressing praise for children who recycle or say no to unnecessary plastic.

Meeusen found some less obvious findings as well including that the gender of the parent did not seem to matter. Mothers and fathers have equal effect on the transmission of environmental concern. In fact, it was a combination of how often the environment was talked about at home and the concern the parents held that predicted a child's environmental concern. SCT might explain this finding because parents who are concerned about the environment might exhibit behaviors (e.g., recycling, taking public transit, using reusable grocery bags) that their children learn to incorporate into their own lives.

PRACTICAL APPLICATIONS AND THINGS TO CONSIDER

The principles of SCT might be at play not only in the everyday family behaviors but also might help shape behaviors that have larger implications. For example, often children learn about religious and political behaviors from watching their families. This could influence not only whether a child grows up to be civilly engaged (e.g., voting, attending political events) but also who they want to represent them. Ultimately, how you behave can have immense implications for those around you.

SOMETHING TO THINK ABOUT

Have you ever caught yourself doing something or saying something that reminds you of a family member? These mimicking behaviors might surprise us, but social cognitive theory helps us understand why we adopt the behaviors and beliefs of our family members.

KEY TERMS

Observation
Reinforcements

Self-efficacy
Social learning

Socialization

IN-CLASS ACTIVITY

Even in the twenty-first century with the majority of women in the workforce, men, on average, do only one-third of the "home work," leaving two-thirds of this work to women (Allen, 2011). Social cognitive theory helps explain why these unequal patterns persist. To illustrate how observing our parents may contribute to unequal division of labor, ask students to journal for five minutes about how they would like household labor to be handled in their future homes. They should imagine who they expect will take care of chores inside the home like cooking, cleaning, and picking up groceries, as well as childcare responsibilities and household maintenance like repairs (on the home and vehicles), lawn care, and landscaping. Next, ask them to recall how the division of labor was handled in their childhood home. They should brainstorm a similar list of tasks and note which family member was responsible for each.

Once they have completed this recall activity, ask them to discuss with a neighbor how their past and future lists are similar and different. Are their expectations for the future based on observed behaviors from the past? Or have they imagined a more equal division of labor for the future? Students should also compare how the division of labor in their childhood homes was similar or different from one another since students' previous experiences will differ. Finally, ask the students to recall any disagreements they remember between their parents or parent-figures concerning household labor. For example, how did their parents decide who would do what? Was there any conflict around this issue at home? After this discussion, students could be taught about the "second shift" many women take on after returning home from their full-time jobs (Hochschild & Machung, 2012).

REFERENCES

Allen, B. J. (2011). Gender matters. In *Difference matters* (2nd ed.). Long Grove, IL: Waveland Press.

Bandura, A. (1989). Human agency in social cognitive theory. *American Psychologist, 44,* 1175–1184. doi:10.1037/0003-066x.44.9.1175

Bandura, A. (2001). Social cognitive theory: An agentic perspective. *Annual Review of Psychology, 52,* 1–26. doi:10.1111/1467-839x.00024

Hochschild, A., & Machung, A. (2012). *The second shift: Working families and the revolution at home.* New York, NY: Penguin.

Kramer, L. (2014). Learning emotional understanding and emotion regulation through sibling interaction. *Early Education and Development, 25,* 160–184. doi:10.1080/10409289.2014.838824

Meeusen, C. (2014). The intergenerational transmission of environmental concern: The influence of parents and communication patterns within the family. *Journal of Environmental Education, 45,* 77–90. doi:10.1080/00958964.2013.846290

RELATED READINGS

Bussey, K., & Bandura, A. (1999). Social cognitive theory of gender development and differentiation. *Psychological Review, 106,* 676–713. doi:10.1037//0033-295x.106.4.676

Kunkel, A., Hummert, M. L., & Dennis, M. R. (2006). Social learning theory: Modeling and communication in the family context. In D. O. Braithwaite & L. A. Baxter (Eds.), *Engaging theories in family communication: Multiple perspectives* (pp. 260–275). Thousand Oaks, CA: Sage.

Segrin, C., Taylor, M. E., & Altman, J. (2005). Social cognitive mediators and relational outcomes associated with parental divorce. *Journal of Social and Personal Relationships, 22,* 361–377. doi:10.1177/0265407505052441

Van Hek, M., & Kraaykamp, G. (2015). How do parents affect cultural participation of their children? Testing hypotheses on the importance of parental example and active parental guidance. *Poetics, 52,* 124–138. doi:10.1016/j.poetic.2015.06.001

Chapter 9

Relational Dialectics Theory

Family relationships are some of the most *meaningful* relationships people have over the course of their lives. But what is meaning and from where does it come? To answer these important questions, family communication scholars often turn to relational dialectics theory (RDT). Originally developed by Baxter and Montgomery (1996) and later rearticulated by Baxter (2011), this **dialogic theory** provides insight into the process of meaning-making. Furthermore, RDT allows researchers to illuminate marginalized and otherwise silenced voices, expose taken-for-granted power structures, and ultimately understand the meaning of any phenomenon in a particular moment in time.

BACKGROUND

Based on the writings of Russian philosopher Mikhail Bakhtin, Baxter and Montgomery introduced a theory that focused attention on the ways competing ideologies produced meaning. For example, Baxter and her colleagues (1997) illustrate how betrayal is only meaningful in light of its counterpart, loyalty. In other words, if no one ever betrayed each other, would we even have to have a term like loyalty? Ultimately, their study described different loyalty demands that people experience in friendships and romantic relationships.

Over time, Baxter grew unsatisfied with the ways scholars were using RDT merely to describe competing ideologies (or what she calls discourses). She realized that not only were discourses competing to make meaning, but they also

Communication in Family Contexts: Theories and Processes, First Edition.
Elizabeth Dorrance Hall and Kristina M. Scharp.
© 2020 John Wiley & Sons, Inc. Published 2020 by John Wiley & Sons, Inc.
Companion website: www.wiley.com/go/dorrance_hall/communication-in-family-contexts

were competing on an unequal playing field. Put simply, some ideas that people value produce advantages whereas ideas that receive less buy-in create marginalizing experiences. In this regard, powerful ideas about the ways things should be and institutional structures like race and gender make it harder for some groups and/or experiences to gain legitimacy. Thus, unlike many of the other theories in this textbook, RDT is a theory focused on power and power inequities. Regardless of how RDT has changed over time, the central proposition of RDT remains: Meaning is made in the interplay of competing, often contradictory, discourses. Below you will find some key concepts that can help shed light on what this means.

KEY CONCEPTS

One of the most demanding aspects of RDT is understanding the theory's key concepts. Indeed, there are many unfamiliar concepts that make RDT one of the most challenging theories to understand and use.

One of the most important things to remember is that people are not making meaning, but rather the discourses that emerge in the text make meaning, and that some texts have more potential for meaning such as stories or rituals. When we mention "texts" we mean anything from transcribed interviews to online stories, blog posts, or even visual signs. Despite the complexity of RDT, it is a valuable theory and will be explained in detail. The following concepts correspond to RDT's new articulation, what Baxter (2011) calls RDT 2.0.

Discourse

A system of meaning; ideology. In any culture, some of these systems of meaning are powerful and guide many of our behaviors. Let's take the discourse of masculinity; this discourse could influence what people wear, the activities in which they participate, and/or how they manage their identities and emotions. For example, in North American culture the discourse of masculinity suggests that men provide for their families or that they should not show too much emotion.

Centripetal Discourse

Dominant or powerful discourses are called centripetal. Centripetal discourses are commonly accepted by a given culture as a way of life. For example, in the United States there is a discourse of intensive mothering that says a mother should intensely care for her child, experience immediate connection with her baby, self-sacrifice, and express unconditional love. When a mother violates this centripetal discourse, she is often punished by other members of the culture and might be labeled as a "bad mother" regardless of the reasons for her behaviors. For example, a mother who does not immediately connect with her child, such as the case of mothers who experience post-partum depression, might be stigmatized by other members of the culture.

Centrifugal Discourse

Some discourses are marginalized in society or sound counter to the norm. Baxter (2011) calls these discourses centrifugal. For example, in the context of marriage, the discourse of rationality (e.g., getting married for financial reasons) is less dominant than a discourse of romanticism (e.g., getting married because it was love at first sight). Voicing a centrifugal discourse allows new meanings to emerge that have the potential to create opportunities for different types of families to exist and encourages the idea that a happy relationship might look a variety of different ways.

Utterance

An utterance is a unit of language marked by the change of who is talking. Thus, an utterance could be one word or even a novel (so long as it is uninterrupted). In other words, an utterance is one turn in talk.

The Utterance Chain

The utterance chain is another term for a web of meaning and illustrates something called intertextuality. This means that communication does not exist independently from the culture or individual relationships. In RDT 2.0, this web of meaning is tied together by four links to create a chain. Each link is defined below.

Distal Links

The distal links of the utterance chain pertain to the discourses that influence the culture at large. They speak to assumptions about the way "things should be" or "the way things are." For example, there is a discourse of politeness that suggests we should respect our grandparents and treat strangers with kindness.

Proximal Links

The proximal links of the utterance chain pertain to the idiosyncratic talk that is particular to a specific relationship with two or more persons. For example, siblings who call each other nicknames (even if it would be rude to call a stranger that nickname) could be engaging in intimacy between family members.

Already-Spoken Links

The already-spoken links of the utterance chain refer to what is culturally under-stood as "the way things are" (distal) or what we might call a relational history (proximal). In other words, already-spoken links are about the conversations we have had and beliefs we hold about the world. The already-spoken links provide the context for people's utterances. For example, people might generally think that identical twins have similar tastes and interests. But it is possible that you know a set of twins who are very different.

Not-Yet-Spoken

The not-yet-spoken links of the utterance chain are the anticipations people make about how anyone (a generalized other) or a particular person might respond to what we say. For example, a family member might have a nickname that they would expect you to use (because you are proximal) but not a stranger (because that is not appropriate at the distal level).

The utterance chain is one of the most essential ideas in understanding RDT. Most often, scholars are more interested in the distal links of the utterance chain because they have more implications for the culture at large.

Contrapuntal Analysis

Contrapuntal analysis is the corresponding method of RDT and falls broadly under the category of critical discourse analysis. What makes contrapuntal analysis a critical method is that it requires researchers to examine the ways discourses vie for power and how people give voice to discourses that resist dominant discourses. Of note, when communication scholars discuss critical theories or critical analyses, they are not referencing criticism. Rather, critical theories and methods are those that focus on power.

In sum, what is important to remember is that RDT researchers are interested in the ways marginalized people communicatively resist the dominant ideologies that oppress them.

WHAT MAKES RELATIONAL DIALECTICS THEORY A COMMUNICATION THEORY?

Many communication scholars adopt theories from other disciplines like psychology and sociology. RDT is unique because it originated from communication scholars and is particularly focused on language and communication. Specifically, people who use RDT as a theoretical framework are interested in how language constitutes reality when competing discourses interplay. When framing research in RDT, researchers should also focus on a specific meaning because multiple meanings might be possible based on emergent discourses and their interplay. Specifically, there are four ways we can think about discursive interplay.

Discursive Interplay

Monologue

Monologue occurs when there is an absence of interplay. This means that one meaning, and one meaning only, dominates an utterance; all other discourses are silent. Monologue is particularly dangerous because it extinguishes alternatives, often marginalizes groups of people, and creates conditions where people have difficulty resisting that which oppresses them. Even discourses that are seemingly "positive" can be dangerous if they are monologic. For example, we have a discourse in our culture that suggests "killing someone else is bad." On its face, it might seem no one would be for endorsing murder, which makes this monologic discourse productive. But on closer inspection, we might be able to identify situations when taking someone's life could be a viable, albeit undesired option (e.g., war, self-defense). Without alternatives like a discourse of self-defense, we might think of a serial killer the same way we think of a small child who defended herself against someone who was trying to abduct her. Thus, it is important to see how monologue might seem attractive at first glance but can be working to create problematic conditions and realities.

Diachronic Separation

The subtlest form of interplay occurs via diachronic separation. This occurs when speakers align themselves with one discourse only to align themselves with a competing discourse as time progresses. Imagine a conversation between two siblings who are trying to decide what they should do one evening. The first sibling suggests that they could meet up with a group of their friends and go to dinner. We might call this a discourse of group inclusivity. Although the other sibling listens to and acknowledges this option, she offers an alternative suggestion where instead of meeting with a large group, the two spend some quality time making dinner and catching up about their social lives. Rather than thinking of this discourse as one of exclusivity, the emphasis is not on leaving others out but rather one of spending quality time together. Thus, we could call this the discourse of one-on-one connection. The first sibling then relates how despite seeing each other often, they never actually get to spend any meaningful time together and thinks that it would be really fun to cook dinner together. Notice that competing here is not about an argument between siblings, but rather a competition between ideologies about how to spend time.

Synchronic Interplay

Unlike diachronic separation where discourses compete over time, synchronic interplay occurs when discourses battle each other within a given utterance. The following terms are strategies and discourse markers that alert a person to synchronic interplay.

Unfolding: This process requires a person to ask, "To what does this utterance respond?" And "What kind of response does this utterance anticipate?" Practically, unfolding helps people make sense of utterances in context.

Negating: Negating occurs when a discourse flat out denies an alternative. Imagine a woman with post-partum depression saying, "I'm not a bad mother!" To understand this utterance, let's practice unfolding. What do we think culturally about mothers who potentially want to harm themselves and their children? Why would a mother with post-partum depression tell people she isn't a bad mother as soon as they hear about her diagnosis? What other discourse might be competing with the discourse of intense mothering here?

Countering: Countering occurs when one discourse replaces another discourse, often marked by words like "but" or "even." For example, a person might say, "I love my spouse but I also need some time to myself." In this example, the discourse of connection is countered by the discourse of autonomy.

Entertaining: Entertaining occurs when one discourse acknowledges the possibility of another. We can see entertaining in this sentence, "He might be a good dad one day." In this example, it is possible that the discourse of bad fathering entertains the discourse of good fathering.

Dialogic Transformation

The most expansive type of interplay comes in the form of dialogic transformation. Expansive interplay means that there is the potential for new meanings to emerge.

Discursive Hybrid

When two or more discourses (still distinct) combine to form a new meaning. An example of a discursive hybrid might be when oil and vinegar form salad dressing. In this sense, a discursive hybrid suspends competition momentarily.

Aesthetic Moment

When two or more discourses fundamentally change and transform into a new meaning. An example of an aesthetic moment might be when water and hydrogen form into water. Whereas discursive hybrids are logical, aesthetic moments are more emotional. This type of dialogic transformation holds the most potential.

Did You Know?

Many family communication scholars use RDT when they want to understand more about discourse-dependent families (see Chapter 14). For example, Beth Suter and her colleagues (2015) used RDT to frame their study about lesbian motherhood. They explored how the discourse of queer motherhood competes with a discourse of essential motherhood to create a space for new possibilities for what it can mean to be a mother. To learn more about LGBTQ families, take a look at Chapter 26.

INTERESTING RESEARCH FINDINGS

Answering Questions Using Relational Dialectics Theory: Exploring the Meaning of the Parent–Child Relationship

Your textbook author has explored meanings in a variety of family contexts such as adoption, cohabitation, and parent–child estrangement. Indeed, scholars who use RDT to frame their studies often are interested in stigmatized experiences (e.g., mental illness, disability) or marginalized family types (e.g., foster adoption, lesbian parents). For example, Scharp interviewed 52 adult children who distanced themselves from their parents because of an ongoing negative relationship or what she calls parent–child estrangement. Along with Lindsey Thomas she engaged in a contrapuntal analysis to see how the competing discourses these adult children voiced gave meaning to the parent–child relationship (Scharp & Thomas, 2016).

First, the authors were interested to see what discourses emerged in the adult children's talk. They identified two groups of themes that combined into two separate discourses. The first group of themes were: (1) parents–children are forever connected through biology, (2) family webs create unending obligations and interactions, and (3) shared history is irreplaceable. These three themes combined to create a discourse of relationship endurance. The second group of themes were: (1) parent–child relationships require maintenance, (2) parents and children support and take care of one another, (3) parents and children love one another, and (4) individual needs outweigh the dyad. These four themes combined to create a discourse of temporal contingency.

After Scharp and Thomas identified the discourses, they then turned to the most important component of a contrapuntal analysis: examining the interplay. They found these two discourses competed through diachronic separation and through synchronic interplay in the forms of negating, countering, and entertaining. They also were encouraged to see dialogic transformation in the form of a discursive hybrid. For example, for some adult children, the only way for them to become close to their parent was by moving further away.

Theoretically, this study helped challenge the idea that (1) biological families are tied together forever, (2) family relationships do not require maintenance because they cannot end, (3) ongoing/unresolved family conflict will be resolved without consequences, (4) family closeness is always positive, and (5) biology and love are synonymous. Specifically, they introduced the idea of relational moral hazard which occurs when family members treat each other worse than other people who they believe might exit the relationship, just like people who engage in riskier behaviors because they have health insurance. Practically, this analysis helped illuminate some of the misconceptions people have about the parent–child relationship and family estrangement more broadly. These misconceptions were then translated to the public via a newspaper article in *The New York Times*. You can read about it here: https://www.nytimes.com/2017/12/20/well/family/debunking-myths-about-estrangement.html

PRACTICAL APPLICATIONS AND THINGS TO CONSIDER

RDT is an important theory not only because it helps shed light on meaning, but also because it draws attention to power disparities such as the example above about debunking estrangement myths. RDT might also help researchers identify target audiences. For example, Baxter and her colleagues (2004) used RDT to develop a community-based public health media campaign on the topic of drinking during pregnancy. Their findings suggest that two competing discourses were voiced in a sample of 60 women's attitudes, beliefs, and behaviors surrounding pregnancy and alcohol consumption. For example, the discourse of individualism represented a belief that pregnant women are in charge of their own bodies and that others should not interfere. Alternatively, a discourse of responsible motherhood sug-gested that women assume responsibility to put their babies' interests above their own. Based on this analysis, the authors created a campaign that spoke to both of these discourses by emphasizing (a) the health risks to the baby and (b) the long-term costs for a mother faced with raising a child with Fetal Alcohol Syndrome. The analysis also revealed a second target audience who might be able to influence the pregnant mothers' behaviors: other women such as mothers, sisters, aunts, close female cousins, and close female friends. These examples illustrate the ways that RDT research reaches the public and the potential influence it has to change people's ideas and behaviors.

THOUGHT ACTIVITY

Think about the TV show *Modern Family*, which features different configurations of what a family can be. What are some of the assumptions the families on this show have to resist? Where do those assumptions come from? Also think about the ways these families respond … Can you identify the ideologies that are competing?

KEY TERMS

Already-spoken links
Centrifugal
Centripetal
Countering
Diachronic separation

Dialogic transformation
Discourse
Distal links
Entertaining
Monologue

Negating
Not-yet-spoken
Proximal links
Synchronic interplay
Utterance

"What's the Worst that Could Happen?" Voicing Discourses of Unintended Pregnancy

CASE STUDY BY LINDSEY J. THOMAS

"You're finally giving up smokes? About damn time! I'm proud of you for making a healthy decis-"

"I'm pregnant," May interrupted, "so I'm pretty sure I don't deserve any accolades at the moment."

"Whoa, dropping a lunch break bombshell! Sounds like you're not thrilled about this. How can I support you?" responded Dani, May's work spouse, without missing a beat.

"I don't know. I wasn't going to tell anyone at work, at least not yet, but, well, you're more than just a coworker. You know my family stuff. Hell, you *are* my family! I'm not thrilled. I'm also not *not* thrilled. I don't know how I should feel about it. Or what to do."

"It makes sense that you have complicated feelings. Do you want to unpack while I listen?" Dani gently prodded.

May contemplated aloud, "Well, when I was little, I saw firsthand how much Abigail struggled as a single mom. I mean, all four of us kids ended up in foster care. I know I'm in a better place than her health-wise though, and I have family now, *real* family, people who are *there* for me. Still, sometimes I see similarities, find myself snapping at someone I love, or a couple years ago when I forgot your birthday, and I worry that there's enough of her in me that I wouldn't be able to handle a kid. If it went well, it would be nice to really see myself in another person though, you know?"

"Nature AND nurture, May. You are not destined to be your biological mother," Dani reminded gently.

"Maybe, maybe not," May responded, "but we come from *somewhere*. Even when I think about my foster parents, there are so many mixed messages. I remember when another girl in one of the houses got pregnant, the foster mom just kept telling her that babies are a gift to be cherished at all costs. She was fifteen and in foster care!"

"The girl or the mom?" Dani asked, trying to lighten the mood.

"Shut up," said May. "This is serious. The mom, who I think was more interested in having a baby around than offering guidance."

"Yikes. No, I know it's serious. I'm sorry. You're not fifteen though. Do *you* think babies are a gift?"

"Not at fifteen! But you're right. I'm a decade older, and you know how much I enjoy working with kids. Plus, I LOVED the babies that stayed at Miss Alice's when I lived there. She used to tell me I'd be a great mom someday, if I ever wanted to." May laughed, "After college, of course – you know she was always my academic champion. But, I also remember worrying I might be pregnant my junior year of college and thinking I'd rather be dead! Those feelings are hard to shake. And, it's not like this was planned – maybe it's STILL the worst thing that could happen to me!" May exclaimed.

Dani's voice was calm. "May," they asked, "do you really think this is the worst thing that could happen to you?"

"Ugh, no," May sighed, "but I don't have a plan. And I really don't know what to do. I wish Miss Alice was here. I almost called Abigail when I found out, but she'd just talk about how much work kids are. Plus, I really don't want her to know that she technically might have a grandchild on the way."

"You have a little time to think about it. What's your gut say?"

"My head says I'm not ready, but my heart says no one ever feels fully ready for the responsibility of a tiny human," May said, as their server approached the table. "My gut says it wants this food."

CASE STUDY DISCUSSION QUESTIONS

1. What meanings could be examined through May and Dani's exchange?
2. Which discourses create meanings (e.g., of pregnancy or babies) that emerge in May and Dani's talk?
3. When May describes her feelings surrounding babies, what are some related ways that others have described babies in the past or might describe babies in the future?
4. How are the discourses you have identified interplaying in May and Dani's conversation?

REFERENCES

Baxter, L. A. (2011). *Voicing relationships*. Thousand Oaks, CA: Sage.

Baxter, L. A., Hirokawa, R., Lowe, J. B., Nathan, P., & Pearce, L. (2004). Dialogic voices in talk about drinking and pregnancy. *Journal of Applied Communication Research*, *32*, 224–248. doi:10.1080/0090988042000240158

Baxter, L. A., Mazanec, M., Nicholson, J., Pittman, G., Smith, K., & West, L. (1997). Everyday loyalties and betrayals in personal relationships. *Journal of Social and Personal Relationships*, *14*, 655–678. doi:10.1177/0265407597145005

Baxter, L. A., & Montgomery, B. M. (1996). *Relating: Dialogues and dialectics*. New York, NY: Guilford.

Scharp, K. M., & Thomas, L. J. (2016). Family "bonds": Making meaning of parent–child relationships in estrangement narratives. *Journal of Family Communication*, *16*, 32–50. doi:10.1080/15267431.2015.1111215

Suter, E. A., Seurer, L. M., Webb, S., Grewe, B., & Koenig Kellas, J. (2015). Motherhood as contested ideological terrain: Essentialist and queer discourses of motherhood at play in female–female co-mothers' talk. *Communication Monographs*, *82*, 458–483. doi:10.1080/03637751.2015.1024702

RELATED READINGS

Sahlstein Parcell, E., & Baker, B. M. A. (2018). Relational dialectics theory: A new approach for military and veteran-connected family research. *Journal of Family Theory & Review, 10,* 672–685. doi:10.1111/jftr.12279

Scharp, K. M., & Thomas, L. J. (2017). "What would a loving mom do today?": Exploring the meaning of motherhood in stories of pre-natal and post-partum depression. *Journal of Family Communication, 17,* 401–414. doi:10.1080/15267431.2017.1355803

Suter, E. A., Baxter, L. A., Seurer, L. M., & Thomas, L. J. (2014). Discursive construction of the meaning of "family" in narratives of foster adoptive parents. *Communication Monographs, 81,* 59–78. doi:10.1080/03637751.2014.880791

Suter, E. A., & Seurer, L. M. (2018). Relational dialectics theory. In D. O. Braithwaite, E. A. Suter, & K. Floyd (Eds.), *Engaging theories in family communication.* (pp. 244–254). New York, NY: Routledge.

Thomas, L. J., Jackl, J. A., & Crowley, J. L. (2017). "Family? … Not just blood": Discursive constructions of "family" in adult, former foster children's narratives. *Journal of Family Communication, 17,* 238–253. doi:10.1080/15267431.2017.1310728

PART II

Family Communication Processes

Foundational Processes

Chapter 10

Caregiving in Families

Caregiving can occur at any stage of life and is one of the primary functions family members fulfill for one another. When humans are young, they are cared for by parents and when parents are old, they are sometimes cared for by their children and/or other family members. In fact, it is not just the beginning and end of life when caregiving is needed. People need support throughout the lifespan, especially when dealing with health issues, caregiving for others, living with disabilities, or experiencing unexpected challenges.

CAREGIVING AND COMMUNICATION

Caregiving is centrally related to communication because it is often done through communication. This is especially true of providing support to those needing care. In fact, caregiving often requires information management for young children and information seeking for older adults (see Chapter 16). Communication in general tends to shift over the life course where middle-aged parents typically initiate communication with their adult children, then over time, the adult children start to initiate more of the communication as their parents age. The same shifts happen for giving care beyond checking in with these family members.

Caregiving is a gendered activity. Though men can be excellent caregivers, these duties still typically fall to women. Kinkeeping, a related concept, tends to be done by women, though not exclusively. Kinkeeping is the work of keeping in touch with and caring for family, and is needed to maintain all family relationships, though especially extended family ones that might be in contact less

Communication in Family Contexts: Theories and Processes, First Edition.
Elizabeth Dorrance Hall and Kristina M. Scharp.
© 2020 John Wiley & Sons, Inc. Published 2020 by John Wiley & Sons, Inc.
Companion website: www.wiley.com/go/dorrance_hall/communication-in-family-contexts

mohamed_hassan/pixabay

often (Leach & Braithwaite, 1996). Kinkeeping work includes planning events like birthday parties and holidays, calling relatives, providing support, and sharing information to keep family members informed. Family storytelling (i.e., telling stories to and about the family) is a primary way for members to kinkeep and pass along important information about the family to younger generations (see Chapter 7 for more about family storytelling). Although an important task, the pressure to maintain the family can be hard emotional, financial, and physical work. Research from the 1990s suggests kinkeeping is linked to distress, especially when it interferes with a person's paid work.

CAREGIVING FOR CHILDREN

Caregiving for children is both rewarding and stressful for new parents. New parents experience stress from lack of sleep, role strain, and household division of labor after having a baby (Pinquart & Teubert, 2010). Women often experience even more stress as they are typically the primary caregivers and are biologically able to perform some tasks such as breastfeeding. Even when both partners have careers, most of the household work falls to the woman in the relationship.

As more evidence that the family is truly a system (see Chapter 6), having a child impacts the spousal relationship. In fact, relationship satisfaction between spouses tends to decrease after having a child as a result of engaging in more conflict and less communication about the relationship. The focus tends to be on the baby instead of maintaining the partnership. It is not all doom and gloom after having a child, though. A good amount of research has been dedicated to what makes the transition to parenthood easier on people. Researchers have found that having high self-esteem, sense of control over one's life, social support from one's partner, friends, and family, sharing ideas about gender roles with one's partner, and having access to childcare classes at local hospitals or community centers, all work to decrease the stress people experience when learning to be a parent.

Parents are not the only people tasked with caregiving for children. It is also common for grandparents to be part-time or primary caregivers for their grandchildren (see Chapter 25). Studies have shown that grandmothers who are primary caregivers are often not provided with enough emotional support and have high levels of depression, anxiety, and stress.

Caregiving does not stop when children turn 18. Most middle-aged parents continue to support their adult children to various degrees after they move away from home. Parents continue to provide emotional support over text, phone, or video chat, give advice, and send money, among other things. Some parents take this support too far and provide developmentally inappropriate support to their adult children in the form of over-parenting or helicopter parenting. You can read more about the trends and outcomes of over-parenting in Chapter 27. It may sound like a burden to continue supporting children after they have grown, but many parents feel great joy in providing support, especially emotional support, to their children.

KEY THEORY

Attachment theory was developed to explain the long-lasting outcomes of different types of caregiving. John Bowlby created attachment theory in the 1960s after observing the reactions of children who were separated from their parents. His theory, along with research by Mary Ainsworth, explains that children attach to their parents naturally, often by physically being near them, to survive. The way their parents provide care in response will shape the way they relate to the world. Specifically, infants are hard-wired to engage in a variety of attachment behaviors such as visual checking, signaling to establish contact, and moving to establish contact (e.g., clinging). If their primary caregiver, whoever that might be, is sufficiently near, attentive, responsive, and approving, children become secure in their attachment. Parents or caregivers who are inconsistent, unpredictable, or unavailable tend to have children who are insecurely attached.

As Bowlby predicted, the attachments children form when they are young continue to be important in adulthood. Yet, people do not always maintain the attachment style they developed in infancy. Indeed, large-scale events might disrupt attachment styles like the death of a family member or a marriage. People might even develop different attachment styles for different kinds of relationships. Furthermore, changes in communication behaviors could also lead to a change in style over time. Although changing styles is not easy or does not happen overnight, certainly people with insecure styles can work toward becoming secure. To learn more about the specific attachment styles, refer to Chapter 27 on parent–child relationships.

CAREGIVING FOR ADULTS

Caregiving for friends and relatives occurs due to illness, a disability, or end-of-life. Caregiving for older adults is becoming more common. In fact, according to the National Health and Aging Trends Study (2011), 15 million Americans provide unpaid care to an older adult. Those same caregivers are more likely to have physical and emotional health problems than people who are not engaged in substantial caregiving. Research has found that supportive, understanding communication and care from family members can lessen the burden of living with an illness.

Caregiving tends to bring out positive and negative feelings in all parties involved. Caregivers might feel positive about the support they are able to provide while also experiencing negative feelings toward the burden and amount of time spent in their caregiving role. Those being cared for might feel close to their caregiver and positive about the time they are able to spend with family, yet feel negatively about their inability to do things for themselves.

Two types of caregivers include hands-on and long-distance. The communication patterns of these two types of caregivers are different. **Hands-on** caregivers likely get to spend more time with the older adult and have a better sense of their health status because they are able to physically see them but might also feel resentment toward the long-distance caregivers as most of the caregiving responsibility falls on them.

Family members might fill the **long-distance** caregiver role when they are involved in caregiving part-time due to living away from the family member in need. Long-distance caregivers depend on their family members who live closer to the aging adult to share important information with them, otherwise they are left reading between the lines to figure out their family members' health status. According to Jennifer Bevan and Lisa Sparks (2011), long-distance caregiving has serious relational and health implications. These types of caregivers might feel guilty for not being closer, not doing enough, or might feel jealous that the family members who live closer are able to provide more care.

Because the family is a system (see Chapter 6), caregiving for a parent affects the lives of more than just the parent and the caregiver. Research has shown that for couples who have had a parent move in with them for caregiving help, husbands felt there was more interference in their day-to-day lives and in the bigger picture (for example, planning for the future). While the elderly parent might be able to help with household duties or caregiving for small children in the family, they often create more work for the couple. Other cultures outside of North America have more experience managing multigenerational households. The increase in life expectancies across the globe will, at the very least, increase communication across generations and will likely result in more multigenerational families living under one roof.

According to Jose Postigo and Rigoberto Honrubia (2010), people have both negative and positive ideas and beliefs about co-residency, or multiple generations of family members living together, usually including elderly people. For example, all three generations they examined believe that grandparents entertain grandchildren with stories of the past and that elderly people can have good quality of life. Grandparents and grandchildren do not believe co-residence with grandparents is very relaxed. The researchers found that the middle adult or parent generation had the most negative outlook on co-residence with elderly family members including that elderly people take up a lot of time and that they use their illness as a defense. For more information about intergenerational relationships, see Chapter 25.

INTERESTING RESEARCH FINDINGS

What is it Like to Caregive for Someone with Alzheimer's Dementia?

Denise Polk (2005) conducted a study to learn more about the uncertainty experienced by caregivers of people with Alzheimer's dementia. She interviewed seven caregivers who were related to the Alzheimer-affected person by blood or marriage once a month for six months and found that caregivers make attributions, or justifications and reasoning to make sense of why someone did or said something, about pleasure and displeasure. In fact, the caregivers felt quite confident in knowing when their loved ones experienced pleasure. They felt less certain about their abilities to assess displeasure. She also identified tools caregivers use for managing uncertainty including gaining knowledge and, as a result, confidence in their attributions and ability to handle future challenges. Distractions were another tool caregivers used to fill time, decrease agitation, and keep up social involvement.

How do People Kinkeep Online?

A team of Malaysian researchers led by Fazillah Kamal (2016) set out to bring the kinkeeper concept into today's digital age by conducting a study about the digital kinkeeper, one who performs kinkeeping duties using mobile social messaging technology. The researchers found that, like offline kinkeepers, most digital kinkeepers are women. They are often the first to communicate to their virtual family group at the beginning of a day through greetings, reminders of events, sending a photo or emoji, or announcing family news.

KEY TERMS

Attachment theory
Caregiving
Hands-on caregiving

Long-distance caregiving
Kinkeeping

IN-CLASS OR OUT-OF-CLASS ACTIVITY

Brainstorm theoretically driven (i.e., based on theory you have learned about in this class) ways you could support someone you know who is currently caregiving for a young child, a sick adult family member (not elderly), and an older adult. Divide a piece of paper into three columns and make three lists, one list with ways to support a caregiver of a young child, one for the sick adult, and one for the caregiver of the older adult who is at the end-of-life.

1. How are the lists similar? Are there some types of support that work for all caregivers?
2. How are the lists different? Are there some supportive actions that only apply to certain situations?

REFERENCES

Bevan, J. L., & Sparks, L. (2011). Communication in the context of long-distance family caregiving: An integrated review and practical applications. *Patient Education and Counseling, 85*, 26–30. doi:10.1016/j.pec.2010.08.003

Kamal, F. M., MdNoor, N., & Baharin, H. (2016, June). *"Silence is golden no more" in family digital environment: Understanding the kinkeeper role through mobile social messaging system.* Paper presented at the Twenty-Fourth European Conference on Information Systems (ECIS), Istanbul, Turkey.

Leach, M. S., & Braithwaite, D. O. (1996). A binding tie: Supportive communication of family kinkeepers. *Journal of Applied Communication Research, 24*, 200–216. doi:10.1080/00909889609365451

National Health and Aging Trends Study. (2011). Retrieved from https://www.nhats.org/

Pinquart, M., & Teubert, D. (2010). A meta-analytic study of couple interventions during the transition to parenthood. *Family Relations, 59*, 221–231. doi:10.1111/j.1741-3729.2010.00597.x

Polk, D. M. (2005). Communication and family caregiving for Alzheimer's dementia: Linking attributions and problematic integration. *Health Communication, 18*, 257–273. doi:10.1207/s15327027hc1803_4

Postigo, J. M. L., & Honrubia, R. L. (2010). The co-residence of elderly people with their children and grandchildren. *Educational Gerontology, 36*, 330–349. doi:10.1080/03601270903212351

RELATED READINGS

Baldassar, L., Wilding, R., & Baldock, C. (2007). Long-distance caregiving: Transnational families and the provision of aged care. In I. Paoletti (Ed.), *Family caregiving for older disabled people*. New York, NY: Nova Science Publishers.

Burton, L. M., & Devries, C. (1992). Challenges and rewards: African American grandparents as surrogate parents. *Generations: Journal of the American Society on Aging, 16*, 51–54.

Collins, N. L., & Feeney, B. C. (2000). A safe haven: An attachment theory perspective on support seeking and caregiving in intimate relationships. *Journal of Personality and Social Psychology, 78*, 1053–1073. doi:10.1037//0022-3514/78.61053

Copeland, D. B., & Harbaugh, B. L. (2010). Psychosocial differences related to parenting infants among single and married mothers. *Issues in Comprehensive Pediatric Nursing, 33*, 129–148. doi:10.3109/01460862.2010.498330

Gerstel, N., & Gallagher, S. K. (1993). Kinkeeping and distress: Gender, recipients of care, and work–family conflict. *Journal of Marriage and the Family, 55*, 598–608. doi:10.2307/353341

Stamp, G. H., & Banski, M. A. (1992). The communicative management of constrained autonomy during the transition to parenthood. *Western Journal of Communication, 56*, 281–300. doi:10.1080/10570319209374417

Wittenberg, E., Buller, H., Ferrell, B., Koczywas, M., & Borneman, T. (2017a). Understanding family caregiver communication to provide family-centered cancer care. *Seminars in Oncology Nursing, 33*, 507–516. doi:10.1016/j.soncn.2017.09.001

Wittenberg, E., Kravits, K., Goldsmith, J., & Ferrell, B. (2017b). Validation of a model of family caregiver communication and caregiver outcomes. *Palliative & Supportive Care, 15*, 3–11. doi:10.1917/S1478951516000109

Chapter 11

Conflict and Forgiveness

Conflict is an inevitable part of any relationship. According to Hocker and Wilmot (2014), conflict is an "expressed struggle between two interdependent parties who perceive incompatible goals, scarce resources, and interference from others in achieving their goals" (p. 13). Given that all families are interdependent systems (see Chapter 6), it might come as no surprise that family members experience conflict both at the interpersonal level (e.g., conflict between two or more members) and the family level (e.g., conflict between members of the family and third parties). When family members want to repair their relationship after conflict, they might seek or grant forgiveness. This chapter focuses on both the processes of conflict and forgiveness.

BACKGROUND

Conflict and forgiveness are studied in a variety of fields and by many different types of scholars including those in Communication Studies. In families, how members engage in conflict often is a product of their family communication environment (see Chapter 5). For example, Koerner and Fitzpatrick (2002) suggest that how open a family is and how much they value shared beliefs and attitudes influences how they handle conflict at home and can even influence how people handle romantic conflict later in life. Research on attachment styles (see Chapter 27) also suggests that the relationship between parent and child (secure or insecure) can influence people's ability to resolve conflict up to 20 years later (Simpson,

Communication in Family Contexts: Theories and Processes, First Edition.
Elizabeth Dorrance Hall and Kristina M. Scharp.
© 2020 John Wiley & Sons, Inc. Published 2020 by John Wiley & Sons, Inc.
Companion website: www.wiley.com/go/dorrance_hall/communication-in-family-contexts

Collins, & Salvatore, 2011). Generally, destructive marital conflict can have negative effects for both the couple and, if present, their children. Research suggests that the presence of ongoing negative conflict can have even worse effects for children than if the parents get a divorce or otherwise dissolve their romantic relationship and the conflict lessens. **Put simply, destructive family conflict affects all members of the family and can have long-lasting effects.** The key concepts below show how some conflict can be destructive whereas other conflict can be an opportunity for positive change. We also discuss key concepts important to the forgiveness process.

KEY CONCEPTS: THE PROCESS OF CONFLICT

Components of Conflict

Based on the definition, there are three ingredients for conflict. Below we discuss each ingredient and what it might look like within the family.

(Perceived) Incompatible Goals

Typically, people engage in conflict over issues that are important to them. Although sometimes people have goals that are mutually exclusive, in other words, they cannot both occur and it is impossible for both people to get what they want, other times merely perceptions of incompatible goals create unsatisfactory situations. People might perceive their goals as incompatible either when they want the same thing or different things. For example, when one sibling wants the attention of her parents and the other sibling wants the attention of his parents, they might experience incompatible goals. Alternatively, two people might want very different things. For example, family members might perceive incompatible goals when one parent wants to save money and the other parent wants to take a vacation. Because people have both primary (e.g., go on vacation) and secondary goals (e.g., maintaining a positive relationship with one's spouse), many opportunities exist for family members to perceive incompatible goals. **In brief, conflict occurs when two people perceive they have incompatible goals.**

(Perceived) Scarce Resources

Resources can either be real or perceived as real. Typically, resources are a positive physical, social, or economic material, behavior, and/or asset. For example, although we typically think of money as a resource, affection might also be a resource for family members. When family members perceive a resource to be scarce, they might engage in conflict. Let's think back to the example of the siblings who are vying for their parents' attention. In this scenario, the siblings might consider attention to be a scarce resource if they think their parents only have so much attention to give. To address perceptions of scarcity, people might try changing others' perception that the resource is scarce or reallocate resources in a more equitable way. Parents might assure these siblings that they have plenty of attention for both of them. Unfortunately, some resources really are scarce. In these cases, people's sense of power and self-esteem are often at stake. In this regard, family members who are in conflict often perceive they have too little power and self-esteem or that another family member has too much.

(Perceived) Interference

When family members obstruct other members' ability to achieve their goals or a third party obstructs a family from achieving its goals, they might find themselves in conflict. Thus, perceived interference is the last ingredient for conflict. Interference can also become problematic for family members when members assume they know why another member interfered with their goals. When people think they know the motives behind someone else's behavior without engaging in conversation, they often commit something called the **fundamental attribution error**. The fundamental attribution error occurs when people place too much emphasis on the characteristics of another person and not enough emphasis on contributing environmental factors. For example, if a family member shows up late to a family event, other members might assume that he did not want to come to the event or that he is simply lazy instead of considering the possibility he was in a traffic jam or helping a coworker in need. Consequently, without honest communication, it is possible that family members will escalate their conflict or repeat the same conflict over and over (i.e., serial arguments).

Distributive and Integrative Conflict

When thinking about conflict distributively, some family members walk away winners whereas others walk away losers. Distributive conflict is characterized by positions, outcomes, and the idea of scarcity. Taking a distributive approach means family members are in a zero-sum game where there are inevitable victors and losers. Alternatively, an integrative approach to conflict is characterized by a win-win mentality and focuses on needs instead of positions, process instead of outcomes, and abundance versus scarcity. An integrative perspective opens up the possibility for collaborative conflict and requires a fundamental shift in how people communicate in and about conflict.

Conflict Styles

Even though we might engage in different communication patterns depending on the person, relationship, and/or situation, research suggests that people often default to particular patterns when they engage in conflict. When thinking about the five conflict styles, most correspond to a distributive approach where there are some winners and some losers. Of note, conflict styles are often dependent on cultural norms and one's own perception of their style might be different from others' perceptions. Based on two axes, (1) concern for self and (2) concern for others, we now discuss the five conflict styles.

1. **Avoiding**: When family members ignore or stay away from conflict they are engaging in avoiding behaviors. Avoiding behaviors might include physically staying away or ignoring important conversations. For example, a son may avoid engaging in conversations about his future with his parents if he knows they often lead to conflict. A grown son may ignore the signs that his father should no longer be driving by avoiding riding with him because he does not want to have to tell his father he should not be on the road. Family members who engage in avoidance behaviors generally think of conflict negatively and have a low concern for both themselves and others since ignoring the problem means that neither side gets what they want (lose-lose). Although avoiding behaviors can be unsatisfying for people in the long term, sometimes, avoiding a conflict can be productive. In fact, some couples are satisfied when they repeatedly avoid conflict. Overall, research suggests that partners of avoiders tend to feel more frustrated and uncomfortable than those who can manage their conflict constructively (Harper & Welsh, 2007). Research also suggests that couples with low levels of commitment are more likely to use the silent treatment, which is one method of avoiding conflict (Wright & Roloff, 2009).

2. **Accommodating/Obliging**: Family members who prefer to accommodate during conflict have low concern for themselves getting what they want and have a high concern for what others want (lose-win). During conflict, obliging members defer to the other member and do not assert their own points of view, desires, or needs. For many accommodators, they might even anticipate the needs of another family member to prevent the conflict altogether without the other member ever knowing the other person would have preferred something different. Although people might like to be in a relationship with someone who has an accommodating style, this can become extremely taxing for the person doing the obliging. In some instances, accommodators might become bitter or sometimes seem to explode with no warning, leaving their relational partners confused.

3. **Competing/Dominating**: People who engage in a competing or dominating style take a win-lose approach to conflict. They are characterized by a high concern for self (and getting what they want) and a low concern for others. Family members with this style might appear like they highly value certain issues but they might also appear to want to win at any cost. To "win" the conflict, family members might engage in indirect strategies designed to punish another member without direct confrontation (i.e., passive aggression). These strategies might include guilt, eye rolling, and/or sarcasm. Other times, someone with a dominating style might be directly aggressive, most often in the form of a threat. These behaviors might also include physical attacks or any number of verbal attacks (e.g., questioning someone's competence, character, physical appearance, swearing). Communication partners of dominators often feel humiliated, desperate, depressed, and/or hopeless. Given that people have multiple goals, winning a battle might ultimately lose family members the war.

4. **Compromising**: Although avoidance might seem like the most obvious lose-lose scenario, compromising is also a style that facilitates a lose-lose outcome. During compromise, both parties must sacrifice part of their goals in a negotiated deal where neither party is completely satisfied. Indeed, compromise is characterized by exchanges and trade-offs. Although compromise can stifle creative solutions by splitting the difference, it can sometimes let parties accomplish important goals when they do not have the time to think of an integrative solution. In fact, when thinking about distributive conflict, compromise can often look like the best solution and is likely the source of relational advice that promotes this style. Despite the idea that getting something might be better than getting nothing, there is another way people can approach conflict that can yield a more satisfactory situation.

5. **Integrating/Collaborating**: Of all the conflict styles, only one is a true integrative approach. Collaborating requires both a high value placed on yourself and a high value placed on others, making sure that both parties get what they want (win-win). Unlike compromising, integration requires an innovative solution where both parties are able to meet their goals in satisfactory ways. In this scenario, relationships are better off as a result of collaboration and neither party feels an imbalance of self-esteem or power. Often considered a prosocial behavior, a primary component of collaborating requires both parties to take responsibility for their part in the conflict. Asking questions (instead of making demands) also facilitates a collaborative process and emphasizes a mutual versus individual orientation to conflict. Researchers agree, mastering an integrative style can lead to benefits for both people and their relational partners. Hocker and Wilmot warn, however, that people should not denigrate others for not using this style, in effect, one-upping them. This can quickly change the power dynamic and stifle the possibility for a satisfactory resolution.

Harmful Conflict Behaviors

For families, especially married couples, certain conflict patterns are strong indicators of relationship dissolution and divorce (see also Chapter 21 on Divorce and Dissolution). Below we discuss just some of the communicative patterns that contribute to and reflect harmful conflict behaviors.

Demand–Withdraw

One relational party seeks change, discussion, or resolutions and the other partner seeks to end or avoid the discussion. In other words, one partner might make demands or nag while the other withdraws from the conversation emotionally or physically. For example, a husband might bring up the idea of taking a vacation several times, and then start mentioning it frequently. Rather than engaging in a discussion about the possibility (or impossibility) of scheduling a vacation, his partner shuts down and leaves the room whenever the topic is broached.

Cross-Complaining Loops

This negative loop occurs when one person voices a complaint only for the other party to issue a completely different complaint. Neither complaint is acknowledged or addressed. For example, "Why did you not take out the garbage?" might be met with "Why did you not do the dishes?"

Four Horsemen of the Apocalypse

Researcher John Gottman has spent decades trying to understand the behaviors that predict divorce. Although discussed in more depth in Chapter 21, we briefly discuss the destructive signs he looks for when predicting a couple's success.

- **Criticism**: Attacks on people's character (instead of their behaviors).
- **Defensiveness**: Denying responsibility for any problems.
- **Stonewalling**: One person withdraws from the interaction, shutting down dialogue or the possibility for resolution. Sometimes this might also look like a refusal to engage with the other person, even if the person is still physically present.
- **Contempt**: Markers of disgust that can be verbal (e.g., belittling or demeaning) or nonverbal (e.g., eye rolling).

Meta-Communication Loops

These negative loops happen when people argue about how they are arguing. For example, "Don't take that tone of voice with me!"

Violence

Verbal aggressiveness and abuse are communicative strategies designed to attack another person's self-concept. This type of violence might look like character attacks, insults, malicious teasing, ridicule, and profanity. Verbal aggressiveness is a common response during conflict and can quickly escalate to intimate partner violence.

Beyond verbal threats and aggressiveness, violence can be any verbal or physical strategy to bring others to your point of view through attempts to convince, control, or compel. On average, 20 people are physically abused by an intimate partner every minute. In her lifetime, one in three women will be a victim of some sort of physical violence with an intimate partner. This number is actually not much different for men (one in four). Ultimately, 15% of all violent crime is intimate partner violence. Below we discuss some patterns of violence based on research conducted by Bartholomew and Cobb (2011). To learn more about these alarming statistics, you can visit the National Coalition Against Domestic Violence here: https://ncadv.org/statistics

- **Pattern 1**: Verbal aggression almost always comes before physical aggression. This does not mean that the presence of verbal aggression means physical aggression is imminent. Rather, it suggests that physical abuse most often does not arise out of nowhere.

- **Pattern 2**: Both people often engage in intimate partner violence. Aggression and violence are often reciprocal. When one person responds in violence, it is likely the other person will respond in violence as well. Of note, however, the effects and seriousness of the violence tend to be different between men and women. For example, 40% of all women who are murdered are killed by a person who is close to them. Patterns of violence more often reflect an attack–counterattack pattern where women are more likely to be seriously victimized.

- **Pattern 3**: Women and children are more likely to suffer injuries. Although men can suffer injury, historical patterns, institutional power structures, and cultural norms often create unviable situations for women and their children that make it more difficult for them to leave their abuser. Leaving an abusive relationship might also be extremely dangerous. More domestic abuse victims are killed when they try to leave their abuser than at any other time.

- **Pattern 4**: Victims of intimate partner violence are in difficult, often no-win situations. Once the cycle of abuse has begun, victims do not often have many viable options for escape. Indeed, partners have already begun to exert control over their victims' lives and the fear of physical threat to themselves or important others like their children precludes many options. Unfortunately, abusers escalate their control tactics once their partners try to leave and most victims who turn to a domestic violence shelter return to their spouses. There is no doubt intimate partner violence is extremely complex and that the risks of leaving are high.

- **Pattern 5**: Different narratives about violence exist for those perpetrating the violence and for those who are victims. Research suggests that perpetrators often see their violent behaviors as a product of external factors that could not be helped. Thus, they often see their behaviors as uncharacteristic whereas victims see the behaviors as harmful patterns with lasting consequences. Furthermore, husbands are more likely than wives to minimize their violent behaviors or see them as acts of self-defense.

Can Conflict be Positive?

Research suggests there are many potentially beneficial outcomes to engaging in conflict, including (1) developing a better understanding of oneself, another family member, or the family relationship, (2) establishing similarities and differences between parties, (3) learning how to engage in constructive conflict in the future, (4) illuminating places to strengthen your relationship, (5) creating healthy boundaries that foster intimacy, and (6) changing conditions that perpetuate perceived incompatible goals, scarce resources, and interference.

KEY CONCEPTS: THE PROCESS OF FORGIVENESS

Forgiveness can be defined in a variety of ways, although most definitions share some common elements: (1) a focus on the present after reflection on the past, (2) a desire to be free of the negative patterns influencing quality of life, (3) a willingness to work on yourself instead of focusing on what another person is willing or able to do, and (4) having compassion for yourself as well as giving up on getting even (Hocker & Wilmot, 2014). In addition to these commonalities, many communication scholars focus on forgiveness as a process. This process is often seen as movement through the following four phases described below.

The Four Phases of Forgiveness

According to Enright (2001), there are four phases of forgiveness: (1) uncovering your anger, (2) deciding to forgive, (3) working on forgiveness, and (4) discovery and release from emotional prison (Figure 11.1).

- **Uncovering**: During this part of the process, people are asked to examine their emotions and psychological defenses. They might become conscious of repetitive thoughts (i.e., rumination), address their emotional pain, and/or recognize the ways their world has changed.

- **Deciding**: During this phase, people begin considering forgiveness as an option, recognize that old ways of behaving might not be working, and commit to the forgiveness process.

- **Working**: This phase asks people to test whether they can see the other person in a different way, empathize, feel compassion, and accept that what happened was painful.

- **Discovering and releasing**: During this last part of the process, people might find meaning in what happened, recognize times when they might have needed forgiveness, recognize that they are not alone, and repurpose their life. Finally, people might find release and freedom from guilt and remorse.

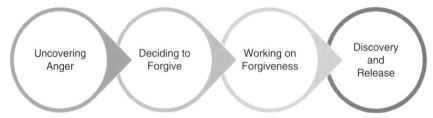

Figure 11.1 The four phases of forgiveness.

Forgiveness and Communication

According to a study by Vincent Waldron and Douglas Kelley (2005), there are five types of forgiveness communication: (1) conditional, (2) minimizing, (3) discussion, (4) nonverbal display, and (5) explicit. Conditional forgiveness communication occurs when one party makes the forgiveness dependent on whether or not their partner will change their behaviors. They found that when adults in romantic relationships engage in conditional strategies they report deterioration after the forgiveness episode. Alternatively, nonverbal strategies (affection, hugs, etc.) are related to relational strengthening. When transgressions are severe, adults in romantic relationships use more conditional and less minimizing strategies. Minimizing strategies emphasize that the transgression is not that big of a deal. Explicit strategies required participants to state, "I forgive you" to repair their relationships. Finally, discussion strategies included an exploration of motives, emotions, and solutions. This research is particularly important considering it emphasizes the central role of communication in the forgiveness process.

What Forgiveness Is Not …

- Forgiveness is not about forgetting. Forgiveness requires that people acknowledge what happened and the resulting outcomes.

- Forgiveness is not indifferent to justice.

- Forgiveness is not a sign of weakness. Forgiveness can have many benefits for a person even if they have experienced extreme hardship.

- Forgiveness is not something someone else can grant on your behalf. Forgiveness is a personal choice.

- Forgiveness and reconciliation are not the same thing. Forgiveness is a process undertaken by one person in relation to another – with or without the other person. Reconciliation is a process of reestablishing a connection and renewing trust to restore harmony. During reconciliation both parties want to reengage and believe the benefits of being in the relationship outweigh the risks.

PRACTICAL APPLICATIONS AND THINGS TO CONSIDER

Do you feel like you are stuck in the same conflict over and over? Communication scholar Clair Canfield finds that people often experience the same conflict because they are stuck in unsatisfying patterns and a justification trap. In this trap, people tell stories about their conflicts where they take on a role of victim, villain, and/or hero. Regardless of the position, each person in this *drama triangle* feels justified in their behaviors. When feelings of justification persist, opportunities for change can be limited.

To overcome these unsatisfying patterns and work toward integrative conflict, Canfield suggests five steps. These steps, outlined below, can also be further explored in his TEDx talk entitled "The Beauty of Conflict": https://www.youtube.com/watch?v=55n9pH_A0O8

- **Vulnerability**: Being vulnerable requires people to access their feelings and think deeply about what the conflict is really about. Even though surface problems can exist (e.g., unwashed dirty dishes), vulnerability requires people to express their needs and articulate their emotions.

- **Ownership**: Sometimes people do not want to take responsibility for their part of the conflict whereas other people take on too much. In this stage of the process, people acknowledge their part in the conflict and do not take ownership of the issues that are not theirs to own.

- **Communication process**: Conflict is inherently a communicative process. In this phase, people seek to ask questions for genuine understanding with the goal of empathizing with the other party.

- **Acceptance**: Acceptance can be a difficult part of the conflict process when people feel the need for control. In this stage, people must come to accept that despite their best efforts, they might not be able to change the other person or the outcome.

- **Boundaries**: Boundaries are important in the conflict process because it helps people and their relational partners understand what is and what is not acceptable. True intimacy requires boundaries.

KEY TERMS

Acceptance
Accommodating
Avoiding
Boundaries
Collaborating
Communication process
Comprising
Cross-complaining loops

Demand–withdraw
Distributive conflict
Dominating
Four Horsemen of the Apocalypse
Incompatible goals
Integrative conflict

Interference
Meta-communication loops
Ownership
Scarce resources
Violence
Vulnerability

Summer on the Farm...

CASE STUDY BY JOSHUA R. PEDERSON

Growing up on a farm, James was always helping out and summertime is the busiest time on the farm. Now that James is living away from home at college, he is experiencing new opportunities and growing his career interests. After taking a few pre-law courses James is considering going to law school. James found an internship at a law firm near his school for the upcoming summer. This would be the first summer away from the farm, but he is hopeful that his parents will be supportive.

A few weeks later James called his parents to share the good news about getting offered the internship. After hearing about the internship his dad jumped in, "I don't think that is going to work. James, we need you on the farm this summer."

"But dad, this is a great opportunity!" he exclaimed. "It will give me a leg up for law school."

"LAW SCHOOL!" His dad was yelling now. "You can't be serious! James, you are a farmer and that's it. I don't want you going off to be some lawyer. What about the farm?!"

James' mom intervened. "Lawrence! Calm down! Let James explain himself."

James was upset. How could his dad not respect his decisions to do something that he wanted to do? He is an adult now, so why does he have to do what his parents want?

"You know what dad, I'm not a kid anymore and you can't tell me what to do!" James fired back. "Screw you and the farm!"

"James!" his mother said in a reprimanding tone.

"I didn't raise you like that, James. In fact, you don't even sound like my son anymore. All this talk about law school and what not!" Lawrence countered.

"Whatever, dad." James scoffed as he hung up the phone.

James exhaled deeply. "Woah, that was not how I wanted that to go," he thought. James was angry and taken aback by his dad's reaction. His dad had always been supportive and even encouraged him to go away for college. But now he was uncertain about what he was going to do this summer and, more importantly, he probably hurt his parents with how he talked to them.

Back on the farm James' dad put the phone down and, looking exhausted, he turned toward his wife as his eyes started to well up with tears. "You know, Lawrence, James has a point," James' mom said softly. "He is not our little boy anymore. We might need to let him do this or at least talk to him about it more."

"I know, honey. It's just that he has always been here to help us and I get worried about the future of the farm. What are we going to do?" Lawrence replied.

"We will figure it out. Let's give it a few days and talk to James again. I think the two of you should find a way to smooth things over."

Over the next few days both James and his parents spent a lot of time reflecting on their conversation. James started to see his dad's perspective about the challenges of keeping the farm going. He felt bad for talking to his parents the way he did. He wanted to apologize for his behavior. His dad just wanted to tell his son that he loves him and he didn't mean what he said about not sounding like his son. James still wants to do the summer internship and his father still wants him to help on the farm. But they are willing to work out a solution that leads to the best outcomes for everyone.

CASE STUDY DISCUSSION QUESTIONS

1. What are the components of the conflict between James and his parents and what conflict styles were displayed by each family member?
2. What were the harmful conflict behaviors used by James and his father? Do you ever catch yourself using these conflict behaviors?
3. How can James and his parents productively resolve this conflict?
4. It looks like James and his dad are starting the process of forgiveness. Talk about what the process of forgiveness looks like in your own experiences.

REFERENCES

Bartholomew, K., & Cobb, R. J. (2011). Conceptualizing relational violence as a dyadic process. In L. M. Horowitz & D. Strack (Eds.), *Handbook of interpersonal psychology: Theory, research, assessment, and therapeutic interventions*. Hoboken, NJ: John Wiley & Sons.

Enright, R. D. (2001). *Forgiveness is a choice: A step-by-step process for resolving anger and restoring hope*. Washington, DC: American Psychological Association.

Harper, M. S., & Welsh, D. P. (2007). Keeping quiet: Self-silencing and its association with relational and individual functioning among adolescent romantic couples. *Journal of Social and Personal Relationships, 24*, 99–116. doi:10.1177/0265407507072601

Hocker, J. L., & Wilmot, W. W. (2014). *Interpersonal conflict* (9th ed). New York, NY: McGraw Hill.

Koerner, A. F., & Fitzpatrick, M. (2002). Toward a theory of family communication. *Communication Theory, 12*, 70–91. doi:10.1111/j.1468-2885.2002.tb00260.x

Simpson, J., Collins, W., & Salvatore, J. (2011). The impact of early interpersonal experience on adult romantic relationships function: Recent findings from the Minnesota longitudinal study of risk and adaptation. *Current Directions in Psychological Science, 20*, 355–359. doi:10.1177/0963721411418468

Waldron, V. R., & Kelley, D. L. (2005). Forgiving communication as a response to relational transgression. *Journal of Social and Personal Relationships, 22*, 723–742. doi:10.1177/0265407505056445

Wright, C. N., & Roloff, M. E. (2009). Relational commitment and the silent treatment. *Communication Research Reports*, *26*, 12–21. doi:10.1080/08824090802636967

RELATED READINGS

Pederson, J. R. (2014). Competing discourses of forgiveness: A dialogic perspective. *Communication Studies*, *65*, 353–369. doi:10.1080/10510974.2013.833526

Waldron, V. R., & Kelley, D. L. (2008). *Communicating forgiveness*. Thousand Oaks, CA: Sage.

Chapter 12
Coping and Resilience in Families

Coping and resilience are fundamental human processes that maintain well-being. Coping and resilience are important functions that family members can fulfill or facilitate for one another. While coping and resilience are related concepts, they are also distinct. Below, each are described in detail.

COPING

Coping is one reaction people can have to stress. Other reactions available to people include ignoring the problem or running away from it. For example, when a parent gets laid off from their job, they may engage in coping with their partner by working together to come up with a plan to make some extra money. The parent might also ignore the impending decrease in income and continue spending as if the problem does not exist. Coping is the most active way to deal with stress and includes attempts to control the situation and other actions that attempt to solve a problem or reduce stress.

As you learned in Chapter 6, family members are **interdependent**. This means that if a child is not coping well with stress, their experience will affect their parents and potentially other siblings. If a parent or both parents are not coping well (or even just one of the parents), it will affect all others. Only when all family members are coping well is family coping effective.

Communication in Family Contexts: Theories and Processes, First Edition.
Elizabeth Dorrance Hall and Kristina M. Scharp.
© 2020 John Wiley & Sons, Inc. Published 2020 by John Wiley & Sons, Inc.
Companion website: www.wiley.com/go/dorrance_hall/communication-in-family-contexts

Coping can be done alone, though it is more effective when others are involved. Dyadic coping strategies are communicative, for example, providing support and joint problem solving. Family members are often the ones people rely on during difficult situations. According to Lynne Webb and Fran Dickson (2011), coping as a family is comprised of three pillars. The first pillar is the need to make sense of challenging situations together. The second pillar involves communication among family members to make sense of the situation. The third pillar is about remaining positive about the survival of the family. The result of effective coping should be transformation or successful adjustment to life post-crisis, which often involves creating a new sense of what is normal for the family.

Kathleen Maguire (2012) takes this focus on communication to the next level and argues that communication is central to every step of the process. For example, she recognizes that communication is used to make sense of a stressful event, which in turn informs our perceptions of the stress. Communication is both a coping strategy in that talking about what we are going through can be helpful, and a resource people can use to cope with stress (for example, social support is a resource). We can also examine communication to determine whether people have been able to successfully cope since healthy communication in our relationships would be indicative of having been able to cope. Figure 12.1 represents the ideas in Maguire's communication-based model of coping in the family.

As you can see in Figure 12.1, coping is a complex process, and communication plays a key role in that process. For instance, communication is both a **source** of stress and a **symptom** of stress. As a source, interpersonal conflict, unexpected or disturbing disclosures, relationship trouble, hurtful messages, or discrimination

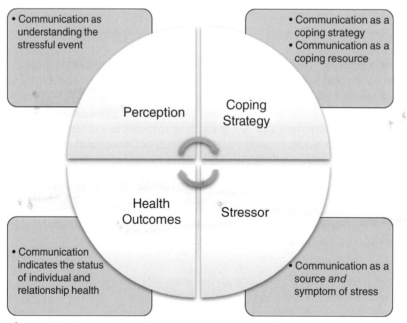

Figure 12.1 Communicative stress and coping. Figure adapted from Maguire (2012).

could all be the source of stress. Communication is also affected by stress. Someone might communicate aggressively as a symptom of stress. Our **perception** of a stressor is also shaped by our communication about it which helps us make sense of what happened.

Communication is also a **strategy** for coping. People might decide to avoid talking about a certain stressor, they might journal about their stress, they might show more or less affection, they seek information to reduce their uncertainty, and this is just the beginning of a long list of ways communication can be used to cope with stress. In fact, Maguire says seeking support from others is a **resource** and one of the most common forms of coping. You can read more about seeking supportive communication in Chapter 17.

Finally, communication can be used as an indicator for **healthy outcomes** of coping. Communication with family, within a given relationship, or just examining how an individual is communicating can show whether a person is successfully coping with stress.

Categories of Coping

- **Problem-focused coping** – Coping behaviors that change the problem that is causing stress. This type of coping is common when we think we are able to make a change.

- **Emotion-focused coping** – Thoughts or behaviors that regulate emotional responses to the stressor. This type of coping is common when we do not think we can change the problem.

- **Meaning-focused coping** – Thoughts and communication that influence our thoughts used to reframe or otherwise manage the meaning we assign to a stressful event or problem.

- **Relationship-focused coping** – Thoughts and behaviors couples use to manage the stress of the problem along with the emotional needs of a partner who is coping. Couples may actively discuss the problem or decide it is best to avoid the topic of the problem or stressor (for example, when talking about the cancer diagnosis only makes things worse).

- **Communal coping** – Related to relationship-focused coping described above, communal coping occurs when a couple decides that a problem is *their* problem. In other words, they are in it together. Continuing from the example above, in this scenario the couple would decide that a cancer diagnosis for one of them is really "their/our" problem instead of just one partner's problem. In this type of coping, partners come together to deal with stress.

RESILIENCE

Resilience is the ability to bounce back and/or move forward after experiencing significant life challenges. Froma Walsh (2003) describes family resilience as more than coping. She says it is a process families go through to restore balance in the face of stress or crisis.

Individual Resilience

Resilience is sometimes treated as an individual trait a person is born with and other times as an outcome people can experience depending on how they were raised or the skills training they have undergone. Patrice Buzzanell, a professor at the University of South Florida, proposed a theory of resilience that, like Maguire, puts communication at the center of the resilience process (Buzzanell, 2010). She claims that resilience is enacted through communication with others and that resilience is based on interaction with others instead of a trait people are born with. In other words, people are not born more or less resilient; instead they use their communication networks and resources to enact resilience with greater or lesser skill or success. Buzzanell's five resilience processes people can use can be found in Table 12.1.

Relationship Resilience

Relationships can also vary in how resilient they are. Tamara Afifi has developed a theory of resilience and relational load (TRRL; Afifi & Harrison, 2017). Her theory describes the process by which couples can maintain their relationships by managing stress, building resilience, and ultimately, thriving. She emphasizes the fact that relationships require maintenance and nourishment to thrive. She describes **resilience** as the process of calibration in relationships where feedback is used by partners to understand how they need to adjust to improve the relationship and be prepared for more stressful times. Because all couples face challenges and stressors, they can invest in the relationship while things are running smoothly to prepare for the harder times. According to Afifi, these harder times can even impact people's personal and relational health, especially when they have not invested in the relationship during the good times. Specifically, she recommends that partners and family members invest in their relationships to develop a communal orientation, in other words, having each other's backs, knowing they are

Table 12.1 Buzzanell's Five Resilience Processes

Crafting normalcy	Insisting that family life is normal, even when there has been a crisis or disruption (e.g., the primary earner has lost their job)
Affirming identity anchors	Playing up identities members value like "son" or "mother"
Utilizing communication networks	Spending time with others outside of the family for support
Reframing	Finding a different way of looking at the problem to allow the family to move forward
Downplaying negative feelings while focusing on positive emotions	Recognizing that bad things have happened while refocusing that energy on positive outcomes of the change or challenge

there for one another, and feeling unified. "Relational partners who have a strong communal orientation and maintain their relationships positively over time are less likely to see events as stressful, and when they are stressful, they appraise and communicate with one

mohamed_hassan/pixabay

another in ways that help manage the stress and promote personal and relational resilience" (Afifi & Harrison, 2017, p. 3). Based on this theory, we learn that investing in and maintaining our relationships is about more than just relationship satisfaction, it is also about how we face and overcome challenges together.

INTERESTING RESEARCH FINDINGS

Coping with Natural Disasters

A research team led by Lauren Smith examined how Haitian adults living in the United States were affected by the earthquake in Haiti in 2010 (Smith et al., 2014). This study is clearly framed in systems theory, based on the assumption that the earthquake in Haiti would affect family members living in the United States. Smith and her team refer to this as **vicarious coping**. The research team surveyed 471 Haitians living in the United States, 417 of whom had family members living in Haiti at the time of the earthquake. Almost all of the participants reported worrying about family members and friends in Haiti, some of whom even reported post-traumatic stress disorder symptoms resulting from the earthquake. In fact, 60% of participants reported a family member in Haiti had either passed away or been injured in the disaster. In terms of coping with the trauma, the researchers noted that family coping strategies were especially important for managing the trauma experienced by family members outside of the disaster zone. Many Haitians have a strong family orientation, which might have buffered some of the stress associated with the earthquake.

Resilience during a Parental Gender Transition

Myrtle Dierckx's research team recently completed a study to understand what it is like for children and parents in families where one of the parents is transgender (Dierckx et al., 2017). The researchers interviewed 13 children and 15 parents from nine families to find out more about the experience of having a parent change their social gender role (with or without medical intervention). They found that these families used a variety of resilience strategies including family continuity, or stability in parenting behavior, which was especially important in light of other changes happening with one parent, open and honest family communication, acceptance by the other parent and the community of the change, and attributing meaning to the parent's new gender and how that will affect the parent–child relationship. The researchers concluded that when families engage in productive resilience strategies by communicating with one another, a parent's gender transition can be accepted by children and the family can thrive.

PRACTICAL IMPLICATIONS AND THINGS TO CONSIDER

Think about a time you or someone in your family has faced a significant challenge. Challenges could include a health scare/diagnosis, losing a job, or a death in the family, among others. How did you cope with the stress of the challenge? How did your family members contribute to and/or detract from your ability to cope?

Do you feel you have been resilient after this challenge? In other words, have you been able to bounce back and move forward, having learned from the challenge? If yes, how? If no, why not? Do any of the ways you've been resilient match the resilience strategies outlined above?

IN-CLASS ACTIVITY

Split the class into four groups of about five people and assign each group one type of coping. Students should work together to define their type, identify pros, cons, and challenges with their type of coping, and each come up with an example of a time they have used that type of coping. Encourage them to explore how things turned out. If they find this too personal, they could also identify a time they saw their type of coping on a television show or in a movie. Each group should report back to the whole class.

IN-CLASS DISCUSSION/WORKSHEET

1. How are the concepts of coping and resilience similar and different?
2. How does communication contribute to coping? Resilience?
3. What is unique about coping in a family?
4. Which of the five resilience strategies seem like it would be easiest for you to do? What about the hardest?

KEY TERMS

Communal coping
Emotion-focused coping
Individual resilience

Meaning-focused coping
Problem-focused coping
Relational resilience

Relationship-focused coping
Vicarious coping

REFERENCES

Afifi, T. D., & Harrison, K. (2017). Theory of resilience and relational load. In J. Lebow, A. Chambers, & D. Breunlin (Eds.), *Encyclopedia of couple and family therapy*. New York, NY: Springer.

Buzzanell, P. M. (2010). Resilience: Talking, resisting, and imagining new normalcies into being. *Journal of Communication, 60,* 1–14. doi:10.1111/j.1460-2466.2009.01469.x

Dierckx, M., Mortelmans, D., Motmans, J., & T'Sjoen, G. (2017). Resilience in families in transition: What happens when a parent is transgender? *Family Relations, 66,* 399–411. doi:10.1111/fare.12282

Maguire, K. C. (2012). *Stress and coping in families.* Cambridge, UK: Polity Press.

Smith, L. E., Bernal, D. R., Schwartz, B. S., Whitt, C. L., Christman, S. T., Donnelly, S., … Kobetz, E. (2014). Coping with vicarious trauma in the aftermath of a natural disaster. *Journal of Multicultural Counseling and Development, 42,* 2–12. doi:10.1002/j.2161–1912.2014.00040.x

Walsh, F. (2003). Family resilience: A framework for clinical practice. *Family Process, 42,* 1–18. doi:10.1111/j.1545-5300.2003.00001.x

Webb, L. M., & Dickson, F. C. (2011). Effective family communication for coping with crises. In F. C. Dickson & L. M. Webb (Eds.), *Communication for families in crisis: Theories, research, strategies* (pp. 1–26). New York, NY: Peter Lang.

RELATED READINGS

Afifi, T. D., Merrill, A. F., & Davis, S. (2016). The theory of resilience and relational load. *Personal Relationships, 23,* 663–683. doi:10.1111/pere.12159

Carr, K., & Koenig Kellas, J. (2018). The role of family and marital communication in developing resilience to family-of-origin adversity. *Journal of Family Communication, 18,* 68–84. doi:10.1080/15267431.2017.1369415

Dorrance Hall, E. (2018). The communicative process of resilience for marginalized family members. *Journal of Social and Personal Relationships, 35,* 307–328. doi: 10.1177/0265407516683838

Theiss, J. A. (2018). Family communication and resilience. *Journal of Applied Communication Research, 46,* 10–13. doi:10.1080/00909882.2018.1426706

Chapter 13

Difficult Family Conversations

Difficult conversations are those that are typically emotionally charged and characterized by uncertainty (Browning, Meyer, Truog, & Solomon, 2007). Yet, what is considered "difficult" will vary from family to family. We do know, however, that some topics are particularly taboo in families (see Chapter 16 on Information Management and Disclosure in Families). According to Baxter and Akkoor (2011), sex and sex communication, addiction and substance abuse, and finances were among the most difficult conversations for families to discuss. We have also included a research study about death and dying given the positive possibilities of end-of-life conversations, despite the potential for the topic to be complicated and uncomfortable (Generous & Keeley, 2014). We recognize that families might have a myriad of other topics that they find difficult to discuss. To equip you with tools that might make these difficult conversations easier, we provide some theoretical frameworks that have the potential to help make any difficult conversation less uncomfortable.

KEY CONCEPTS

Even though families might engage in a variety of conversations about difficult topics, research is fairly consistent that open communication can yield positive outcomes. We now provide a brief summary of some of the most difficult topics for families to discuss. For more general information about taboo topics, secrets, and information, refer to Chapter 16.

Communication in Family Contexts: Theories and Processes, First Edition.
Elizabeth Dorrance Hall and Kristina M. Scharp.
© 2020 John Wiley & Sons, Inc. Published 2020 by John Wiley & Sons, Inc.
Companion website: www.wiley.com/go/dorrance_hall/communication-in-family-contexts

Addiction/Substance Abuse

Extensive research has established that substance abuse leads to negative psychological, physiological, relational, and economic problems (see Kam & Miller-Day, 2017). According to a 2013 national survey, 1.3 million adolescents (aged 12–17) and 20.3 million adults had a substance abuse disorder in the past year (Center for Behavioral Health Statistics and Quality, 2014). Research suggests the important role parents play in the substance abuse prevention and reminds parents that communicating about substance abuse can have a big influence even thought it might not seem that way. Yet, not all communication is productive communication. Research also has illustrated the ways parents' inconsistent behaviors can create conditions where they unintentionally encourage the very behavior they are trying to prevent or stop through inconsistent patterns of reinforcement and punishment (this is explained further in inconsistent nurturing as control theory; LePoire, 1995).

The research of family communication scholar Michelle Miller-Day (2002), in particular, has been pivotal in centering communication in the context of addiction and substance abuse within the family. Her research focuses on the ways parents talk to their children and whether those conversations are effective. Researchers agree that when it comes to discussions about substance abuse, parents should talk with their children early and often. This is true even when a family member has already started to abuse a substance. A study by Middleton, Pusateri, and Caughlin (2017) found that when substance abuse has already become a problem, most parents avoid discussing intervention attempts even though some turn to third parties for help. Unfortunately, substance abuse problems are not only difficult between parents and children. Research from Glowacki (2017) found that siblings can escalate problematic drinking through inconsistent nurturing. Regardless, communication scholars agree **one size does not fit all when it comes to family member substance abuse** (Kam & Miller-Day, 2017).

Death and Dying/End-of-Life Conversations

Talking about the end of life is complex given the many factors a family must contend with such as completing legal documentation, treatment plans, and choosing a place of care. When these conversations do not happen, there are risks that a person could receive unwanted or even unnecessary medical procedures. But research suggests that simply having a conversation is not enough. A study by Allison Scott and John Caughlin (2014) found that the perceptions of the quality of conversation adults have with their (adult) children about the end of life matters with regard to their conversation satisfaction and feelings of hope. Furthermore, when people perceive that their end-of-life conversations with their family were high quality, they report fewer hurt feelings and less relational distancing. These findings correspond with research that suggests that family communication about the end of life decreases mental health issues such as anxiety and depression not only for the patients, but also for other family members (Weiner & Roth, 2006). **Taken together, when it comes to family communication about**

the end of life, the quality of the conversation might be just as important as the quantity for multiple members of the family.

Finances

To achieve financial stability in the future, people often need to learn about how to manage their finances. Parents are children's primary source of financial education, which ultimately influences their long-term financial beliefs. For example, research suggests that parent communication about finances is related to both children's ability to manage money, actual financial behaviors, and their economic stress. Lynsey Romo (2014, 2017) has conducted a variety of studies pertaining to parent–child communication about finances and has found that where things like saving are not a taboo topic, more personal financial matters such as income, debt, and net worth are more difficult conversations. Specifically, Romo (2014) found that children are rather attuned to financial talk and that their perceptions of financial topics their parents shared about are extremely similar to what parents report talking with them about. Although she warns that full disclosure at any age might be problematic, Romo still contends that even discussing financial mistakes could help children learn valuable lessons and prevent economic hardship in the future. Another added bonus of discussing finances is that parents can stop children from having unwarranted uncertainties which might help them better prepare to handle their own financial difficulties later in life. **Despite the topic of money being potentially uncomfortable, children benefit from parents engaging in financial discussions.**

Sex/Sex Communication

No matter what kind of relationship, sex and sex communication often emerge as the number one taboo topic. This is extremely problematic, considering approximately half of the pregnancies in the United States are unintended (mistimed or unwanted; Finer & Zolna, 2011) and statistics suggest that young adults between the ages of 13 and 24 are the second highest group of people to be newly diagnosed with HIV (CDC, 2010; see Chapter 31 for more information about HIV/AIDS). In addition, half of all new sexually transmitted infection (STI) diagnoses occur in emerging adults between the ages of 15 and 24 (CDC, 2008). It is clear that talking to children about sex is an important process by which parents and children can co-construct shared sexual values, beliefs, and attitudes. Consequently, the National Campaign to Prevent Teen and Unplanned Pregnancy (2011) suggests:

1. **Talking with your children**. Just like you read about in Chapter 5, families with open communication environments experience a variety of different positive outcomes. Parents and children should both feel free to engage in conversation. Parents should especially consider the possibility that their children want to contribute to the conversation.

2. **Talking with your children about sex**. Just because parents find talking about sex difficult does not mean their children are not seeking other avenues to learn more information about sex. Indeed, if parents want to

limit the possibility that their children are seeking unreliable sources, they should be open to conversation.

3. **Beginning discussions with your children when they're young**. Starting young does not mean sharing explicit details with young children. Rather, age-appropriate conversations can be had very early on. These conversations might even be less difficult because younger children are often less judgmental.

4. **Continuing discussions over time**. Having a conversation once might not be enough to help children co-construct values, attitudes, and beliefs about sex. Thus, communication should happen often and over time.

5. **Involving both parents in a two-parent family**. When in a two-parent household, both parents should take responsibility for communicating about sex. This helps children see multiple perspectives and does not unnecessarily burden mothers, who are often the ones to speak with children about sex.

6. **Talking to all children**. Just as both parents should engage in conversation, all children should also be involved. In the past, parents had focused on talking with their daughters, which can have some negative outcomes. Sons also need to know about sex and their responsibilities as a partner.

7. **Establishing a mutual dialogue**. Parents should be open to questions and mutual discussion about sex. When parents prescribe rules, children are more likely to shut down and stop listening.

8. **Creating a supportive environment**. Finally, parents should work to create a nonjudgmental environment both in what they say and what they do (i.e., verbally and nonverbally).

Taken together, parents should discuss sex with their children early, often, and interactively. Indeed, research suggests that parents who discuss sex with their children generally have children who come to expect more specific conversations later on. This expectation can help reduce the discomfort around talking about sex. Furthermore, children who report having satisfying conversations about sex with their parents are more predisposed to having conversations about sex with the romantic partners in the future as well as have generally caring and nonpromiscuous attitudes about sex.

OVERCOMING DIFFICULT CONVERSATIONS WITH THEORY

Some theories help us craft messages that will be better received by family members and may ease the burden of having difficult conversations.

Politeness Theory

Politeness theory was created by Brown and Levinson (1987) to capture what seemed to be universal needs of all humans: the need to be liked and the need to make our own choices.

Positive face captures that first need, the need to be liked by others, approved of, or appreciated. Any time a difficult conversation implies we are not happy with the other person or we dislike what they are doing, positive face is threatened. We can support others' positive face by reminding them that we do like them, and that is why we are having this difficult conversation in the first place.

Negative face is all about autonomy. Autonomy is basically independence, or the right to make your own decisions. People tend to like having options and not being told they must do something by others. We can support others' autonomy by giving them options, asking them questions, and putting the ball in their court, so to speak. We can also acknowledge that what we are asking them to do is threatening.

Face-threatening acts, or messages that threaten positive or negative face, are common in difficult conversations since difficult conversations usually involve indicating someone is doing something you do not want them to do or you do not think they should be doing (likely threatening their negative face), or they involve a disclosure or judgment that might threaten their positive face. You can combine a face-threatening message with positive and negative politeness strategies (discussed above with each type of face) to lessen the threat of your message. For example, you might tell your sister you do not want to go along with her plan for the weekend by first telling her how much you appreciate her enthusiasm for planning to make sure everyone has a good time. Appreciating her enthusiasm should attend to her positive face needs. To lessen the blow to her negative face you might say that you recognize how much time and effort she put into the plan, and suggest you work together to compromise and make some changes, giving her options for what to change. Giving her options and recognizing the work she put into the plan should attend to her negative face needs.

In brief, all people have positive and negative face needs and face-threatening acts typically do not feel good. We can work to attend to face needs and avoid face-threatening acts by being mindful of our messages and use perspective-taking to predict what might feel threatening to others.

Confirmation Theory

Confirmation theory, developed by Rene Dailey (2010), offers two dimensions to draw from when creating messages that will be better received by family members during difficult conversations.

The first dimension is called **acceptance**. Messages high in acceptance are warm, nice, and express how much we like the other person. Messages like "I love you" and "I care about you" are high in acceptance. To use this in a difficult conversation you might remind your family member that the reason you are having this conversation in the first place is because of how much you care about them.

Challenge is the second dimension of confirmation theory. Messages high in challenge push others to examine their behaviors and emotions to see if there is something they could have done differently in the past or might do differently in the future. You can think of this as a gentle push for others to improve.

The best messages include a combination of acceptance and challenge. For example, if your brother is having a hard time finding a job, you might remind him how much you care and admire him for his job-related skills while encouraging him to think about his job interview performance and where he could improve or offer to look at his resume with him to identify places he could add or rewrite to better showcase those skills.

Person-Centered Messages

While not a fully articulated theory like the first two ways to craft messages in difficult conversations (i.e., politeness theory and confirmation theory), this approach to message creation says that the messages people tend to like best validate the concerns a person is having, show awareness of that person's feelings, encourage discussion about concerns and possible solutions, and adapt to the particular circumstance and the particular person facing those concerns (High & Dillard, 2012). **In other words, people tend to like messages that are kind, caring, empathetic, and tailored to the particular needs of the person.**

These types of messages are high on person-centeredness and are called **high person-centered messages**. For example, if you needed to encourage your best friend to seek counseling for depression, you might validate that depression is a common experience for people going through major life transitions. You might also discuss ways she could seek help including taking an online therapy workshop, going to see a university counselor, or seeing a trusted family psychiatrist. You might also tailor the message to her life and personality by describing how happy and enthusiastic she once was and that you know she could get back to that state with some help.

It might be useful to contrast this high person-centered message with other types of messages so you can see the difference. **Low person-centered messages** minimize the feelings of others, do not validate what they are going through, and do not encourage reflection of the behaviors that might have led to the problem. For example, you might tell your friend to just "shake off" the blues and move on with her life. A medium person-centered message might implicitly recognize the person's feelings and promote distraction. This type of message might encourage your friend to go out and party to take her mind off the stress she is experiencing. Neither of these low or medium person-centered messages encourage your friend to actually get help and deal with what is causing her problems in the first place. High person-centered messages are not right for every difficult conversation, but across people, they tend to be the most effective and well liked.

INTERESTING RESEARCH FINDINGS

How Do We Make Sense of Nonverbal Communication at the End of Life?

Communicating about the end of life is an extremely difficult conversation. Valerie Manusov and Maureen Keeley (2015) enhanced our understanding of these conversations when they explored the accounts of 55 people who had participated in end-of-life conversations with a family member. They focused on nonverbal communication and found that nonverbal behaviors served a variety of functions, including:

1. relational messages
2. emotional expression
3. interaction management
4. social support
5. transitioning

Relational messages highlighted how participants felt about each other through expressions of either love and/or connection. **Emotional expression** communicated how participants who had the end-of-life conversations were feeling and the intensity and effect of that expression. **Interaction** described the way conversations were managed through a variety of nonverbal signals that indicated a person's presence, greetings, and everyday goodbyes. **Social**

mohamed_hassan/pixabay

support communicated support availability by illustrating that the participants were "here for" the other person. This was accomplished through assistance, care, comfort provision, and companionship. Finally, the **transition** function emphasized the dying person's desire to be remembered and ultimately communicated final goodbyes and spiritual experiences. In sum, these authors' findings suggest that nonverbal communication is a meaningful part of the end-of-life experience that can be a meaningful part of the sense-making process. Nonverbal messages make up a large part of any conversation, but can be especially useful during difficult conversations like these.

PRACTICAL APPLICATIONS AND THINGS TO CONSIDER

When faced with having a difficult conversation with a family member, review the theories above and think about how you might best frame your messages so they are polite, confirming, and person-centered. You might also pick a strategic location for the conversation. This location might be a pleasant park or restaurant that your family member likes. You might also bring along another family member or

friend your family member likes. Having these challenging conversations in a pleasant atmosphere, with people you and your family member love and enjoy, might
take away some of the unpleasantness. According to Dan Ariely, psychologists refer
to this as "reward substitution," which occurs when a positive activity is paired with
a dreaded one.

IN-CLASS ACTIVITY

Think back to when you were growing up. Did anyone in your family talk to you
about drug and alcohol use? What were some memorable messages? Why do you
think those messages stuck with you after all this time? Did you find any of their
messages particularly persuasive?

KEY TERMS

Acceptance
Challenge
Confirmation

Difficult conversations
Face-threatening acts
Negative face

Person-
centered messages
Positive face

REFERENCES

Baxter, L. A., & Akkoor, C. (2011). Topic expansiveness and family communication.
  Journal of Family Communication, 11, 1–20. doi:10.1080/15267431003773523
Brown, P., & Levinson, S. C. (1987). *Politeness: Some universals in language usage*
  (Vol. 4). Cambridge, UK: Cambridge University Press.
Browning, D. M., Meyer, E. C., Truog, R. D., & Solomon, M. Z. (2007). Difficult
  conversations in health care: Cultivating relational learning to address
  the hidden curriculum. *Academic Medicine, 82*, 905–913. doi:10.1097/
  ACM.0b013e31812f77b9
Center for Behavioral Health Statistics and Quality. (2014). *Results from the 2013
  National Survey on Drug Use and Health: Summary of national findings* (HHS
  Publication No. 14–4863, NSDUH Series H-48). Rockville, MD: Substance Abuse
  and Mental Health Services Administration.
Centers for Disease Control (CDC). (2008). *Sexually transmitted disease
  surveillance, 2007* [Pamphlet]. Atlanta, GA: Department of Health and
  Human Services.
Centers for Disease Control (CDC). (2010). *Diagnoses of HIV infection and AIDS in
  the United States and dependent areas, 2010 HIV surveillance report*. Retrieved
  from http://www.cdc.gov/hiv/surveillance/resources/reports.2010report/
  pdf/2010_HIV_Surveillance_Report_vol_22.pdf
Dailey, R. M. (2010). Testing components of confirmation: How acceptance
  and challenge from mothers, fathers, and siblings are related to adolescent

self-concept. *Communication Monographs, 77*, 592–617. doi:10.1080/03637751
.2010.499366

Finer, L. B., & Zolna, M. R. (2011). Unintended pregnancy in the United States:
Incidence and disparities, 2006. *Contraception, 84*, 478–485. doi:10.1016/j.
contraception.2011.07.013

Generous, M., & Keeley, M. P. (2014). Creating the final conversation scale: A measure of end-of-life relational communication with terminally ill individuals.
Journal of Social Work in End-of-Life & Palliative Care, 10, 257–281. doi:10.1080/
15524256.2014.938892

Glowacki, E. M. (2017). Examining sibling communication about problematic
drinking: An application of inconsistent nurturing as control theory. *Journal of
Family Communication, 17*, 65–87. doi:10.1080/15267431.2016.1251919

High, A. C., & Dillard, J. P. (2012). A review and meta-analysis of person-centered
messages and social support outcomes. *Communication Studies, 63*, 99–118. doi:
10.1080/10510974.2011.598208

Kam, J. A., & Miller-Day, M. (2017). Introduction to special issue. *Journal of Family
Communication, 17*, 1–14. doi:10.1080/15267431.2016.1251922

Le Poire, B. A. (1995). Inconsistent nurturing as control theory: Implications for
communication-based research and treatment programs. *Journal of Applied
Communication Research, 23*, 60–74. doi:10.1080/00909889509365414

Manusov, V., & Keeley, M. (2015). When family talk is difficult: Making sense of nonverbal communication at the end-of-life. *Journal of Family Communication,
15*, 387–409. doi:10.1080/15267431.2015.1076424

Middleton, A. V., Pusateri, K. B., & Caughlin, J. P. (2017). A normative approach to
parent–young adult child communication in the context of substance use disorders: Explicating parents' communication challenges and strategies. *Journal of
Family Communication, 17*, 49–64. doi:10.1080/15267431.2016.1251918

Miller-Day, M. (2002). Parent–adolescent communication about alcohol,
tobacco, and other drug use. *Journal of Adolescent Research, 17*, 604–616.
doi:10.1177/074355802237466

National Campaign to Prevent Teen and Unplanned Pregnancy. (2011). *Counting
it up – The public cost of teen childbearing: Key data* [Pamphlet]. Washington,
DC: Author.

Romo, L. K. (2014). Much ado about money: Parent–child perceptions of financial disclosure. *Communication Reports, 27*, 91–101. doi:10.1080/08934215
.2013.859283

Romo, L. K. (2017). A review of family financial communication. In A. V. Laskin (Ed.),
The handbook of financial communication and investor relations. Hoboken, NJ:
Wiley-Blackwell.

Scott, A. M., & Caughlin, J. P. (2014). Enacted goal attention in family conversations
about end-of-life health decisions. *Communication Monographs, 81*, 261–284.
doi:10.1080/03637751.2014.925568

Weiner, J. S., & Roth, J. (2006). Avoiding iatrogenic harm to patient and family
while discussing goals of care near the end of life. *Journal of Palliative Medicine,
9*, 451–463. doi:10.1089/jpm.2006.9.451

RELATED READINGS

Burleson, B. R. (1982). The development of comforting communication skills in childhood and adolescence. *Child Development, 53*, 1578–1588. doi:10.2307/1130086

Choi, H. J., Miller-Day, M., Shin, Y., Hecht, M. L., Pettigrew, J., Krieger, J., … Graham, J. W. (2017). Parent prevention communication profiles and adolescent substance use: A latent profile analysis and growth curve model. *Journal of Family Communication, 17*, 15–32. doi:10.1080/15267431.2016.1251920

Goffman, E. (1959). *The presentation of self in everyday life*. Garden City, NY: Doubleday.

Holman, A., & Koenig Kellas, J. (2018). "Say something instead of nothing": Adolescent perceptions of memorable conversations about sex-related topics with their parents. *Communication Monographs, 85*, 357–379. doi:10.1080/03637 751.2018.1426870

Kam, J. A. (2011). Identifying changes in youth's subgroup membership over time based on their targeted communication about substance use with parents and friends. *Human Communication Research, 37*, 324–349. doi:10.1111/ j.1468-2958.2011.01408.x

Warren, C., & Warren, L. K. (2015). Family and partner communication about sex. In L. H. Turner & R. West (Eds.), *The Sage handbook of family communication* (pp. 184–202). Thousand Oaks, CA: Sage.

Chapter 14
Discourse Dependence

All families are discourse dependent. This means that every family requires communication to create a shared family identity. Yet, some families are more discourse dependent than others. When families lack blood or legal ties and/or deviate from cultural expectations, they require more communication to construct what it means to be a family both for themselves and for people outside of the family. Earlier in this textbook you can read about theories that explain how families communicate to create a shared family identity. Later in this textbook you can read about many types of families that tend to be more discourse dependent than others (e.g., stepfamilies in Chapter 22, adoptive families in Chapter 23, and LGBTQ families in Chapter 26).

BACKGROUND

Kathleen Galvin (2006) was the first communication scholar to introduce the idea of discourse dependence. Since then, a number of communication scholars have used this perspective to frame their research. For example, some of the first and most prevalent discourse dependence research is about adoptive families (Galvin, 2006; Nelson & Colaner, 2018; Suter, 2012). All members of the **adoption triad** (birth parents, adoptive parents, and adoptees) have to rely on communication to explain questions like "Why would a person give up her child for adoption?", "Why did you decide to adopt?" or "Are you ever interested in reconnecting with your birth parents?" Based on this definition, other discourse-dependent family types might include, but are not limited to, child-free couples, foster families, families

Communication in Family Contexts: Theories and Processes, First Edition.
Elizabeth Dorrance Hall and Kristina M. Scharp.
© 2020 John Wiley & Sons, Inc. Published 2020 by John Wiley & Sons, Inc.
Companion website: www.wiley.com/go/dorrance_hall/communication-in-family-contexts

headed by same-sex partners, non-engaged cohabiting couples, half-siblings, and voluntary kin families.

In response to the emerging research on discourse-dependent families, Leslie Baxter (2014) highlighted a myriad of different types of families who deviate from expectations in her book, *Remaking the Family Communicatively*. She argues that constructing a family's identity requires three Rs: (1) remaking, (2) resistance, and (3) resilience. Remaking emphasizes the action of family construction. In other words, family is something you do through engaging in a variety of activities. Resistance acknowledges the ways that certain family types are marginalized or stigmatized and the burden these families bear in legitimating themselves. Finally, resilience pertains to families' abilities to bounce back from crisis and adversity. Taken together, the three Rs illustrate the complex process of meaning-making certain families must negotiate to construct their internal and external identities.

Although the majority of discourse dependence research has focused on how families come together, Galvin also argues that a discourse dependence approach might be valuable in understanding how family members gain distance from one other such as in the case of family estrangement or marginalization. In other words, if communication has the power to construct families, then it also has the power to deconstruct them (see Chapter 15 on Family Distancing).

KEY CONCEPTS

Discourse: The word "discourse" can have many meanings. From a discourse dependence perspective, discourse refers simply to communication or talk.

Internal boundary management: Sometimes, family members talk about themselves and to each other in ways that help solidify what it means to be a part of a particular family. To do so, family members can engage in a variety of communication strategies, which include:

- **Naming** – Choosing titles and names for non-biologically related kin.
- **Discussing** – Talking about the ties that bind families together.
- **Narrating** – Telling stories about the family.
- **Ritualizing** – Involving members in family enactments/traditions/holidays.

External boundary management: Sometimes, family members find themselves in situations when they have to talk about their families to people outside of their family. Often, they engage in these sets of communication strategies:

- **Labeling** – Creating titles or positions to show how people are connected.
- **Explaining** – Helping others understand the relationship by giving reasons for it or describing how it works.

- **Legitimizing** – Invoking the law to justify the validity of the relationship. Legitimizing might also describe the work families must do to help others recognize the family as authentic.
- **Defending** – Justifying or defending the relationship against attack.

WHAT MAKES THE DISCOURSE DEPENDENCE PERSPECTIVE COMMUNICATIVE?

The discourse dependence perspective emphasizes how communication constructs a family's identity. This is different from other ways people tend to think about how families form because it does not privilege blood or legal ties. Communication construction corresponds to a social constructionist framework. This framework requires that scholars ask how communication defines and constructs the social world, which includes our selves, our families, and our personal relationships. Communication scholars who use a social constructionist framework believe that relationships get spoken into being (and presumably nonbeing) as opposed to an alternative where communication is found "in" our relationships. Thus, communication plays a central role in a discourse dependence perspective, suggesting that it is not only important *that* families communicate but also important *how* they communicate to make meaning of themselves.

mohamed_hassan/pixabay

INTERESTING RESEARCH FINDINGS

Understanding Family Identity After Diagnosis

In addition to instances when families lack blood or legal ties, researchers have also introduced the idea of disability as a reason why a family might be more discourse dependent, especially when that disability is invisible such as autism, hearing loss, or post-partum depression. For example, Alexie Hays and Colleen Colaner (2016) conducted a study with 19 parents of children, teens, and adults with mild, moderate, and severe autism. Their findings suggest that parents engage in all eight internal and external boundary management practices. Specifically, families construct an internal identity by using the name "autism," discussing both their emotions and everyday life happenings, telling stories, and creating rituals. When communicating with members outside of the family, parents tried to help others understand by educating them, showing their family loyalty, and to illustrate their family's normalcy. Theoretically, this study helped illustrate that the absence of blood and legal ties is not the only criterion that makes a family discourse dependent. Instead, health issues might also create communicative burdens for families. Practically, expanding the framework of discourse dependence to include health contexts sheds light on the difficulties with which families must negotiate when a member has a chronic health condition.

To better understand the birth family relationship, Haley Kranstuber Horstman and her colleagues (2018) took a closer look at the management processes of naming and connecting. Based on the accounts of 298 open adoptive parents, six terms of address for birth families emerged. Although some adoptive parents did not have a way to address the birth family, many parents addressed the birth parents informally (e.g., Mama, Grandpa C.). Sometimes, the address took on a word from another culture (e.g., Madre). Finally, sometimes the address was more formal (e.g., birth father). Based on a quantitative analysis, these authors determined that there were four contact types: (1) controlled, (2) social, (3) constant, and (4) concise. Controlled types reported low levels of connection and use of technology whereas social types reported high levels of social media use and moderate levels of contact. Constant types spent the most time communicating with birth families using a variety of media but hardly ever communicated through the adoption agency. Finally, concise types were apt to use texting and email but were less involved in using other types of communication channels (i.e., more synchronous).

Practical Applications and Things to Consider

A discourse dependence perspective shifts the focus from blood ties to emphasize the importance of communication in defining the family. By doing so, different types of families might gain more legitimacy. For example, do you have anyone in your life that is "like a mother, like a sister, like a grandparent?" If so, how do you talk about these people to your families and to others? Based on the discourse dependence strategies, what communicative practices could you enact to help include them into your family better?

Discourse dependence highlights the importance of names and labels. What does it mean when we describe certain family members as "real," "step," or "half"? What could be some implications of labels like these? How can we communicate in ways that celebrate different types of families?

KEY TERMS

Defending
Discourse
Discussing
Explaining

External boundary
management
Internal boundary
management
Labeling

Legitimizing
Naming
Narrating
Ritualizing

Haven't You Heard? Her "Real" Dad's In Jail

CASE STUDY BY KRISTINA M. SCHARP

Ellie couldn't wait for Spring Break. She finally was going to New York City after dreaming about seeing its sights since she was a little girl. Her dad promised if she made good grades during college, he would take her somewhere special in her last year. She couldn't believe how lucky she was to have a dad who was also becoming her friend instead of just a parent. Now, the time had finally come for just the two of them to go on an adventure.

Ellie packed three bags full of clothes, shoes, and accessories and brought them to the spot where her dad planned to pick her up. While she was waiting, she ran into Sarah and Katie who were also waiting for rides. "Hey Ellie!" they chirped in unison. "Where are you headed?" With a smile, she told them she was going to see the Statue of Liberty and the Empire State Building.

Finally, her dad pulled up. "Put those bags in the trunk and get in!" Taking a look at her giant suitcases, her dad reconsidered and said, "Never mind, I'll grab them."

Katie began looking around frantically so Ellie went over. "Are you okay?"

"No – are you okay?" whispered Katie. "Are you being kidnapped?"

"What? No, that's my dad." Ellie tried to respond so her dad wouldn't hear.

"But you look nothing like!" Katie said, shocked.

"Oh." Ellie started to get nervous. "Actually, that's Jeff. He adopted me when I was just a kid. But he's always been dad to me."

"What happened to your real dad?" Katie wondered aloud.

"Let's catch up when I get back from New York!" Ellie deflected.

Throughout the talk Sarah eyed Katie with disbelief ... After Ellie and her dad got into the car, Sarah said to Katie, "Haven't you heard? Her real dad's in jail."

"Shhh!" Katie said, "The windows are open."

"Oh no, I hope she didn't hear."

Ellie began to put her seatbelt on and tried to hide her horror. Her dad turned to her and said, "Anything you want to talk about, Ellie?"

CASE STUDY DISCUSSION QUESTIONS

1. What communication strategies did Ellie use to create her external family identity?
2. How might Ellie's dad continue the conversation to create a sense of internal family identity?
3. What other types of families might be particularly discourse dependent?
4. How have you used these communication strategies creating your own family identity?

REFERENCES

Baxter, L. A. (Ed.). (2014). *Remaking the family communicatively.* New York, NY: Peter Lang.

Galvin, K. M. (2006). Diversity's impact on defining the family: Discourse-dependence and identity. In L. H. Turner & R. West (Eds.), *The family communication sourcebook* (pp. 3–20). Thousand Oaks, CA: Sage.

Hays, A., & Colaner, C. (2016). Discursively constructing a family identity after an autism diagnosis: Trials, tribulations, and triumphs. *Journal of Family Communication, 16*, 143–159. doi:10.1080/15267431.2016.1146722

Kranstuber Horstman, H., Colaner, C. W., Nelson, L. R., Bish, A., & Hays, A. (2018). Communicatively constructing birth family relationships in open adoptive families: Naming, connecting, and relational functioning. *Journal of Family Communication, 18*, 138–152. doi:10.1080/15267431.2018.1429444

Nelson, L. R., & Colaner, C. W. (2018). Becoming a transracial family: Communicatively negotiating divergent identities in families formed through transracial adoption. *Journal of Family Communication, 18*, 51–67. doi:10.1080/15267431.2017.1396987

Suter, E. A. (2012). Negotiating identity and pragmatism: Parental treatment of international adoptees' birth culture names. *Journal of Family Communication, 12*, 209–226. doi:10.1080/15267431.2012.686940

RELATED READINGS

Baxter, L. A., Henauw, C., Huisman, D., Livesay, C., Norwood, K., Su, H., ... Young, B. (2009). Lay conceptions of "family": A replication and extension. *Journal of Family Communication, 9*, 170–189. doi:10.1080/15267430902963342

Baxter, L. A., Norwood, K. M, Asbury, B., & Scharp, K. M. (2014). Narrating adoption: Resisting adoption as "second best" in online stories of domestic adoption told by adoptive parents. *Journal of Family Communication, 14*, 253–269. doi:10.1080/15267431.2014.908199

Baxter, L. A., Scharp, K. M., Asbury, B., Jannusch, A., & Norwood, K. M. (2012). "Birthmothers are not bad people": A dialogic perspective of online birth mother narratives. *Qualitative Communication Research, 1*, 53–82. doi:101525/qcr.2012.1.1.53

Braithwaite, D. O., Bach, B. W., Baxter, L. A., DiVerniero, R., Hammonds, J. R., Hosek, A. M., … Wolf, B. M. (2010). Constructing family: A typology of voluntary kin. *Journal of Social & Personal Relationships, 27*, 388–407. doi:10.1177/0265407510361615

Breshears, D. (2011). Understanding communication parents and their children regarding outsider discourse about family identity. *Journal of GLBT Family Studies, 7*, 264–284. doi:10.1080/1550438X.2011.564946

Docan-Morgan, S. J. (2014). "They were strangers who loved me": Discussions, narratives, and rituals during Korean adoptees' initial reunions with their birth families. *Journal of Family Communication, 14*, 352–373. doi:10.1080/15267431.2014.946033

Galvin, K. M. (2014). Blood, law, and discourse: Constructing and managing family identity. In L. A. Baxter (Ed.), *Remaking families communicatively* (pp. 17–32). New York, NY: Peter Lang.

Harrigan, M. M., & Braithwaite, D. O. (2010). Discursive struggles in families formed through visible adoption: An exploration of dialectical unity. *Journal of Applied Communication Research, 38*, 127–144. doi:10.1080/000909881003639536

Scharp, K. M., & Dorrance Hall, E. (2017). Family marginalization, alienation, and estrangement: A review of and call for research that questions the nonvoluntary status of family relationships. *Annals of the International Communication Association, 41*, 28–45. 10.1080/23808985.2017.1285680

Suter, E. A. (2008). Discursive negotiations of family identity: A study of U.S. families with adopted children from China. *Journal of Family Communication, 8*, 126–147. doi:10.1080/1526743070185706

Chapter 15
Family Distancing

Despite a cultural belief that family relationships last forever, seeking or gaining relational distance is a fairly common occurrence in families. Distance in families might look like two family members who no longer speak or family members who intentionally create space in their relationships though they are still part of one another's lives. Because distance in families is not seen as normative in the United States, families experiencing distance are discourse dependent. In this chapter, we discuss the processes of family member marginalization, parent–child alienation, and parent–child estrangement. These three communication processes illustrate the communicative burden family members take on as they reimagine their family identity and explain their situation to outsiders (see Chapter 14 on Discourse Dependence). Even though family distancing, at first glance, might seem problematic, research suggests that family distancing could be a healthy solution to an unhealthy family environment.

BACKGROUND

Although family distancing is not a new concept, researchers have only just begun exploring the ways family members attempt and maintain distance from other members. Some of what we know about these processes comes from the psychologists and social workers who interact with these families, but the majority of what we know actually comes from researchers in the field of Communication Studies. Furthermore, the majority of what we know pertains to the parent–child relationship although marginalization and estrangement might happen with a myriad of family relationships, including but not limited to siblings, grandparents, and aunts and uncles. Uncovering how family distancing processes unfold is an

Communication in Family Contexts: Theories and Processes, First Edition.
Elizabeth Dorrance Hall and Kristina M. Scharp.
© 2020 John Wiley & Sons, Inc. Published 2020 by John Wiley & Sons, Inc.
Companion website: www.wiley.com/go/dorrance_hall/communication-in-family-contexts

important step in understanding what a family is and what communicative behaviors might be necessary to keep a family together.

In this chapter, we focus on family member marginalization, parent–child alienation, and parent–child estrangement. Even though each of the three distancing processes is distinct, they are **voluntarily** enacted (as opposed to third-party removal such as incarceration or foster care) and initiated because of a presumably **negative relationship** or perceived negative behaviors. These processes also carry stigma, can be difficult to explain to others, and sometimes even carry legal ramifications. Below we discuss each process.

KEY CONCEPTS
Family Member Marginalization

Marginalization of one family member is sometimes known as the family "black sheep." **Marginalized family members feel disliked, disapproved of, excluded, and different from the rest of the family**. Marginalization in families is fairly common, with as many as 80% of families having a member they consider a "black sheep."

The label of *black sheep* is problematic, but the origins of the term are worth mentioning. Black wool, caused by a recessive gene in sheep, cannot be dyed and therefore was not worth as much as white wool at market. Black sheep were therefore less desirable to farmers.

There are three main types of marginalized family members: those who are **dissenting**, or hold and express views and goals that are the opposite of their family members; **diverging**, or family members who are excluded and disapproved of by family but are more similar than different from their family; and **questioning**, or those who derive some sense of self from their family membership but are most likely to question why they are the black sheep of the family. Being a questioning marginalized family member may be especially hard if the person does not know why they are treated differently than others in the family and therefore live with uncertainty about their family relationships.

Communication is the way in which family members are told they are different, but it is also the way marginalized family members can stay strong and resilient despite having challenging family relationships to work with. One of your textbook authors, Dorrance Hall (2018), found that marginalized family members have a variety of resilience strategies they can use to cope with their status in the family (for more on coping and resilience, see Chapter 12). Marginalized family members can:

1. Seek support from their communication networks.
2. Create and negotiate boundaries with family members.
3. (Re)build their lives while recognizing past negative experiences with family.
4. Downplay what it is really like to be excluded.
5. Stay true to themselves despite the disapproval of family.

Marginalized family members are different from others in their family and likely feel disapproved of and excluded at times. There are a variety of ways they can feel better about their family relationships and can also create new family relationships with others outside of their family of origin.

Parent–Child Alienation

Parent–child alienation results after divorce when one parent intentionally (or unintentionally) persuades his or her children to distance themselves from or reject the other parent. A concept often used in court custody decisions, 13.4% of parents report being alienated by at least one or more of their children. Research from Kelly and Johnston (2001) suggests that parent–child alienation exists on a five-point spectrum following separation and divorce. Anchoring one end of the spectrum is a **positive relationship** with both parents. Next is a point called **affinity** in which children have a closer relationship to one parent but still seek contact with both parents. The third point, **alliance**, describes children who have a consistent preference for one parent but who also do not completely reject the other. The fourth point, **estrangement**, occurs when children reject a parent because of abuse. Finally, **alienation** depicts an open rejection of the parents without ambivalence and/or guilt.

Although older ideas about parent–child alienation circulated in the mid-1980s through the early 2000s, the limited research being conducted today has moved away from focusing on outcomes experienced by the children to focusing on the communicative and alienating behaviors enacted by the parents. According to Jaffe, Asbourne, and Mamo (2010), four priorities have emerged:

1. Protect children from ongoing destructive parental conflict and litigation.
2. Protect the security and stability of the children's relationships with the primary parent while respecting the right of that parent to direct his or her own life.
3. Respect the right of the children to have a meaningful relationship with both parents.
4. Promote the positive outcomes for children of having a healthy relationship with a co-parenting team.

Parent–child alienation requires communication to begin the process of alienation, maintain the distance, as well as resolve the alienation.

Parent–Child Estrangement

Estrangement occurs when at least one family member voluntarily and intentionally distances himself or herself from another because of an ongoing negative relationship. According to your textbook author Scharp (2019), there are eight characteristics of estrangement that family members might manipulate to create distance: (1) communication quality, (2) communication quantity, (3) physical distance, (4) presence/absence of emotion, (5) positive/negative affect, (6) role reciprocity, (7) desire for reconciliation/to be a family, and (8) legal action. For example, to gain more distance, a person might consider moving away, holding on to negative feelings, and taking away durable power of attorney. In a different family, there might be a completely different set of behaviors. Regardless of the combination, these family members could still fall somewhere along the estrangement continuum.

So how does estrangement happen? Adult children who gained distance from their parents typically report some form of psychological, physical, or sexual abuse and sometimes gross neglect or indifference. As a result, they either came to an internal realization that they needed distance or experienced a "last straw" event that helped them to begin the estrangement process. After they initiated distance, adult children discussed feeling pressure from either their social network (e.g., other family members, friends, coworkers) to reconcile or an internal sense of guilt that they should give their parents another chance. Although some adult children were able to resist these pressures and maintain distance (i.e., **continuous estrangement**), most entered into an on-again/ off-again relationship until they were finally able to maintain the amount of distance that worked for them (i.e., **chaotic disassociation**). Indeed, gaining distance is often very difficult at both a cultural and tangible level for adult children. For example, many children have to wait until they become an adult to have the financial means to gain and maintain distance from their parents.

Research suggests that some parents, however, tell a very different story. Unlike adult children who typically can explain exactly why they sought distance, some parents have a much more difficult time providing a reason for why the distance occurred. Parents on the receiving end often also express a desire for reconciliation whereas adult children typically do not. Although sometimes parents also want distance, they experience different cultural pressures above and beyond those experienced by adult children. For example, parents who want to distance themselves from their children also must overcome cultural beliefs that suggest parents should unconditionally love their children and sacrifice anything for them. In sum, these differing accounts illustrate that the estrangement process can be extremely distressing even if distance might be healthier for all the family members involved.

Similarities and Differences

Despite all being chronic, chaotic, and dynamic, distinctions remain among these family distancing processes. For example, people engage in distancing behaviors to varying degrees, over different lengths of time, and make sense

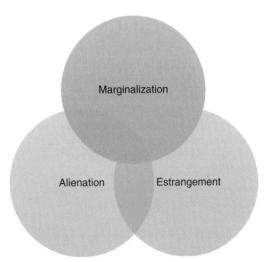

Figure 15.1 Marginalization, alienation, estrangement.

of their experiences in different ways. Briefly we discuss some similarities and differences (Figure 15.1).

Commonalities

All three processes are marked by emotional volatility, impact the family system at large (see Chapter 6), require a significant amount of communication to explain both within and outside of the family (see Chapter 16), and are not part of a common pattern where parents and children become more and less close over the life course. In other words, family distancing processes do not happen over one fight and are not a product of children wanting more autonomy as they grow older.

Distinctions

Parent–child alienation is always initiated by children whereas marginalization and estrangement might be initiated by any member of the family. Marginalized members feel fundamentally different from the other members of their family although this is not necessarily the case of people in the alienation or estrangement process. Alienation and estrangement have legal ramifications whereas marginalization does not. Specifically, courts differentiate between whether a child "irrationally" wants distance from a parent (i.e., alienation) or because of abuse (i.e., estrangement). Marginalization and estrangement could be positive and/or negative for parties involved although alienation is typically more ubiquitously negative. Finally, whereas marginalized family members and those on the receiving end of estrangement and alienation often want to reconcile with their families, that is mostly untrue of those who initiated the estrangement and alienation processes.

INTERESTING RESEARCH FINDINGS

What Kinds of Family Events are Especially Marginalizing?

Dorrance Hall (2017), interviewed 30 adults who felt they were the black sheep of their family about the process of becoming marginalized from family. She asked them to tell her about an event in the past 10 years that was the most marginalizing experience they had. She also asked them to think about times when they felt really included with family. Some participants had an easier time talking about times they felt included than others. Some of the events marginalized family members talked about that were times when they felt especially different or excluded were family weddings, graduations, changing jobs, and moving away from family. Sometimes participants talked about these same events as making them feel included. For example, one of the participants talked about walking his sister down the aisle at her wedding as being a time he felt really included in his family. At that same wedding he was not included in a large group photo of the family, making him feel really marginalized. Other marginalizing events included times people were lied to, conversations they had with family members about ceasing all contact, and crisis events like health issues or deaths in the family. Communication was a theme that ran through all of these events because communication from family is how people know they are different or disapproved of, especially when the family uses hurtful communication.

What Are the Uncertainties Adult Children Must Manage When They Distance Themselves from their Parents?

The process of estrangement can be extremely confusing, even for those who initiated the distance. A study based on 52 in-depth interviews revealed that adult children who distanced themselves from their parents yielded six types of uncertainty (Scharp & McLaren, 2018). Specifically, they discussed: (1) parental love uncertainty, (2) identity uncertainty, (3) safety uncertainty, (4) cycle of abuse uncertainty, (5) self-uncertainty (whether they wanted to be in the relationship), and (6) network uncertainty, which pertained to their concern about how distancing themselves would influence other people in their network. Unlike some communication research that assumes people always want to reduce their uncertainty, adult children managed their concerns in a variety of ways which included: (1) contrasting themselves to their parent, (2) trying to keep themselves safe, (3) limiting other close relationships so cycles of abuse would not continue, (4) sharing their story with others, (5) managing their social network, and (6) making external attributions for why their parents behaved the way they did. For example, many adult children blame drug/alcohol addiction or mental illness for their parents' perceived abusive behavior. Perhaps one of the most interesting findings was that adult children did not want to reduce their parental love uncertainty (i.e., questions about whether or not their parents loved them). Although this sounds counterintuitive, neither answer to the question is particularly satisfying. For adult children, either their parents loved them and treated them terribly or they wondered what child is not loved by their parents. This finding reiterates the general practical advice that network members should refrain from attempting reconciliation or providing reassurances until those in the estrangement process are clear about what would be supportive.

PRACTICAL APPLICATIONS AND THINGS TO CONSIDER

Family distancing is more common than you might think. Do you know a family member who has created distance between themselves and your family? Try to take their perspective and think about why they might desire some distance. Alternatively, is there a family member your family may have pushed away? Why did the family find it necessary to do this? Do any of your reasons for wanting distance or the family pushing a member away line up with the research we covered above?

KEY TERMS

Chaotic disassociation
Discourse dependence
Family distancing

Family member
marginalization
Parent–child alienation

Parent–child
estrangement

OUT-OF-CLASS ACTIVITY

Identify a marginalized/black sheep family member from a TV or movie family. Rewatch an episode/movie that contains such a character and analyze how others react to them. Who does the character blame, if anyone, for their challenging relationship with family? How do they explain their family situation to others? Does their family show evidence of discourse dependence?

COMMUNICATION IN FAMILY CONTEXTS PODCAST

Podcast with Elizabeth Dorrance Hall (Michigan State University) and Kristina Scharp (University of Washington): www. familycommlab.com/podcasts

Elizabeth Dorrance Hall and Kristina Scharp define, compare, and contrast the concepts of marginalization and estrangement. They explore reasons people give for marginalization and estrangement in their families and overview research on both topics.

DORRANCE HALL & SCHARP PODCAST REFLECTION QUESTIONS

1. How are marginalization and estrangement different from one another?
2. What are nonvoluntary family relationships as defined by Dr. Scharp?
3. How do people go about distancing themselves from their family relationships? (Hint: the podcast mentions eight markers of estrangement or ways people gain distance from family.)
4. Define and describe the three dimensions of marginalization. Do all marginalized family members score high on all three dimensions?
5. What is an example of an event that could make someone feel both marginalized and included? Have you ever felt both of these ways at a family function? If yes, describe.
6. What reasons do people give for why they are marginalized from their families? What reasons do people give for family estrangement?
7. What does Dr. Scharp suggest social network members, like friends, should (and should not) do to support people who are estranged from their families?
8. Name and describe at least two of the resilience strategies marginalized people use.

REFERENCES

Dorrance Hall, E. (2017). The process of family member marginalization: Turning points experienced by "black sheep." *Personal Relationships*, *24*, 491–512. Doi:10.1111/pere.12196

Dorrance Hall, E. (2018). The communicative process of resilience for marginalized family members. *Journal of Social and Personal Relationships*, *35*, 307–328. doi:10.1177/0265407516683838

Jaffe, P. G., Asbourne, D., & Mamo, A. A. (2010). Early identification and prevention of parent-child alienation: A framework for balancing risks and benefits of intervention. *Family Court Review*, *48*, 136–152. Doi:10.1111/j.1744–1617.2009.01294.x

Kelly, J. B., & Johnston, J. R. (2001). The alienated child: A reformulation of parental alienation syndrome. *Family Court Review*, *39*, 249–266. Doi:10.1111/j.174–1617.2001.tb00609.x

Scharp, K. M. (2019). "You're not welcome here": A grounded theory of family distancing. *Communication Research*. Advanced online publication. doi:10.1177/0093650217715542

Scharp, K. M., & McLaren, R. M. (2018). Uncertainty issues and management in adult children's stories of their estrangement with their parents. *Journal of Social and Personal Relationships*, *35*, 811–830. doi:10.1177/0265407517699097

RELATED READINGS

Blake, L. (2017). Parents and children who are estranged in adulthood: A review and discussion of the literature. *Journal of Family Theory & Review, 9*, 521–536. doi:10.1111/jftr.12216

Scharp, K. M. (2016a). Parent–child alienation. In C. Shehan (Ed.), *Encyclopedia of family studies*. Hoboken, NJ: Wiley-Blackwell. doi:10.1002/9781119085621.wbefs457

Scharp, K. M. (2016b). Parent–child estrangement: Conditions for disclosure and perceived social network member reactions. *Family Relations, 65*, 688–700. doi:10.1111/fare.12219

Scharp, K. M., & Dorrance Hall, E. (2017). Family marginalization, alienation, and estrangement: A review of and call for research that questions the nonvoluntary status of family relationships. *Annals of the International Communication Association, 41*, 28–45. doi:10.1080/23808985.2017.1285680

Scharp, K. M., & Dorrance Hall, E. (2019). Reconsidering family closeness: A review and call for research on family distancing. *Journal of Family Communication, 19*, 1–14. doi:10.1080/15267431.2018.1544563

Scharp, K. M., & Thomas, L. J. (2016). Family "bonds": Making meaning of parent–child relationships in estrangement narratives. *Journal of Family Communication, 16*, 32–50. doi:10.1080/15267431.2015.1111215

Scharp, K. M., & Thomas, L. J. (2018). Making meaning of the parent–child relationship: A dialogic analysis of parent-initiated estrangement narratives. *Journal of Family Communication, 18*, 302–316. doi:10.1080/15267431.2018.1484747

Scharp, K. M., Thomas, L. J., & Paxman, C. G. (2015). "It was the straw that broke the camel's back": Exploring the distancing processes communicatively constructed in parent–child estrangement backstories. *Journal of Family Communication, 15*, 330–348. doi:10.1080/15267431.2015.1076422

Chapter 16

Information Management and Disclosure in Families

Family members must manage a variety of information about themselves and their family as a whole. Often, family members openly share stories about their lives that both reflect and construct their identity (see Chapters 7 and 14), but other times they need to make decisions to disclose or withhold certain types of information. In this regard, managing information is an important process that serves a variety of functions. In this chapter, we discuss some of the fundamental issues in the information management process.

BACKGROUND

Unlike some theories you might read about in this textbook, the body of information management research does not originate with one scholar in particular. Instead, many communication scholars have contributed to what we know about information management topics and some even have their own theories related to processes like the decision to disclose information (e.g., the theory of motivated information management, TMIM; Afifi & Weiner, 2004, see

Communication in Family Contexts: Theories and Processes, First Edition.
Elizabeth Dorrance Hall and Kristina M. Scharp.
© 2020 John Wiley & Sons, Inc. Published 2020 by John Wiley & Sons, Inc.
Companion website: www.wiley.com/go/dorrance_hall/communication-in-family-contexts

Chapter 18; the disclosure decision-making model, DDMM; Greene, 2009; the revelation risk model, RRM; Afifi & Steuber, 2009) or how to manage private information (communication privacy management theory; Petronio, 2013; see Chapter 4 of this textbook). Furthermore, sometimes scholars focus on related phenomena or processes pertaining to information management such as taboo topics (Baxter & Wilmot, 1985), family secrets (Vangelisti & Caughlin, 1997), or deception (Buller & Burgoon, 1996).

Traditionally, much of the information management literature grew out of a focus on self-disclosure. **Self-disclosure** is the process of revealing personal information about the self. This research focused on the benefits of disclosing information to others which includes building new relationships and restoring psychological well-being. As more researchers gained an interest in disclosure processes, new information emerged that pointed to potential benefits of withholding information such as creating intimacy or avoiding destructive conflict. **Self-disclosure can have both positive and negative outcomes for people**. Below are some important concepts related to managing information within and/or about the family.

KEY CONCEPTS

Deception

Deception occurs when people knowingly and intentionally communicate messages and information to foster false beliefs and conclusions. People choose to hide, manipulate, misrepresent, and/or omit sharing information through a variety of tactics such as bending the truth, not telling the whole story, sharing irrelevant information, speaking ambiguously, exaggerating, and/or communicating indirectly. When engaging in deception, people might need to manage both their verbal and nonverbal behaviors. Indeed, the most common deception indicators include: (1) short responses, (2) increased speech errors, (3) increased blinking, and (4) increased fidgeting (Ekman & Friesen, 1969).

Private Information

Private information is information that is personal. Of note, the concepts of private information and secrets overlap and are not mutually exclusive (this means that private information can also be secret). Private information might include information about a family's financial situation.

Secret

Information that people are purposefully trying to conceal from others is secret. This definition emphasizes people's *decision* that the information should not be public and the *behaviors* they enact to keep that information private. As such, secrets are not merely the absence of disclosure; rather, they involve purposeful concealment. A couple, for example, may actively conceal the fact that one of them had an affair when speaking with their parents. Instead, they may put up a façade and act like they are happily married at family gatherings like Thanksgiving in order to keep up appearances and preserve their reputation. In families, secrets shared among the family can serve to help bond members, maintain relationships, keep information private, and defend the family against people who might use the information against its members (Vangelisti, 1994).

Self-Presentation

Self-presentation is the ways people convey a desired impression to others. The couple from the earlier example kept the affair a secret so that others would believe they had a happy marriage. Although self-presentation might be about an individual, families might also disclose information about other members of their family to create an impression of them or their family as a whole (i.e., family identity). For example, a mother might share her daughter's scholastic achievement with others so that people believe she is a good mother and has an intelligent and successful family.

Taboo Topic

Taboo topics are topics that at least one family member perceives to be "off limits." A topic is "taboo" if it is avoided because someone anticipates negative outcomes from its discussion. Research suggests that within families, sexual activity/issues and another cluster of difficult conversation topics (e.g., drinking/drugs/smoking, money matters, and educational progress) were the most taboo or at least the topics parents and children feel less comfortable discussing within the family (Baxter & Akkoor, 2011).

Topic Avoidance

This refers to the idea that people steer clear of certain topics in conversations with their relational partners. This avoidance is strategic and plays a role in people's ability to maintain their relationships. For example, if a person knows that talking about finances always causes conflict in his/her relationship, s/he may avoid bringing up the topics of money, budgets, and spending. If those topics come up naturally, s/he may redirect the conversation elsewhere.

FAMILY SECRETS AND THE FUNCTIONS THEY SERVE

Communication scholars Anita Vangelisti and John Caughlin (1997) conducted an important study about families and the secrets they keep. Specifically, they set out to examine the association between (1) the topic of the secret, (2) the function of the secret, (3) family satisfaction, and (4) the quality of the relationship with the potential target of the disclosure and the likelihood a person would disclose a family secret.

The researchers found that family secrets consist of three overarching types: (1) taboo topics, (2) rule violations, and (3) conventional secrets. Taboo topics were the most commonly cited secrets and were activities that are stigmatized or condemned by the larger society and included marital problems and divorce, substance abuse, finances, sexual preferences, illegal activities, mental health, extramarital affairs, and physical/psychological abuse. Rule violations were instances when a family member broke a rule common to most families in North American culture such as premarital pregnancy, cohabitation, drinking/partying, sexual relations, and breaking specific family rules. Finally, conventional secrets were comprised of information that is not necessarily wrong but often considered inappropriate for sharing like physical health problems, death, religion/ideology, personality conflict, tradition/stories, dating partners, and grades or achievement in school.

Next, the authors turned their attention to whether people were likely to reveal these secrets. Vangelisti and Caughlin found that secrets were kept for the following six reasons: (1) evaluation, (2) maintenance, (3) defense, (4) privacy, (5) bonding, and (6) communication. Thus, in addition to the four functions identified by Vangelisti (1994), the fear of negative evaluation and inability to communicate the secret emerged as concerns for two separate populations of 236 and 257 people respectively. Furthermore, people who strongly endorse evaluation, maintenance, privacy, and defense as functions for concealing secrets were more likely not to reveal them. Of note, the level of stigma associated with the taboo topics did not influence whether people felt they were more important to conceal.

Finally, the data suggest that the function of secrets, family satisfaction, and the relationship people had with the potential target of the disclosure influenced whether a person was likely to reveal a family secret. Specifically, family members who feel satisfied in their relationships are less likely to disclose family secrets. Perhaps the opposite of what you might think, people who perceived themselves as similar to the person about whom the secret was being kept were more likely to reveal that secret. Results from a second analysis with 386 people also suggest that perceptions concerning the intimacy of a secret determined whether people were more or less likely to reveal that secret.

SOME TRUTHS ABOUT LIES

Based on decades of research by communication scholars Judee Burgoon and Tim Levine (2010), certain results consistently reoccur in research findings:

- People can only detect deception slightly more than half of the time.
- People overestimate their ability to detect someone else's lies.
- People have a truth bias; that is to say, they (want to) believe others are telling the truth.

- Even with training, people hardly improve in their ability to detect deception (about 4%).
- Most detection research is conducted as an experiment. This means that people do not have contextual information when they try to determine whether someone is telling the truth. Consequently, estimations of deception detection ability could be exaggerated.

PRACTICAL APPLICATIONS AND THINGS TO CONSIDER

Managing information is a fundamental part of initiating, maintaining, and exiting relationships. For example, consider the types of information you might want or not want to share with an in-law. When might you share your family secrets? How about when trying to become closer to someone? Research suggests we follow a **norm of reciprocity** whereby people have a strong tendency to respond in similar ways to how they are treated. This often means that people might disclose similar information to you that you disclose to them. This reciprocity might take the form of topic or even depth (i.e., similar level of personal information).

Managing information also has implications for maintaining relationships. For example, disclosure is often the first step to seeking supportive communication (see Chapter 17). Disclosing information might also be a way to increase closeness, or alternatively, sharing someone's information might be a way to break trust.

Finally, managing information might also be important during break-ups like divorce. When and how should parents tell their children that they have decided to get a divorce? What type of information, if any, should they share with their children? In some families, one parent might disclose such negative information that the child no longer wants to have a relationship with the other parent (i.e., parent–child alienation). Indeed, managing information could be a major factor in the health of a family system.

KEY TERMS

Deception

Norm of reciprocity

Private information

Secret

Self-disclosure

Self-presentation

Taboo topic

Topic avoidance

IN-CLASS ACTIVITY

The instructor comes to class with a story about something memorable that happened when they were growing up. Throughout the story, the instructor includes parts of the truth and adds in some deceptive elements. Meanwhile, students observe the instructor's nonverbal communication, trying to detect the deception. After the story, students are allowed to ask some questions to ferret out the truth. This also gives the instructor a chance to engage in more deception. Then the class can discuss if they observed any verbal/nonverbal indicators and what types of deception the instructor used.

Private Affairs: Information Management When Communicating About Marital Problems

CASE STUDY BY JENNY L. CROWLEY

Rachael was not looking forward to attending her childhood friend's wedding. When she RSVPed months ago, naturally she listed her husband as her date. Now the marriage seemed headed for divorce and her husband Nathan refused to attend the wedding with Rachael. Because she couldn't bear the thought of going alone, Rachael asked her mom Christina to be her date instead. Rachael was starting to regret that decision, because she was worried her mom would use the time together as an opportunity to pry into Rachael's personal life.

The wedding venue was an hour's drive away, which gave Rachael and Christina plenty of time to catch up. Rachael distracted herself and her mother by telling Christina about a new project at work, but Christina eventually steered the conversation to Rachael's marriage.

"How have you and Nathan been doing lately?"

"Not great," Rachael said vacantly.

"I know the last few months have been difficult, but Nathan is such a sweet guy. I'm not sure why you two can't just get along," Christina chirped.

"Some people are not as sweet as they appear," Rachael shot back. Rachael was annoyed because her mom implied that she was the problem, but she knew that wasn't true. In fact, Nathan had recently crossed a line when he called Rachael a "bitch" during an argument.

"I'm not sure what you mean by that," responded Christina. "Has something happened that I should know about?"

"Actually, something did happen. I didn't want to tell you because I believe what happens in a marriage is private. But if you must know, Nathan has started acting disrespectful towards me. I'm contemplating asking him for a divorce."

"I'm sorry to hear he hasn't been treating you well," her mom said sadly. "You know, when your father and I were having marital problems I almost asked him for a divorce."

"You and dad? I had no idea...."

"I remember that time well. Waking up every morning wondering whether or not we should continue our marriage felt like a slow torture. It was a very difficult period for both me and your father." After a pause,

Christina turned to Rachael. "I understand why you want to keep your marriage private. Just know that no matter what happens or what you decide, I'm here for you."

They chatted about other things for the rest of the car ride, but Rachael could not stop thinking about what might have happened between her parents. Even though she didn't have all the information about her parents' relationship, she felt comforted knowing that her mom had been through a similar experience.

As soon as they arrived at the church, they ran into her childhood friend's mother. "Rachael! It's so good to see you again. Christina, I didn't realize you would be here. Where's Nathan?"

Christina immediately responded, "Nathan got called into work this weekend. Although I'm sure Rachael's missing her husband, I'm so delighted that I got to come instead. And who doesn't love a mother–daughter day?"

CASE STUDY DISCUSSION QUESTIONS

1. What strategies did Rachael and Christina use to manage information?
2. What motivations do Rachael and Christina have for managing information?
3. How is Rachael and Christina's relationship impacted by information management?
4. How might the family system be impacted by Rachael and Christina's various attempts at managing information?

REFERENCES

Afifi, T. D., & Steuber, K. (2009). The revelation risk model (RRM): Factors that predict the revelation of secrets and the strategies used to reveal them. *Communication Monographs, 76*, 144–176. doi:10.1080/03637750902828412

Afifi, W. A., & Weiner, J. L. (2004). Toward a theory of motivated information management. *Communication Theory, 14*, 167–190. doi:10.1111/j.1468-2885.2004.tb00310.x

Baxter, L. A., & Akkoor, C. (2011). Topic expansiveness and family communication. *Journal of Family Communication, 11*, 1–20. doi:10.1080/15267431003773523

Baxter, L. A., & Wilmot, W. W. (1985). Taboo topics in close relationships. *Journal of Social and Personal Relationships, 2*, 253–269. doi:10.1177/0265407585023002

Buller, D. B., & Burgoon, J. K. (1996). Interpersonal deception theory. *Communication Theory, 6*, 203–242. doi:10.1111/j.1468-2885.1996.tb00127

Burgoon, J. K., & Levine, T. (2010). Advances in deception detection. In S. W. Smith & S. R. Wilson (Eds.), *New directions in interpersonal communication research* (pp. 201–220). Thousand Oaks, CA: Sage.

Ekman, P., & Friesen, W. V. (1969). Nonverbal leakage and clues to deception. *Psychiatry: Interpersonal and Biological Processes, 32*, 88–106. doi:10.1080/00332747

Greene, K. (2009). An integrated model of health disclosure decision-making. In T. D. Afifi & W. A. Afifi (Eds.), *Uncertainty, information management, and disclosure decisions* (pp. 226–253). New York, NY: Routledge.

Petronio, S. (2013). Brief status report on communication privacy management theory. *Journal of Family Communication, 13*, 6–14. doi:10.1080/15267431.2013.743426

Vangelisti, A. L. (1994). Family secrets: Forms, functions, and correlates. *Journal of Social and Personal Relationships, 11*, 113–135. doi:10.1177/026540759411107

Vangelisti, A. L., & Caughlin, J. P. (1997). Revealing family secrets: The influence of topic, function, and relationships. *Journal of Social and Personal Relationships, 14*, 679–705. doi:10.1177/0265407597145006

RELATED READINGS

Afifi, T. D., & Afifi, W. A. (2009). *Uncertainty, information management, and disclosure decisions.* New York, NY: Routledge.

Crowley, J. L. (2017). A framework of relational information control: A review and extension of information control research in interpersonal contexts. *Communication Theory, 27*, 202–222. doi:10.1111/comt.12115

Kam, J. A., Gasiorek, J., Pines, R., & Steuber Fazio, K. (2018). Latina/o adolescents' family undocumented-status disclosures directed at school counselors: A latent transition analysis. *Journal of Counseling Psychology, 65*, 267–279. doi:10.1037/cou0000259

Chapter 17

Supportive Communication in Families

Family support can provide members with comfort, reassurance, and help with problem solving. **Support can be any verbal or nonverbal behavior done to assist others when they are in need.** A primary type of support families typically provide is material support, including a warm and safe place to live, food to eat, and clothes to wear. Family support often goes beyond material support with family members providing advice, expressing comfort, and connecting members to others who can help them.

Research has established how important receiving and giving social support is for our health and happiness. For example, support is related to lower depression, improved physical health, higher self-esteem, and reducing upsetting emotions.

People indicate they *need* support in different ways, including simply asking for it, crying, hinting, or even sulking. These behaviors indicate someone is in need of support. There are even more ways people can *give* support. The types of support are listed in Table 17.1.

Support reciprocity refers to exchanges of support where person A provides support to person B, and in return person B provides support back to person A. In other words, if a person supports her sister, does her sister provide supportive communication in return? If the answer is yes, then they are experiencing support reciprocity in their relationship. Support reciprocity is important for maintaining healthy relationships.

Communication in Family Contexts: Theories and Processes, First Edition.
Elizabeth Dorrance Hall and Kristina M. Scharp.
© 2020 John Wiley & Sons, Inc. Published 2020 by John Wiley & Sons, Inc.
Companion website: www.wiley.com/go/dorrance_hall/communication-in-family-contexts

Table 17.1 Types of Support

Support Type	Examples
Emotional	Offering comfort, empathy, concern, affection, encouragement, intimacy
Esteem	Reassurance of worth, enhancing how others feel about themselves
Informational	Advice, sharing information, offering guidance, making suggestions
Network	Expressions of connection, introductions to other people who can help
Tangible	Financial ($), material goods, housing, transportation, or other services
Social presence	Letting someone know you are there for them if they need you

Support gaps occur when there is a difference between how much support a person wants and how much they actually receive (Xu & Burleson, 2001). Gaps can be problematic as they leave someone either over-supported or under-supported. A good way to resolve support gaps is to have a conversation about the support you need with the person you would like to support you. Oftentimes that person simply does not know and would appreciate knowing how to better provide you with support. The **matching hypothesis** is related to experiencing support gaps. The matching hypothesis describes the need for the provider to match the amount of desired support of the recipient, regardless of whether they think the recipient actually needs more or less support. One of the most important things to remember about social support is that it does not matter how much support people are getting if they do not perceive it.

SEEKING SUPPORTIVE COMMUNICATION

It isn't always easy to ask for support. Indeed, people cannot often seek support until they disclose their problems to others. Dana Goldsmith (1992) was perhaps the first family communication scholar to recognize that supportive interactions could be costly. She argued that even though people's primary goal might be to gain assistance, people can only achieve that goal if they attend to their face needs (see Chapter 13 for more about face needs). Specifically, when people ask for help or comfort, they might fear what others will think of them. They could think that needing help makes them look weak or incompetent. When people fear seeking supportive communication because they feel bad about not being able to solve a problem for themselves, we call this an **intrapersonal cost**. Intrapersonal costs affect people's ego by damaging their pride, vanity, or esteem. Alternatively, people might also feel like a burden on others, fear people will judge them negatively, or fear that others will not be able to keep their problem private. This type of concern is called an **interpersonal cost**. Interpersonal costs reflect the

mohamed_hassan/pixabay

threat that corresponds to not meeting others' expectations. Together, these two types of costs might explain why people, even though they need some sort of assistance, do not seek it when they are in need.

SUPPORT PROCESSING

Dual-process models of cognition and persuasion also apply to the way we process supportive messages. When applied to support, the dual-process model suggests that people cannot process support unless they have the ability and motivation to do so. This model also suggests that it matters who the message comes from. For example, if someone you really trust and think of as a wise expert on the problem you are experiencing offers you support or advice, it might not matter as much what they say. The fact that they reached out and provided support might be enough. For more on this line of thinking based on dual-process theories of persuasion, check out Petty and colleagues (2004).

ADVICE

Advice is a form of informational support where one person makes a recommendation about what the other might think, say, or do to manage a problem. Giving advice to others has benefits for the person who gives the advice, including raising that person's self-esteem. It might also enhance the relationship between the person getting and the person receiving the advice. Getting useful information and recommendations might make the receiver feel better and reduce their stress. On the other hand, giving advice might do the opposite. Advice can damage a relationship and increase the receiver's stress if they are being told to do something they won't be able to do. In this case, the time spent giving advice could be spent simply providing support instead.

ADVICE RESPONSE THEORY

Advice response theory (ART) was developed by Erina MacGeorge and her colleagues to explain perceptions of advice, advice processing, and how advice influences future actions, like whether or not advice is implemented by receivers (MacGeorge, Guntzviller, Hanasono, & Feng, 2016). ART makes predictions about how message features (i.e., efficacy, feasibility, and absence of limitations) influence advice outcomes such as advice quality, facilitation of coping, and the receivers' intention to implement the advice. Let's break down each of those message features and advice outcomes.

- **Efficacy** refers to a person's belief that they can indeed do the recommended action.
- Advice is **feasible** when the recommended action is easily doable by the advice recipient.
- **Absence of limitations** means that there are not significant road blocks or barriers to doing the recommended action.
- Advice is rated as **high quality** when it is seen as helpful, appropriate, sensitive, and supportive by the receiver.
- Advice **facilitates coping** when the receiver thinks the advice has helped them cope with their problem.
- **Intent to implement** advice refers to whether the receiver plans to actually do or enact the advice they are given.

The theory also identifies important advisor characteristics such as **expertise**, **trustworthiness**, **likability**, and **similarity**. Finally, ART recognizes that the way advice is said (e.g., utilizing **politeness** strategies, see Chapter 13), whether advice confirms the receivers' existing plans, and the context in which the advice is given are all important elements that change the way advice is perceived and received. The model provides a theoretical order of influence starting with advisor characteristics, followed by message features as mediating variables, and ending with advice outcomes. For example, people who perceive that the advice they have been given is efficacious, feasible, low in limitations, and polite are more likely to implement the recommendation, think of the advice as higher in quality, and report that it helped them cope. When that advice comes from someone with expertise, and is well liked and trusted by the recipient, this will influence how people evaluate the messages which may then positively influence whether they implement the advice, think it is high quality, and whether it helped them cope (Guntzviller, 2018).

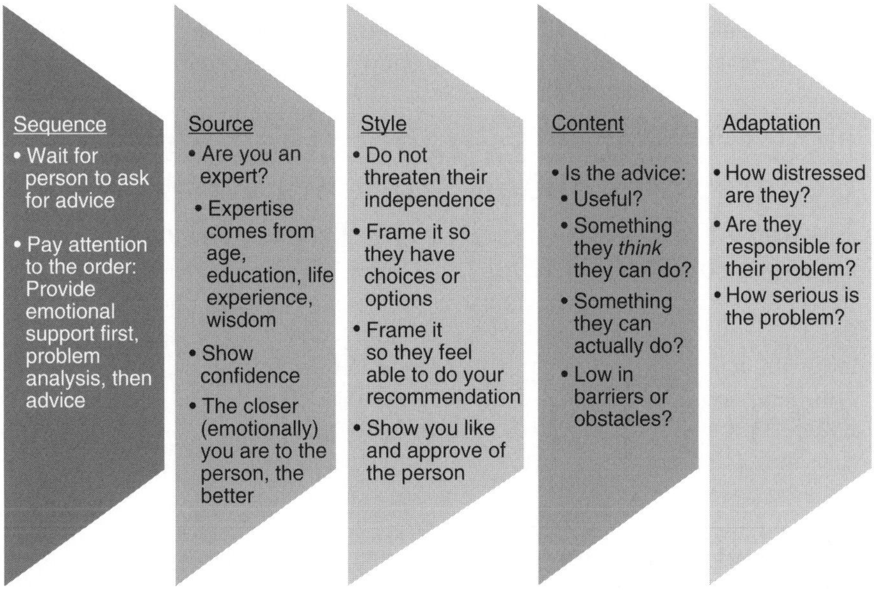

Figure 17.1 Good advice.

Decades of research led by scholars like MacGeorge have determined what makes for good and bad advice. Good advice is advice that the recipient likes, increases their ability to cope with their problem, and is likely to be taken and implemented by the recipient. Figure 17.1, based on a compilation of good advice characteristics by MacGeorge, lays out what good advice sounds like.

INTERESTING RESEARCH FINDINGS

What Kind of Advice Do Military Couples Give about Deployment and Reintegration?

Leanne Knobloch and her team (2016) surveyed 118 service members and their partners who had recently experienced military deployment and reunion. She asked them about the challenges and benefits of deployment and reunion, and also asked them about advice they would give others about reintegrating their service member back into family life. Service members and their partners recommended other couples communicate openly and listen closely to understand how other family members are feeling. They advised being patient, not rushing the reintegration processes, and focusing on family during this time. Participants suggested other couples try to have realistic expectations of what reintegration will be like and to seek help from people outside of the family if they need it. The researchers did note that despite the advice the couples would give to others, they often struggled with the same issues. For example, while they encouraged other couples to communicate openly, they mentioned it was difficult for them to be open with each other.

How Can Parents Support their First-Generation College Students When They Haven't Been to College Themselves?

Julienne Palbusa and Mary Gauvain (2017) asked 344 first-year college students to complete a survey about how they communicate with their parents about grades. The researchers chose to focus on comparing first-generation students, or students who are the first in their families to attend college, and non-first-generation students, or students who had parents who attended college. Part of the reason why they chose to do this comparison is because first-generation students tend to have less social support available to them at home since their parents do not have direct experience with what they are going through as they transition to college.

The researchers note that first-generation students are at higher risk of leaving college before finishing and tend to have lower grades than non-first-generation students. The researchers found that first-generation students spoke to their parents about the same amount as non-first-generation students. However, first-generation students did not find those conversations to be as helpful or as high quality as the non-first-generation students. Both groups of students perceived their parents as providing them with emotional support, yet non-first-generation students indicated their parents were available as a resource when they had concerns about college while first-generation students did not see their parents that way. The authors suggest colleges could better support first-generation students by providing and encouraging attendance of other sources of support for students such as information sessions about how to prepare for and succeed in college.

Did You Know?

People also need support when they experience good things in life too. When someone does something commendable, people could offer them **celebratory support**. This support recognizes people's achievements.

PRACTICAL APPLICATIONS AND THINGS TO CONSIDER

Who in your life provides you with support when you need it? What qualities do you think make for a good support provider? Make a list of the qualities good support providers need to have based on what you learned above and what you know from personal experience receiving support at just the right time, or maybe times when you needed support but didn't receive it. Based on what you wrote down, how might you become a better support provider to others? You can dive deeper into these questions by completing the activity about support gaps below.

IN-CLASS OR HOMEWORK ACTIVITIES

Support on Social Media

On their own at home or with a partner or two in class, ask students to define and find examples of each type of support on social media (e.g., Facebook, Twitter). Students should be sure to examine the comments people make to others' posts. Take a screen shot and copy paste the example into a Word doc along with your definitions. This Word doc can be emailed to the instructor or submitted online.

To debrief, ask students to speculate on why it was easier to find some types of support on social media than others. Are some types of support more appropriate than others online? Why?

Family Support Worksheet

Pick a family or romantic relationship you feel provides you with some level of support. Next, fill out the measures below to identify how reciprocal the support giving and receiving is in this relationship.

1. In the first box, indicate how much of the behavior you actually receive from this relationship.

2. In the second box, indicate how much of the behavior you wish you received from this relationship.

3. In the third box, indicate how much of the behavior you actually give to the other person in this relationship. These questions are adapted from Yan Xu and Brant Burleson.

   For support given: (1 = don't give at all, 5 = give a great deal)

   For support desired: (1 = don't desire at all, 5 = desire a great deal)

   For support received: (1 = don't receive at all, 5 = receive a great deal)

4. In the fourth box, calculate your support gap by subtracting what you have received from what you desire (D – R). The higher the value here (positive or negative) indicates more of a support gap.

5. In the fifth box, calculate the reciprocity of support in your relationship by subtracting received from given (R – G). The higher the number here, the less reciprocal the support in the relationship.

Bonus: Can you identify which type of support each question is referring to? For example, question one is about emotional support. Write the support type below each question.

Support Question	Received 1–5	Desired 1–5	Given 1–5	Gap (D – R)	Reciprocity (R – G)
1. Showing physical affection (e.g., hugs) to comfort you when you are upset. Support type:					
2. Expressing respect for a personality trait or quality. Type:					
3. Giving advice about what to do. Type:					
4. Making connections to people who can help. Type:					
5. Offering to lend money when needed. Type:					
6. Expressing they are there for you if you need them. Type:					
7. Making connections to people who share your interests. Type:					
8. Reminding you that you are a valuable and worthwhile person. Type:					
9. Expressing "I love you" or feelings of closeness. Type:					
10. Telling you that you are not alone. Type:					
11. Offering to help do something that needs to be done. Type:					
12. Teaching something that you do not know how to do. Type:					

Reflection: Where are there support gaps in this relationship? Which types of support do you wish you got more of from them? Which types of support do you get more of than you need?

Would you describe the support in this relationship as reciprocal? Are some types reciprocal while others are not? What patterns do you see here?

BONUS ANSWERS

1. Emotional
2. Esteem
3. Informational
4. Network
5. Tangible
6. Social Presence
7. Network
8. Esteem
9. Emotional
10. Social Presence
11. Tangible
12. Informational

KEY TERMS

Advice
Advice response theory
Celebratory support
Emotional support
Esteem support

Informational support
Intrapersonal costs
Interpersonal costs
Matching hypothesis
Network support

Reciprocity
Social presence support
Social support
Support gap
Tangible support

The Freshman 15

CASE STUDY BY LISA M. GUNTZVILLER

Britney just finished her first semester in college. Her older sister is getting married and Britney ordered her bridesmaid dress before she started college. The bridesmaid dress has arrived, so Britney, her sister, and her mother go to the dress shop. When Britney tries on the dress, she discovers the dress size she ordered is now too small.

From the dressing room, Britney cries, "Oh no, I can't believe it! I always said I would never be one of those people who went away to college and got fat, but I've already gained weight!"

Britney comes out of the dressing room to show her mother and sister that the dress is slightly too tight.

Her mom says, "You're not fat. Stop being dramatic. It's normal to gain weight when you go to college because you're no longer playing sports and are eating more pizza and unhealthy meals. You just need to start working out regularly again."

Britney continues to look at herself in the mirror. "Ugh, I just can't believe that I need to get a bigger dress size!"

"Just start going to the gym a couple of times a week," her mom says. "Don't you have one on campus that's free for students?"

"That's not the point, Mom!" Britney whines.

Britney's sister speaks up. "You still look great and you can't even tell. The dress sizes aren't that different anyway. You won't have any problem losing the extra weight if you want to."

"Thank you! At least someone understands me."

"That's exactly what I said!" her mom exclaims. "Why don't you ever listen to me?"

CASE STUDY DISCUSSION QUESTIONS

1. The chapter describes different types of social support. What types of support was Britney seeking? What types of support did Britney's mother and Britney's sister offer?
2. Looking at Figure 17.1 on advice response theory, how would you rate the mother's advice on each of the elements in the figure (i.e., sequence, source, style, content, and adaptation)? What elements did the mother do well? What elements did she not do well?
3. Why did Britney reject her mother's advice but accept what her sister said?
4. What were Britney's face concerns in this interaction? What were her mother's face concerns?
5. How could Britney and her mother change what they said to make a more successful support interaction?

REFERENCES

Goldsmith, D. J. (1992). Managing conflicting goals in supportive interaction: An integrative theoretical framework. *Communication Research*, *19*, 264–286. doi:10.1177/0093650920

Guntzviller, L. M. (2018). Advice messages and interactions. In E. L. MacGeorge & L. M. Van Swol (Eds.), *The Oxford handbook of advice*. New York, NY: Oxford.

Knobloch, L. K., Basinger, E. D., Wehrman, E. C., Ebata, A. T., & McGlaughlin, P. C. (2016). Communication of military couples during deployment and reunion: Changes, challenges, benefits, and advice. *Journal of Family Communication*, *16*, 160–179. doi:10.1080/15267431.2016.1146723

MacGeorge, E. L., Guntzviller, L. M., Hanasono, L. K., & Feng, B. (2016). Testing advice response theory in interactions with friends. *Communication Research*, *43*, 211–231. doi:10.1177/0093650213510938

Palbusa, J. A., & Gauvain, M. (2017). Parent–student communication about college and freshman grades in first-generation and non–first-generation students. *Journal of College Student Development, 58*, 107–112. doi:10.1353/csd.2017.0007

Petty, R. E., Rucker, D. D., Bizer, G. Y., & Cacioppo, J. T. (2004). The elaboration likelihood model of persuasion. In J. S. Seiter & R. H. Gass (Eds.), *Perspectives on persuasion, social influence, and compliance gaining* (pp. 65–89). Boston, MA: Allyn & Bacon.

Xu, Y., & Burleson, B. R. (2001). Effects of sex, culture, and support type on perceptions of spousal social support: An assessment of the "support gap" hypothesis in early marriage. *Human Communication Research, 27*, 535–566. doi:10.1093/hcr/27.4.535

RELATED READINGS

Feng, B. (2009). Testing an integrated model of advice giving in supportive interactions. *Human Communication Research, 35*, 115–129. doi:10.1111/j.1468-2958.2008.01340.x

Haverfield, M. C., Leustek, J., & Timko, C. (2018). Social support strategies in online forums among adult offspring of parents with harmful alcohol use. *Alcoholism Treatment Quarterly, 36*, 86–100. doi:10.1080/07347347324.2017.1387035

Holmstrom, A. J., & Burleson, B. R. (2011). An initial test of a cognitive-emotional theory of esteem support messages. *Communication Research, 38*, 326–355. doi:10.1177/0093650210376191

Jones, S. M., Bodie, G. D., & Koerner, A. F. (2017). Connections between family communication, person-centered message evaluation, and emotion regulation strategies. *Human Communication Research, 43*, 237–255. doi:10.1111/hcre.12103

Lim, V. K., Teo, T. S., & Zhao, X. (2013). Psychological costs of support seeking and choice of communication channel. *Behaviour & Information Technology, 32*, 132–146. doi:10.1080/0144929X.2010.518248

MacGeorge, E. L., Feng, B., & Thompson, E. R. (2008). "Good" and "bad" advice. In M. T. Motley (Ed.), *Studies in applied interpersonal communication*. Los Angeles, CA: Sage. doi:10.4135/9781412990301.n7

Mortenson, S. T. (2009). Interpersonal trust and social skill in seeking support among Chinese and Americans. *Communication Research, 36*, 32–53. doi:10.1177/00936502 08326460

Thomas, L., Scharp, K. M., & Paxman, C. G. (2014). Stories of postpartum depression: Exploring health constructs related to mothers' help-seeking behaviors. *Women & Health, 54*, 373–387. doi:10.1080/03630242.2014.896442

Chapter 18

Uncertainty Management

Uncertainty is a fundamental part of the human experience. As Brashers (2001) describes, **uncertainty** occurs "when details of situations are ambiguous, complex, unpredictable, or probabilistic; when information is unavailable or inconsistent; and when people feel insecure about their own state of knowledge or the state of knowledge in general" (p. 478). Almost anything can be the source of uncertainty (Berger & Bradac, 1982). You likely experience uncertainty when doing something for the first time or meeting someone new. Family members experience uncertainty in all sorts of ways, for example, when they are unsure how a member may react to news or when trying to figure out why a family member said something hurtful. In this chapter, we discuss communication theories that address uncertainty in relationships in addition to some important key concepts about uncertainty and its management.

KEY CONCEPTS

Ambiguity: Even though the words ambiguity and uncertainty are often used interchangeably, they are two different concepts. Ambiguity refers to the quality of being open to more than one interpretation. Situations might be ambiguous.

    Uncertainty is about the doubt and confusion resulting from ambiguity. Where ambiguity emphasizes the situation, uncertainty emphasizes people's thoughts and their reaction.

Communication in Family Contexts: Theories and Processes, First Edition.
Elizabeth Dorrance Hall and Kristina M. Scharp.
© 2020 John Wiley & Sons, Inc. Published 2020 by John Wiley & Sons, Inc.
Companion website: www.wiley.com/go/dorrance_hall/communication-in-family-contexts

RELATIONAL TURBULENCE THEORY

The relational turbulence theory (RTT) emerged out of the research conducted on the relational turbulence model. Denise Solomon, a professor at the Pennsylvania State University, and her colleagues were interested in why romantic relationships were rocky (i.e., experienced turmoil) at medium levels of intimacy. Over time, these scholars began to identify the communicative markers of this turmoil such as topic avoidance (see Chapter 13), poor supportive communication (see Chapter 17), and conflict (see Chapter 11).

mohamed_hassan/pixabay

Overall, the theory suggests that changes in relational environments, or the context surrounding the relationship, trigger relational uncertainties and can disrupt a relational pair's ability to function interdependently. When people experience relational uncertainty and disrupted interdependence, their thoughts, emotions, and communicative behaviors can become polarized in specific interactions. Polarization occurs when people have opposing views/emotions/behaviors, such as when one family member wants to spend more time together and another wants to have more free time to spend in other ways. When this polarization is frequent and ongoing, people consider their relationships to be turbulent. We now discuss the key concepts of this theory.

Relational Uncertainty

This refers to the level of confidence people have in their involvement in their relationship and comes from doubts about relational partners' own involvement (Solomon & Knobloch, 2004). According to the theory, there are three components that make up relational uncertainty: self, partner, and relationship uncertainty. These are sometimes referred to as the sources of relational uncertainty.

- **Self-uncertainty**: The uncertainty people experience about whether they want to be in the relationship.

- **Partner uncertainty**: The uncertainty people experience about whether they think their partner wants to be in the relationship.

- **Relationship uncertainty**: The uncertainty people experience about the relationship itself.

Research on relational uncertainty suggests that it is associated with biased thoughts, intensified emotions, and communication that polarizes people in specific interactions. When people feel uncertain, they tend to make more assumptions about why people are behaving in certain ways and even might have trouble making sense of everyday interactions.

Interdependence

As we discussed in Chapter 6, interdependence is the idea that people are interconnected in ways that mean what happens to one person influences the other.

Partner Interference

When one partner's life influences another in a negative way, we think of that as interference. In other words, partners interfere when they block their relational partners from achieving their goals. For example, if a father refuses to let his son borrow the car, he is interfering with his goals.

Partner Facilitation

Alternatively, when one partner's life influences another in a positive way, we call that partner facilitation. Even though there might be a disruption to people's lives, the disruption functions to help relational partners achieve their goals. For example, a romantic partner decides to stop eating sweets because her partner wants to lose weight.

Responses to Specific Interactions

To recall, RTT suggests that experiences of relational uncertainty and disrupted interdependence can lead to changes in emotions, thoughts, and communicative behaviors during specific interactions. According to Solomon and her colleagues, there are two primary dimensions of communication that influence how people respond to specific interactions: communication engagement and valence.

- **Communication engagement**: This concept refers to the extent people directly or indirectly avoid or talk about a communication episode or event between partners.
- **Communication valence**: Refers to the tone of an interaction. Some interactions can be friendly whereas other can be hostile.

Relational Turbulence

When responses to specific interactions are consistently negative, relational partners experience turbulence. This turbulence might influence a variety of different communicative outcomes (e.g., conflict, support, disclosure). There are different ways this happens:

- **Cognitive construal**: Refers to the psychological distance with which people perceive their environment. This means that turbulence makes it difficult for people to see the long-term possibilities of the relationship. In this regard, they become fixated on what is right in front of them.
- **Dyadic synchrony**: Refers to the degree of coordination in partners' interactions. Relational turbulence makes it harder for people to pay attention to their micro communication in specific interactions. This means people become focused on the things that are immediately hindering their progress, which makes it harder for them to coordinate with their partners.

In sum, the RTT is a useful theory when making sense of family transitions. Let's look at a research study by Keli Steuber. With Denise Solomon, Steuber explored the experiences of infertile couples (Steuber & Solomon, 2008). They found that couples facing infertility experienced both relational uncertainty and partner interference. Specifically, they found that couples felt uncertain because their partners did not validate their relationship because of mismatched priorities. Couples also felt uncertain around questions of blame. When fertility treatments appeared more important than personal or relational goals, couples perceived interference. This was also true when partners violated each other's expectations about how committed they were to becoming pregnant. Overall, this study illustrates how family contexts might be a rich site for the application of RTT.

THEORY OF MOTIVATED INFORMATION MANAGEMENT

Walid Afifi and his colleague Judith Weiner (2004) developed the theory of motivated information management (TMIM) to recognize both the role of efficacy and the dyadic nature of the uncertainty and information management processes (see also Chapter 16). Specifically, they developed this theory to explain uncertainty management within specific interpersonal interactions. The process involved three phases: (1) interpretation, (2) evaluation, and (3) decision.

Interpretation Phase

This phase emphasizes that there can be a discrepancy between how much uncertainty people have and how much they want. When a discrepancy exists, people experience anxiety. Note, uncertainty does not inherently produce anxiety; rather, the difference in what a person wants and what a person has is what produces anxiety. Imagine a person who feels they are the "black sheep" of her family (for more on "black sheep," see Chapter 15). If that person was not sure why her family members treated her differently and excluded her from family events and wanted to understand why (i.e., she wanted less uncertainty), she would experience a discrepancy in the amount of uncertainty she has and the amount she wants to have.

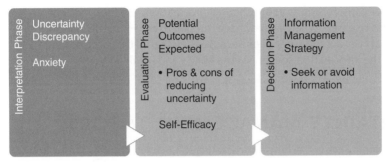

Figure 18.1 Theory of motivated information management model.

Evaluation Phase

At this phase, people need to consider the potential outcomes if they search for information to manage their uncertainty (i.e., **outcome expectancy**) and whether they have the ability to gather and cope with that information (i.e., **efficacy**). TMIM distinguishes between three different types of efficacy: (1) communication efficacy – skill to seek information, (2) target efficacy – whether the target of the search has the information and would share it, and (3) coping efficacy – whether one could emotionally, relationally, and/or financially deal with the outcome of learning the information. For example, learning new information about a health condition might be hard to cope with emotionally or financially if it meant having to undergo expensive medical treatment. In the black sheep example, the woman would need to weigh the outcomes of seeking information about why her family treats her the way they do. She'd need to think about how it would make her feel to know more about why they exclude her; for example, would she learn something that would make her feel worse than if she had just never known?

Decision Phase

Both considerations of outcome expectancy and efficacy factor into whether people will seek information to manage their uncertainty. They are more likely to decide to seek information when they expect positive outcomes and have the confidence to manage the outcomes of the information. Alternatively, they are more likely to avoid the information if they expect negative outcomes and do not have the efficacy to cope with the outcomes. The black sheep family member from above may decide that if she seeks information from her family about why they exclude her, she might have to face the truth about how they feel about her. She might ultimately decide to maintain her uncertainty and not seek new information because the uncertainty she feels is better than having to cope with knowing how her family really thinks of her.

The final consideration of TMIM is about the potential information provider. Specifically, the theory suggests that the potential information provider goes through similar considerations about sharing information. The information provider needs to assess whether they have the skill to respond, the ability to cope with whatever outcome happens because they shared the information, and whether the information seeker has the ability and is willing to manage the information.

UNCERTAINTY MANAGEMENT THEORY

When family members experience uncertainty, they have choices about how to respond. According to the scholarship of Dale Brashers (2001), people might respond in one of three ways to uncertainty: (1) reduce uncertainty, (2) maintain uncertainty, or (3) increase uncertainty. To respond in any of these three ways, people must engage in a variety of communicative strategies. For example, people might choose to seek out or even avoid certain information. This information could either reinforce previously held ideas or refute ideas. Sometimes, people come to accept that certain situations in life come with uncertainty. Asking for supportive communication (see Chapter 17) might be one way to help ease the discomfort of uncertainty. Yet, it is also important to consider that people might want to maintain or even increase their uncertainty. As Brashers argues, uncertainty is not inherently good or bad. For example, people might perceive uncertainty as an opportunity for new possibilities or the only thing standing in the way of bad news. One important thing to remember about this theory is that uncertainty is a dynamic concept and when it is reduced in one area, new uncertainties could arise. Let's continue with the example of a health diagnosis. Even when a person finds out he has a health diagnosis (i.e., reducing uncertainty), new uncertainties about how to proceed with treatment, who to tell, and what to do next might create additional concerns.

PRACTICAL APPLICATIONS AND THINGS TO CONSIDER

Can you think about a time when maintaining or increasing your uncertainty was preferable to reducing it? Family communication scholars Leslie Baxter and Dawn Braithwaite (2009) argue that absolute certainty should be guarded against and avoided. They claim that when thinking about meaning, **absolute certainty eliminates the possibility for change**. What if people were absolutely certain about what job they were going to have, who they would marry, when they would die? Placing a value on people's ability to change has many implications for who we do and think we can become. Let's think about the opportunity uncertainty affords college students ... How can uncertainty be liberating? How can uncertainty help you become someone new?

IN-CLASS ACTIVITY

Step 1: Think about a time when you experienced a discrepancy between the information you had and the information you wanted. Write down the source of your uncertainty and identify the pieces of information you had and the pieces of information you wanted, or, if ambiguity was causing uncertainty, what information did you have that was not clear? How anxious did the uncertainty make you feel on a scale of 1–10?

Step 2: Once you have your example written down, share it with a partner. Together, follow each of your examples through the TMIM phases (see Figure 18.1). Would knowing the information potentially make you feel worse? How did you weigh the pros and cons of finding out more? Do you feel you had the ability, or efficacy, to learn more information and reduce your uncertainty? What did you end up doing about the discrepancy in information you experienced? Did you seek more information? How?

Step 3: Continue to reflect on the situation with your partner. At the time, what did you think you might find out if you sought information? For example, if I was uncertain about how a job interview turned out, the potential outcomes would be: (1) got the job or (2) didn't get the job. My mind might come up with other potential outcomes that might keep me from seeking additional information: didn't get the job because other candidates were better, didn't get the job because I did a terrible job interview. How hard would it have been to cope with the different potential outcomes of learning more information in your situation? How do you feel now about the uncertainty you experienced?

KEY TERMS

Ambiguity
Cognitive construal
Communication engagement

Communication valence
Dyadic synchrony
Facilitation
Interdependence

Interference
Turbulence
Uncertainty (self, partner, relationship)

REFERENCES

Afifi, W. A., & Weiner, J. L. (2004). Toward a theory of motivated information management. *Communication Theory*, *14*, 167–190. doi:10.1111/j.1468-2885.2004.tb00310.x

Baxter, L. A., & Braithwaite, D. O. (2009). Reclaiming uncertainty: The formation of new meanings. In W. Afifi & T. Afifi (Eds.), *Handbook of uncertainty and information regulation* (pp. 26–44). New York, NY: Routledge.

Berger, C. R., & Bradac, J. J. (1982). *Language and social knowledge: Uncertainty in interpersonal relationships*. London, UK: Edward Arnold.

Brashers, D. E. (2001). Communication and uncertainty management. *Journal of Communication, 51*, 477–497. doi:10.1111/j.1460-2466.2001.tb02892.x

Solomon, D. H., & Knobloch, L. K. (2004). A model of relational turbulence: The role of intimacy, relational uncertainty, and interference from partners in appraisals of irritations. *Journal of Social and Personal Relationships, 21*, 795–816. doi:10.1177/0265407504047838

Steuber, K. R., & Solomon, D. H. (2008). Relational uncertainty, partner interference, and infertility: A qualitative study of discourse within online forums. *Journal of Social and Personal Relationships, 25*, 831–855. doi:10.1177/0265407508096698

RELATED READINGS

Afifi, T. D., & Schrodt, P. (2003). Uncertainty and the avoidance of the state of one's family in stepfamilies, post-divorce single-parent families, and first-marriage families. *Human Communication Research, 29*, 516–532. doi:10.1111/j.1468-2958.2003.tb00854.

Hogan, T. P., & Brashers, D. E. (2009). The theory of communication and uncertainty management: Implications from the wider realm of information behavior. In W. Afifi & T. Afifi (Eds.), *Handbook of uncertainty and information regulation* (pp. 45–66). New York, NY: Routledge.

Knobloch, L. K., Solomon, D. H., Theiss, J. A., & McLaren, R. M. (2018). Relational turbulence theory: Understanding family communication in times of change. In D. O. Braithwaite, E. A. Suter, & K. Floyd (Eds.), *Engaging theories in family communication: Multiple perspectives* (pp. 255–266). New York, NY: Routledge.

Merry, U. (1995). *Coping with uncertainty: Insights from the new sciences of chaos, self-organization, and complexity*. Westport, CT: Praeger.

Powell, K. A., & Afifi, T. D. (2005). Uncertainty management and adoptees' ambiguous loss of their birth parents. *Journal of Social and Personal Relationships, 22*, 129–151. doi:10.1177/0265407505049325

Rauscher, E. A. (2017). Investigating uncertainty in genetic counseling encounters: Managing information about genetic cancer risk. *Journal of Health Communication, 22*, 896–904. doi:10.1080/10810730.2017.1373875

Solomon, D. H., Knobloch, L. K., Theiss, J. A., & McLaren, R. M. (2016). Relational turbulence theory: Explaining variation in subjective experiences and communication within romantic relationships. *Human Communication Research, 42*, 507–532. doi:10.1111/hcre.12091

Solomon, D. H., Weber, K. M., & Steuber, K. R. (2010). Turbulence in relationship transitions. In S. W. Smith & S. R. Wilson (Eds.), *New directions in interpersonal communication research* (pp. 115–134). Thousand Oaks, CA: Sage.

Major Family Transitions

Chapter 19

Cohabitation and Marriage

When in a romantic relationship, one way to become a family starts with cohabitation and/or marriage. Recent statistics show that two-thirds of all first marriages begin with cohabitation (Payne, 2013). Furthermore, 7% of children (i.e., 5 million) live with cohabiting parent families. As for marriage, half of Americans ages 18 and older were married in 2016 although that number has been steadily decreasing. One reason for the decline is that people, particularly men, are staying single longer. In 2017, the median age for people's first marriage was approximately 30 for men and 27 for women (see Geiger & Livingston, 2018). In this chapter, we focus on these important transitions in family formation.

KEY CONCEPTS

Cohabitation

Cohabitation, or living together without legally marrying, is a common part of many romantic relationships. In fact, it has become so common that there is increased uncertainty surrounding what living together means for the status and future of the relationship. Indeed, cohabiting couples often do not share the same understanding of their future together and this ambiguity can translate to poorer relational quality for those who choose to cohabit without set plans for the future (Manning & Smock, 2005). Because of the uncertainty surrounding this transition, research often looks at the processes of *sliding* versus *deciding* (Priem, Bailey, & Fazio, 2015; Stanley, Rhoades, & Markman, 2006).

Communication in Family Contexts: Theories and Processes, First Edition.
Elizabeth Dorrance Hall and Kristina M. Scharp.
© 2020 John Wiley & Sons, Inc. Published 2020 by John Wiley & Sons, Inc.
Companion website: www.wiley.com/go/dorrance_hall/communication-in-family-contexts

- **Sliding** is characterized by a slow transition into cohabitation without a deliberate conversation about the transition. Couples who slide may "take the next step" and move in together without really talking about what it means for their relationship. Sliding can be problematic for couples because of the inertia effect. The inertia effect happens when couples get married after cohabiting because the constraints of and investments in cohabiting make leaving the relationship more difficult.

- **Deciding** is a communicative process by which couples discuss living together and then decide to do so. Couples who actively decide to cohabitate talk through options and make an intentional decision to integrate their lives and live together.

In their research, Jennifer Priem and her colleagues found that the majority of people (85%) had some conversation with their partner about living together and remembered that conversation fairly well. Specifically, these conversations focused on relational topics, logistics, and justifications. Relational topics included issues such as consequences, commitment, and social support. Logistical topics related to the tangible aspects of living together such as how much space the couple would need and who would pay the bills. Finally, justifications were the reasons people gave for why cohabitation was the best choice for them. Common justifications included saving money, convenience, and that it just "made sense."

Whether a couple slides into or decides on cohabitation matters.

The Cohabitation Effect

Although cohabitation has been studied less than dating or marriage, researchers have started to connect cohabitation with a variety of negative relational outcomes such as poor communication, low relational satisfaction, increased uncertainty, increased domestic violence, and increased rates of divorce (see Brown & Bulanda, 2008; Stanley et al., 2006). Sometimes called the **cohabitation effect**, researchers have come up with three reasons why outcomes of living together without being married tend to be negative.

1. The first explanation suggests that the time couples spend in the relationship could be what leads to instability (Cohen & Kleinbaum, 2002). Indeed, marital satisfaction tends to decline in the beginning of the committed marital relationship and cohabiters are further along that declining trajectory when they enter marriage. Therefore, because they have been together longer than newlyweds who moved in together post-marriage, they report lower relationship satisfaction.

2. The second accounts for something called a **selection effect**. This means that people who choose to cohabitate might be more likely to possess other characteristics that put them at risk for negative outcomes such as financial instability or certain personality traits.

3. The third explanation is that the experience of cohabitating influences how stable a couple's relationship is and increases people's acceptance of divorce.

Despite the negative outcomes associated with cohabitation, it's important to note that the cohabitation effect does not hold true for engaged cohabiting couples.

In light of multiple explanations for why cohabiting can lead to poor outcomes, people in cohabiting relationships resist social assumptions that cohabiting is inferior to marriage. Specially, cohabiting partners provide three counter-narratives (i.e., stories that challenge the social norm): (1) cohabiting relationships as normal, (2) cohabitation as an easy relationship, and (3) cohabiting relationships as a worthwhile struggle (Thomas & Scharp, 2015). When discussing cohabitation as normal, people justified that cohabitation was just like marriage or at least a step toward marriage. Those who discussed cohabitation as easy were more inclined to discuss the positive aspects of living together and the lack of problems. Finally, some cohabiters acknowledge the difficulties of living together but emphasized that the benefits outweighed the costs.

Stepfamily Cohabitation

Even though we often think of cohabitation as happening between two unmarried people without children, stepfamily cohabitation has become increasingly more common. In fact, over half of children living in an unmarried partner household are those who live with a biological parent and their parent's unmarried partner (Manning, 2006). Specifically, cohabiting stepfamilies include both premarital and nonmarital stepfamilies

mohamed_hassan/pixabay

who live together. Because cohabiting stepfamilies lack, in some instances, both legal and blood ties, they are particularly discourse dependent (see Chapter 14). Based on the accounts of 28 stepchildren, a study by Nuru and Wang (2017) revealed that stepchildren experienced three types of challenges: (1) challenges of commitment, (2) challenges of legitimacy, and (3) challenges of morality. Commitment challenges occurred when people questioned family members' loyalty to one another whereas legitimacy challenges occurred when people questioned whether members were a family at all. Finally, challenges to a cohabiting stepfamily's morality pertained more to the virtue of the relationship between the parents as opposed to being directed at the whole family. Required to make sense of these challenges, the stepchildren discussed having to justify their family to others, refuse to acknowledge the challenge, respond preemptively, and/or directly respond to the challenges.

Marriage

The transition to marriage is often a turbulent time, full of relational uncertainty, partner interference, and partner facilitation (see Chapter 18). Once married, there are four criteria people use to assess marital quality: (1) stability, (2) satisfaction, (3) adjustment, and (4) commitment. Leslie Baxter (2010) argues, however, that marriage is not steady along these dimensions but rather is characterized by the push and pull of many factors. She says that married couples have to negotiate the following six tensions: (1) identity of the marriage as dyadic versus socially embedded, (2) marriage as an institution versus a private relationship, (3) marital love as romantic versus pragmatic, (4) marriage as a bond of commitment versus a personal choice, (5) marriage as two individuals versus a unity of one, and (6) marriage as a site of candor versus a site of discretion.

Specifically, marriage as dyadic versus socially embedded is tension about couple identity. In other words, is marriage just about the two people who are in it or is it about a larger community of people? This might be particularly important in arranged marriages where a union has implications not just for the couple but also for both of the people's families. The next tension couples often have to negotiate is the extent to which couples think of their marriage as a private relationship or something regulated and sanctioned by the state (i.e., an institution). Although couples might easily think of their marriage as both, it can become problematic when some people do not have access to the formal recognition afforded to others by the law. Next, one of the most interesting negotiations is how partners talk about their love. For some, romantic love focuses on what is rewarding to the self, ease, and exclusivity (e.g., love at first sight, one true love) versus pragmatic love which is more focused on realistic obligation and the work both partners must perform to overcome challenges. How people discuss their love might have implications for the expectations they have for the other person. Indeed, people who enter into a marriage with the belief that it will take work are less likely to get divorced than those people who only subscribe to a romantic notion of love. Competing ideas about commitment and choice also can influence how a couple behaves during tough times. For example, the idea of choice emphasizes that a person is in a relationship because it is rewarding to them. When viewing marriage as a lifelong commitment, divorce when the relationship is no longer rewarding seems like less of a viable option. This view of marriage means that spouses are responsible not only for themselves but also for their partners. The transition to marriage also requires partners to decide the extent to which they are two individuals versus a unified entity. Decisions such as legal name changes or whether to refer to yourself as an "I" or a "we" illustrate the meaningfulness of this tension. For example, couples who speak in "we" talk are more likely to be satisfied than those who speak in "me" talk. Finally, Baxter argues that married couples face decisions about the extent to which they are more open (e.g., complete honesty) or exercise discretion as a form of interpersonal protection.

Marriage Rituals

As we have discussed in previous chapters, part of our identity is both reflected and constructed by what we do. For married couples, rituals are an important part of the couple identity. Rituals are repetitive communicative performances that pay tribute to a valued object, person, or phenomenon. Although common in relationships, they are a significant part of family functioning. Based on a study by Carol Bruess and Judy Pearson (1997), 20 married couples described the following seven marriage rituals: (1) couple time, (2) symbolic rituals, (3) daily routines and tasks, (4) intimacy expressions, (5) communication rituals, (6) patterns/habits/mannerisms, and (7) spiritual rituals. Couple time included enjoyable activities, togetherness rituals, and escape episodes (i.e., desire for couple to be alone). Idiosyncratic or symbolic rituals had to do with couple favorites, private codes (e.g., inside jokes), play, and celebration rituals. Taken together, these rituals contribute to the success of a marriage and the extent to which partners find meaning in their marriages.

Same-Sex Marriage

Public support for gay marriage has grown over the past 10 years. Indeed, compared to 2007 when more Americans opposed gay marriage than approved of it, recent statistics suggest that in 2017 more people (62%) favored marriage between members of the gay and lesbian community (Geiger & Livingston, 2018). Based on an online survey of 288 lesbian, gay, bisexual, and transgendered/queer (LGBTQ) people, Pamela Lannutti (2005) found that the vast majority of her participants perceived legal equality as a positive step for the LGBTQ community. Specifically, her participants believed that legal equality was a marker of first-class citizenship that signified the end of protecting some people more than others and legal recognition. Legal equality also came with financial benefits and family security. In her study, Lannutti also highlighted the ways LGBTQ people thought legal equality would promote people to take marriage more seriously but were also concerned that they might get married for the "wrong reasons." Another interesting contradiction emerged in beliefs that the LGBTQ community would simultaneously get stronger and weaker. For example, some people believed that same-sex marriage would help decrease homophobia because they had the same rights whereas other people worried that their community would weaken through a process of assimilation. Finally, people were encouraged that legal equality could be a way to heal some relationships between the LGBTQ community and the heterosexual community.

INTERESTING RESEARCH FINDINGS

Did You Know?

The transition into a cohabiting relationship is a turbulent time where both partners might have many concerns. Keli Steuber, Jennifer Priem, Kristina Scharp, and Lindsey Thomas (2014) found that based on 103 nonengaged cohabiting couples (206 people total), 12 different issues make them feel uncertain:

- Relational Sustainability (will we make it in the long term?)
- Relational Trust (will my partner cheat?)
- Relational Compatibility (what if there is someone better for me?)
- Relational Steps (will my partner's annoying habit annoy me forever?)
- Relational Norms (is my partner satisfied with me working and him doing the chores?)
- Personal Growth (is my partner holding me back from personal growth?)
- Family Planning (does my partner want kids, and if so, how many?)
- Communication (are our communication styles compatible?)
- Social Network Issues (will my partner's family ever accept me?)
- Finances (will we be able to pay off our debt?)
- Sexual Satisfaction (do I satisfy my partner sexually?)
- Health and Well-Being (what will happen with my partner's mental health issues?)

Did You Know?

Do you know what reasons people give for getting married? To find out, the Pew Research Center (Cohn, 2013) conducted a survey and found that there are seven common reasons people get married:

- Love (88%)
- Making a lifelong commitment (81%)
- Companionship (76%)
- Having children (49%)
- A relationship recognized in a religious ceremony (30%)
- Financial stability (28%)
- For legal rights and benefits (23%)

Practical Applications and Things to Consider

Transitioning to both cohabitation and marriage can be stressful but communication often goes a long way in making the transition go smoothly. Indeed, we know from the relational turbulence theory (see Chapter 18) and the literature reviewed above that partners can feel uncertain about how they feel, uncertain about how their partner feels, and uncertain about where the relationship is headed. Cohabiting partners also experience a variety of uncertainties, especially with regard to where the relationship is headed. Toward reducing some of these uncertainties, romantic couples might consider regularly discussing their decisions, plans, and feelings.

KEY TERMS

Cohabitation effect
Deciding

Selection effect
Sliding

THOUGHT ACTIVITY

Think about a couple in your life who is happily married. How do you know? What is it about their behaviors and communication that makes you think they have a happy relationship? What communicative practices are they engaging in? Do they ever have conflict? What kind of conflict do they engage in (see Chapter 11)? How do they resolve conflict?

REFERENCES

Baxter, L. A. (2010). The dialogue of marriage. *Journal of Family Theory and Review*, *2*, 370–387. doi:10.1111/j.1756-2589.2010.00067.x

Brown, S. L., & Bulanda, J. R. (2008). Relationship violence in young adulthood: A comparison of daters, cohabiters, and marrieds. *Social Science Research*, *37*, 73–87. doi:10.1016/j.ssresearch.2007.06.002

Bruess, C. J. S., & Pearson, J. C. (1997). Interpersonal rituals in marriage and adult friendship. *Communication Monographs*, *64*, 25–46. doi:10.1080/03637759709376403

Cohen, C. L., & Kleinbaum, S. (2002). Toward a greater understanding of the cohabitation effect: Premarital cohabitation and marital communication. *Journal of Marriage and Family*, *64*, 180–192. doi:10.1111/j.1741-3737.2002.00180.x

Cohn, D. (2013). Love and marriage. *Pew Research Center*. Retrieved from https://www.pewsocialtrends.org/2013/02/13/love-and-marriage/

Geiger, A., & Livingston, G. (2018). 8 facts about love and marriage in America. Pew Research Center. Retrieved from http://www.pewresearch.org/fact-tank/2018/02/13/8-facts-about-love-and-marriage/

Lannutti, P. J. (2005). For better or worse: Exploring the meaning of same-sex marriage within the lesbian, gay, bisexual and transgendered community. *Journal of Social and Personal Relationships, 22*, 5–18. doi:10.1177/0265407505049319

Manning, W. (2006). Cohabitation and child well-being. *Gender Issues, 23*, 21–34. doi:10.1007/BF03186775

Manning, W., & Smock, P. J. (2005). Measuring and modeling cohabitation: New perspectives from qualitative data. *Journal of Marriage and the Family, 67*, 989–1002. doi:10.1111/j.1741-3737.2005.00189.x

Nuru, A. K., & Wang, T. R. (2017). "He's my dad because he just is!": Cohabiting (step)children's responses to discursive challenges. *Journal of Divorce & Remarriage, 58*, 227–243. doi:10.1080/10502556.2017.1299452

Payne, K. K. (2013). Children's family structure. National Center for Family and Marriage Research, Bowling Green, OH: Bowling Green State University.

Priem, J. S., Bailey, L. C., & Fazio, K. S. (2015). Sliding versus deciding: A theme analysis of deciding conversations of non-engaged cohabiting couples. *Communication Quarterly, 63*, 533–549. doi:10.1080/01463373.2015.1078388

Stanley, S. M., Rhoades, G. K., & Markman, H. J. (2006). Sliding versus deciding: Inertia and the premarital cohabitation effect. *Family Relations, 55*, 499–509. doi:10.1111/j.1741-3729.2006.00418.x

Steuber, K. R., Priem, J. S., Scharp, K. M., & Thomas, L. (2014). The content of relational uncertainty in non-engaged cohabiting relationships. *Journal of Applied Communication Research, 42*, 107–123. doi:10.1080/00909882.2013.874569

Thomas, L. J., & Scharp, K. M. (2015). Exploring the meaning of cohabitation: A relational dialectics perspective. *Iowa Journal of Communication, 47*, 73–95.

RELATED READINGS

Cao, H., Fine, M., Fang, X., & Zhou, N. (2019). Chinese adult children's perceived parents' satisfaction with adult children's marriage, in-law relationship quality, and adult children's marital satisfaction. *Journal of Social and Personal Relationships.* Advanced Online Publication. doi:10.1177/0265407518755319

Kennedy-Lightsey, C. D., Martin, M. M., LaBelle, S., & Weber, K. (2015). Attachment, identity gaps, and communication relational outcomes in marital couples' public performances. *Journal of Family Communication, 15*, 232–248. doi:10.1080/15267431.2015.1043430

Martinez, L. V., Ting-Toomey, S., & Dorjee, T. (2016). Identity management and relational culture in interfaith marital communication in a United States context: A qualitative study. *Journal of Intercultural Communication Research, 45*, 503–525. doi:10.1080/17475759.2016.1237984

Chapter 20

Delaying, Forgoing, and Transitioning to Parenthood

BACKGROUND

About 1.2 million people become new parents every year in the United States (Livingston, 2018). People can become parents through the birth or adoption of a child, or through partnership to someone with children. No matter how people become parents, a new child disrupts life and changes the structure of the family system. As communication scientists, we know that the transition to parenthood is rife with communication challenges as partners renegotiate their roles and relationship as parents and support networks work to assist and encourage sleep-deprived new moms and dads. These support networks can help to relieve the pressure to be a "good parent" by offering support and normalizing the challenges of parenthood. In fact, 52% of millennials report being a good parent is one of the most important goals of their lives. **New parents face myriad changes in their personal, family, social, and professional lives.**

THE RELATIONSHIP DURING THE TRANSITION TO PARENTHOOD

The transition to parenthood is often a joyous and stressful time in the life course. It represents a transition to a new family of origin, when a partnership becomes

Communication in Family Contexts: Theories and Processes, First Edition.
Elizabeth Dorrance Hall and Kristina M. Scharp.
© 2020 John Wiley & Sons, Inc. Published 2020 by John Wiley & Sons, Inc.
Companion website: www.wiley.com/go/dorrance_hall/communication-in-family-contexts

a triad. Many couples have their first child within the first five years of marriage. These first five years of marriage are also the years the couple is most likely to get divorced. With this in mind, it is interesting that most couples experience a fairly dramatic decrease in marital satisfaction following the birth of their first child.

Brian Doss and his team (2009) conducted an eight-year study to determine the effect of the transition to parenthood on the parents' relationship quality. His study found a quick decline in marital satisfaction and relationship functioning after the birth of the first child. The lower levels of satisfaction appeared to persist for the remainder of the eight years of the study. Mothers experienced larger declines in their ability to manage conflict than fathers did. Interestingly, he found that marital satisfaction also gradually declined in couples without children, though it declined more slowly.

The decline in marital satisfaction is related to the amount of stress the couple endures during the transition. There are several "protective factors" that can help new parents through this challenging time. According to Tomlinson and Irwin (1993), couples who came from a happy or average family of origin, have similar views about sex-role expectations (like who is going to change the diapers), and share interests, goals, and background had an easier time with the transition to parenthood. Supporting one another and engaging in relational maintenance before and during the transition are other important stress-reducing factors.

Marital satisfaction is closely linked to the couple's communication patterns including whether they engage in healthy conflict and relational maintenance. Those patterns are detailed in Chapters 11 and 28. Communication is critical at this stage of the life course because the quality of the partners' relationship has effects on how well the child develops psychologically, socially, and academically (Doss et al., 2009).

Couples tend to also decrease their supportiveness of one another after having a baby and increase their conflict. If support can be kept high, it might protect against the decrease in relationship satisfaction during the transition. A study by Alexandra Chong and Kristin Mickelson (2016) found that perceptions of how supportive one's spouse is are linked to relationship satisfaction. They also found that how childcare and household responsibilities are split between the partners matters in predicting marital satisfaction after having a baby. Perceived fairness of childcare and household chores increased perceptions of spousal support, which in turn increased new parents' relationship satisfaction.

The transition to parenthood and the stress that goes with it begin before the baby is born. Based on the finding that a lack of support during pregnancy is related to low birth weight in babies, Christine McKee, Peta Stapleton, and Aileen Pidgeon (2017) explored the role stress and support play during pregnancy. The researchers found that a lack of support was a cause of stress for expecting parents. They advocate for support as an adaptive coping strategy that can be achieved through pre- and perinatal parenting programs.

According to Glen Stamp (1994), new moms and dads go through a process of taking on the role of parent. This process consists of learning and adjusting role expectations, enacting their new roles while facilitating or inhibiting their own and their partner's ability to do so, and negotiating those roles with their partner. Parents experience tensions related to each of the parts of the process. For example, parents have to adjust their role expectations depending on whether their ideas about what parenthood would be like were accurate or inaccurate. New parents cannot know exactly what parenthood will be like, yet they do their best to try to make predictions. Some of those predictions are unrealistic or inaccurate and need to be adjusted, often through conversation with others. Role negotiation with one's partner is also dependent on communication. Couples talk about parenting techniques and sift through the wealth of parenting advice and information available from books, media, doctors, and their support networks. Many of these discussions happen on the fly, when an issue arises during parenting. For example, parents have to decide what to do when the baby cries, who will go pick the baby up, and how long they should let him/her cry. They have to figure out what to do when they have used every trick in the book and the baby is still crying. These pivotal moments are highly dependent on effective communication.

Stamp (1994) highlights the effects of becoming a parent that go beyond the parent–child dyad by explaining that new parents must renegotiate the reality of their marriage because of two major changes: the presence of a child and their new roles as parents. The construction of this new reality is based in communication since it is accomplished and maintained through conversation.

In brief, the transition to parenthood initiates change in all family relationships as partners become parents and new members (i.e., children) are introduced to the family system. This change tends to be hard on the partner–partner sub-system of the family and is marked by a decline in marital satisfaction that typically recovers over time.

LGBTQ PARENTS

An increasing number of people identify as LGBTQ and are raising children in the United States. Much of the parenting research suggests children with gay or lesbian parents are just as happy, intelligent, adaptable, and well behaved as children with mixed-sex parents. According to Biblarz and Stacey (2010), lesbian parents might have better parenting skills than mixed-sex parents due to women typically investing more energy in children and household tasks and ranking higher on parenting skills tests than men. For more on same-sex couples and parents, see Chapter 26.

A research team led by Bérengère Rubio (2017) examined the transition to parenthood for gay, lesbian, and heterosexual couples who conceived through assisted reproduction (i.e., in vitro fertilization, sperm donation, egg donation, embryo donation, and surrogacy). LGBTQ and heterosexual couples who conceive using assisted reproduction technology typically differ in their reasons for turning to assisted reproduction. Same-sex couples indicate wanting to raise a child from birth and wanting to have a biologically related child (as opposed to adopting). Mixed-sex couples typically use assisted reproduction because they are unable to have children without it (i.e., infertility). Utilizing reproductive technologies can be challenging. For example, couples who have struggled with infertility often experience psychological distress and lowered self-esteem (Ellison & Hall, 2003; Gibson, Ungerer, Tennant, & Saunders, 2000). Same-sex couples might feel stigmatized.

SINGLE PARENTS

Single-parent families are more common than ever before. In fact, 28% of children lived with only one parent in 2010 (U.S. Census Bureau, 2010). Most single parents are mothers, but a significant number are also fathers. Single-parent families face unique challenges compared to two-parent families including learning how to parent alone, role overload (i.e., one person doing the work of two parents), financial constraints, social isolation, stigma, and a lack of social support (Amato, 2000). Single parents can experience more ego-depletion than partners with children because they are handling all of the parenting on their own. According to Baumeister (2002), **ego-depletion** refers to a state of overwhelm when it is difficult to make decisions or process new information due to too much information. Ego-depletion causes stress, which makes it more difficult to parent effectively. Certain types of coping, like communal coping, might not be possible without a partner to lean on for support, though many single parents are embedded in strong support networks of their own siblings, parents, and extended family. Single-parent families are discourse dependent, meaning they often have to explain to others their family situation (e.g., other children asking "Where is your dad? Why don't you live with him?"). Despite these challenges, many single-parent families survive and thrive by learning to cope and be resilient and by creating their own communication patterns for successful family functioning.

mohamed_hassan/pixabay

ADOPTIVE PARENTS

Adoptive parents have a unique transition to parenthood as children might not be babies when they enter the family. Adoption represents a small but significant percentage of the transition to parenthood; around 2% of children in the United States are adopted. Adoptive parents might choose to adopt domestically, internationally, or from foster care. Especially in the case of domestic adoption, adoptive parents not only need to negotiate a new child but also might have to negotiate relationships with birth families. For more on adoptive parents and adopted children, see Chapter 23.

UNDERGRADUATE STUDENT PARENTS

Becoming a parent during college can be especially challenging as parenting stress is coupled with academic and often financial stress. Your textbook authors have done research on a special, but significant population of undergraduate students: undergraduate student parents (Scharp & Dorrance Hall, 2019). Gathering data from undergraduate students who also had children, we set out to discover how the costs of seeking social support influenced the health of the student parents. Undergraduate student parents experienced both interpersonal and intrapersonal costs to seeking support, perhaps because they wanted to appear confident and like they had their lives under control, even when they needed network support. We also wondered whether the amount of support a student parent desired influenced his/her physical health. Desiring social presence support (described in detail in Chapter 17) was linked to higher parenting stress. We also found that college-based stress and parenting-based stress were both linked to student parents getting less sleep, having more headaches, and exercising less. Friends and family can make a significant difference in the lives of college students who are also parents. Student parents who feel supported and are not afraid to ask for help are less stressed and in better physical health.

DELAYING OR OMITTING THE TRANSITION TO PARENTHOOD

Increasingly, people are delaying the transition to parenthood. In a recent *New York Times* survey, adults aged 20–45 reported a variety of reasons for waiting longer to have children or choosing to be "childfree." Childfree refers to adults or couples who make a conscious choice to not have children. These families are sometimes called "childless by choice." Those reasons are depicted in Figure 20.1. The bigger boxes indicate larger percentages of people who reported that reason. For example, 36% of people reported wanting more leisure time as a reason for not having or delaying children whereas 14% reported working too much or being worried about population growth as reasons.

Figure 20.1 Reasons to delay parenthood.

Research by Laura Scott (2009) found similar motivations for choosing to be childfree including enjoying life in its current state without kids, and valuing freedom and independence. A difficult communication task comes along with making the choice to be childfree, that is, explaining to others how they are a complete family without children. According to Scott's research, childfree couples are sometimes viewed by others as being too focused on their careers or even considered selfish. Some childfree couples struggle with stress or guilt about their decision and feel frustrated that they have to explain their choice to others (Durham, 2008). Childfree couples are an example of a discourse-dependent family. See Chapter 14 for further discussion on discourse dependence.

Young adults are also having fewer children than they consider "ideal." The reasons given for this are similar to waiting to have children and include thinking childcare is too expensive or they are unable to afford more children, wanting more time for the children they already have, feeling worried about the economy, and wanting more leisure time. Some of the reasons reflect US and individual corporation policy on family leaving including having no paid family leave or not having enough leave available to them.

INTERESTING RESEARCH FINDINGS

Parent–Grandparent Relationships

The transition to parenthood affects more than just the new parents and the baby. Tim Dun (2010) examined turning points in the relationship between new parents and their parents (grandparents of the baby). Turning points are events that change a relationship, typically bringing people closer or further apart. Refer to Chapter 29 for more on turning points including an activity to assess your own relationship turning points with a sibling. Dun interviewed first-time parents about how their relationships with their parents have changed as they themselves have become parents and found 10 major turning points, some of which were good for the relationship and some of which were negative. Positive turning points include connections, gifts, other talk, and disclosure. Negative turning points include conflict and face-threatening advice. Still other turning points were sometimes positive and sometimes negative. Those turning points included "babies here," communication, and separation (giving new parents space versus new parents feeling isolated).

New Parent Interventions

Researchers and clinicians have been using interventions to help couples cope with the decline in marital satisfaction after the birth of a child. In a 2015 study, Alyson Shapiro, John Gottman, and Brandi Fink examined how an intervention could help couples improve their communication and decrease relationship conflict after having a baby. The intervention, called "Bringing the Baby Home," teaches couples how to maintain and strengthen their intimacy, change their conflict patterns so they are more constructive, increase father involvement in the family, and co-parent successfully. The workshop was developed by examining what couples whose marital satisfaction did not decline after having a baby did differently than those whose satisfaction did decline. The workshop taught parents that a **firm relationship foundation** was an important place to start. A firm relationship foundation is based on appreciation of each other and responsiveness to one another's communication. The workshop also taught conflict management, self-soothing, and positive communication. **Positive communication** includes openly discussing things rather than disagreeing and always communicating in respectful ways. The researchers found that couples who took the workshop had improved their communication and lowered conflict in just 3 months, and that communication continued to improve 1 year after the workshop.

PRACTICAL APPLICATIONS AND THINGS TO CONSIDER

New parents benefit greatly from support from their social networks. How might you support new parents you know? Refer back to Chapter 17 where the following types of support are listed and defined: emotional, esteem, informational, network, tangible, social presence. How could you enact each type of support for a friend with a new baby? If you are considering having children, how could you solicit support from others while protecting yourself from face threats (e.g., admitting you do not know everything about parenting from day one)?

IN-CLASS ACTIVITY

Research has found that active, problem-focused coping is best for decreasing new parent stress and increasing involvement with the new baby. Which of the following coping strategies do you think have been found to be more helpful versus less helpful for new parents? Refer back to Chapter 12 and try to place each strategy into one of the four types of coping.

1. Doing things with children
2. Seeking support from social networks
3. Having realistic expectations
4. Crying
5. Trusting your partner
6. Investing in children
7. Watching TV
8. Maintaining family stability
9. Believing life would be better without the baby
10. Taking advantage of economic benefits
11. Shopping with friends
12. Providing mutual support
13. Being thankful
14. Sharing responsibilities
15. Reliving the past
16. Wishing the baby wasn't there
17. Getting up together in the middle of the night

Answer key: helpful (1, 2, 3, 5, 6, 8, 12, 13, 14, 17), less helpful (4, 7, 9, 10, 11, 15, 16), based on research by Ventura and Boss (1983) and Ahlborg and Strandmark (2006).

IN-CLASS DISCUSSION

Apply Afifi's theory of resilience and relationship load to the transition to parenthood (Afifi, Merrill, & Davis, 2016). Refer to Chapter 12 for more about this theory. Answer the following based on the theory: How can soon-to-be parents invest in their relationship before the baby comes to have more reserves to draw from when the sleepless nights hit?

Other questions to consider: How would your family react if you made the decision to be childfree? What communication strategies would you use to convince others your family is "complete" without children?

KEY TERMS

Childfree
Firm relationship
foundation

Positive communication
Protective factors
Role appropriation

REFERENCES

Afifi, T. D., Merrill, A. F., & Davis, S. (2016). The theory of resilience and relational load. *Personal Relationships, 23*, 663–683. doi:10.1111/pere.12159

Ahlborg, T., & Strandmark, M. (2006). Factors influencing the quality of intimate relationships six months after delivery – First-time parents' own views and coping strategies. *Journal of Psychosomatic Obstetrics & Gynecology, 27*, 163–172. doi:10.1080/01674820500463389

Amato, P. R. (2000). The consequences of divorce for adults and children. *Journal of Marriage and Family, 62*, 1269–1287. doi:10.1111/j.1741-3737.2000.01269.x

Baumeister, R. F. (2002). Ego depletion and self-control failure: An energy model of the self's executive function. *Self and Identity, 1*, 129–136. doi:10.1080/152988602317319302

Biblarz, T. J., & Stacey, J. (2010). How does the gender of parents matter? *Journal of Marriage and Family, 72*, 3–22. doi:10.1111/j.1741-3737.2009.00678.x

Chong, A., & Mickelson, K. D. (2016). Perceived fairness and relationship satisfaction during the transition to parenthood: The mediating role of spousal support. *Journal of Family Issues, 37*, 3–28. doi:10.1177/0192513X13516764

Doss, B. D., Rhoades, G. K., Stanley, S. M., & Markman, H. J. (2009). The effect of the transition to parenthood on relationship quality: An 8-year prospective study. *Journal of Personality and Social Psychology, 96*, 601–619. doi:10.1037/a0013969

Dun, T. (2010). Turning points in parent–grandparent relationships during the start of a new generation. *Journal of Family Communication, 10*, 194–210. doi:10.1080/15267431.2010.489218

Durham, W. T. (2008). The rules-based process of revealing/concealing the family planning decisions of voluntarily child-free couples: A communication privacy management perspective. *Communication Studies, 59*, 132–147. doi:10.1080/10510970802062451

Ellison, M. A., & Hall, J. E. (2003). Social stigma and compounded losses: Quality-of-life issues for multiple-birth families. *Fertility and Sterility, 80*, 405–414. doi:10.1016/S0015-0282(03)00659-9

Gibson, F. L., Ungerer, J. A., Tennant, C. C., & Saunders, D. M. (2000). Parental adjustment and attitudes to parenting after in vitro fertilization. *Fertility and Sterility, 73*, 565–574. doi:10.1016/S0015-0282(99)00583-X

Livingston, G. (2018, May 4). More than a million Millennials are becoming moms each year. Retrieved from http://www.pewresearch.org/fact-tank/2018/05/04/more-than-a-million-millennials-are-becoming-moms-each-year/

McKee, C., Stapleton, P., & Pidgeon, A. (2017). Support during pregnancy as an influencing factor on the transition to parenthood. *Journal of Prenatal & Perinatal Psychology & Health, 32*, 99–127.

Rubio, B., Vecho, O., Gross, M., van Rijn-van Gelderen, L., Bos, H., Ellis-Davies, K., ... & Lamb, M. E. (2017). Transition to parenthood and quality of parenting among gay, lesbian and heterosexual couples who conceived through assisted reproduction. *Journal of Family Studies*. doi:10.1080/13229400.2017.1413005

Scott, L. S. (2009). *Two is enough: A couple's guide to living childless by choice.* Berkley, CA: Seal Press.

Scharp, K. M., & Dorrance Hall, E. (2019). Examining the relationship between undergraduate student parent social support seeking factors, stress, and somatic symptoms: A two-model comparison of direct and indirect effects. *Health Communication, 34*, 54–64. doi:10.1080/10410236.2017.1384427

Shapiro, A. F., Gottman, J. M., & Fink, B. C. (2015). Short-term change in couples' conflict following a transition to parenthood intervention. *Couple and Family Psychology: Research and Practice, 4*, 239–251. doi:10.1037/cfp000051

Stamp, G. H. (1994). The appropriation of the parental role through communication during the transition to parenthood. *Communications Monographs, 61*, 89–112. doi:10.1080/03637759409376327

Tomlinson, P. S., & Irwin, B. (1993). Qualitative study of women's reports of family adaptation pattern four years following transition to parenthood. *Issues in Mental Health Nursing, 14*, 119–138. doi:10.3109/01612849309031612

U.S. Census Bureau. (2010). Current population survey: Definitions and explanations. Retrieved from http://www.census.gov/cps/about/cpsdef.html

Ventura, J. N., & Boss, P. G. (1983). The family coping inventory applied to parents with new babies. *Journal of Marriage and the Family, 45*, 867–875. doi:10.2307/351799

RELATED READINGS

Bramlett, M. D., & Mosher W. D. (2001). *Advance data from vital and health statistics; no. 323.* Hyattsville, MD: National Center for Health Statistics.

Cain Miller, C. (2018, July 5). Americans are having fewer babies. They told us why. *The New York Times.* Retrieved from https://www.nytimes.com/2018/07/05/upshot/americans-are-having-fewer-babies-they-told-us-why.html

Cowan, C. P., & Cowan, P. A. (2000). *When partners become parents: The big life change for couples.* Mahwah, NJ: Lawrence Erlbaum Associates.

Dun, T., & Sears, C. (2017). Relational trajectories from parent and child to grandparent and new parent. *Journal of Family Communication, 17*, 185–201. doi: 10.1080/15267431.2017.1281281

Gates, G. J. (2013). LGBT parenting in the United States. *The Williams Institute.* Retrieved from https://escholarship.org/uc/item/9xs6g8xx

Howard, K. S., & Brooks-Gunn, J. (2009). Relationship supportiveness during the transition to parenting among married and unmarried parents. *Parenting: Science and Practice, 9*, 123–142. doi:10.1080/15295190802656928

Huston, T., & Holmes, E. K. (2004). Becoming parents. In A. Vangelisti (Ed.), *Handbook of family communication* (pp. 105–133). Mahwah, NJ: Lawrence Erlbaum Associates.

Pew Research Center. (2010, February 24). Millennials: Confident. Connected. Open to change. *Pew Research Center.* Retrieved from http://www.pewsocialtrends.org/2010/02/24/millennials-confident-connected-open-to-change/

Roy, R. N., Schumm, W. R., & Britt, S. L. (2014). *Transition to parenthood.* New York, NY: Springer.

Chapter 21

Divorce and Dissolution

Despite vows that often include phrases such as "until death do us part," in the last 50 years divorce has become increasingly common in the United States. Approximately half of marriages end in divorce (see Amato, 2010). Recent research has shown that the divorce rate among millennials is lower than the generations that preceded them due, in part, to the millennial age cohort taking a different approach to relationships than past generations (Cohen, 2018). Specifically, millennials are waiting longer to get married, often completing their education and starting careers well before marriage.

Although many societal and individual risk factors such as age at first marriage make divorce more likely for certain people, marital communication plays a key role in whether a couple will stay together and how well the family adjusts in the event of a divorce. The ability to engage in constructive conflict communication (see Chapter 11) is an especially important protective factor that can help couples avoid divorce. In this chapter, we discuss factors that contribute to divorce, the process of divorce, and some outcomes of divorce. To learn more about when family members seek to gain distance from other members (with whom they are not romantically involved), see Chapter 15 on family distancing.

Communication in Family Contexts: Theories and Processes, First Edition.
Elizabeth Dorrance Hall and Kristina M. Scharp.
© 2020 John Wiley & Sons, Inc. Published 2020 by John Wiley & Sons, Inc.
Companion website: www.wiley.com/go/dorrance_hall/communication-in-family-contexts

KEY CONCEPTS

Factors that Predict Divorce

Unhappy married couples might not always get divorced (Caughlin, Huston, & Houts, 2000). Beyond dissatisfaction with the relationship, societal and individual factors influence the risk of getting a divorce. Societal factors include unrealistic assumptions about what marriage will entail, a growing emphasis on individualism in American culture, and gender expectations. Individual factors include those such as age, race/ethnicity, religion, parental divorce, and socio-economic status. Factors such as premarital pregnancy and cohabitation before marriage also increase the likelihood of divorce for a variety of reasons. Research suggests that couples who choose to live together before marriage have less traditional views of marriage, are more likely to suffer from substance abuse issues, are more likely to approve of divorce, and are more likely to experience problems with the law (see Chapter 19 for more on cohabitation). Thus, it is possible that cohabitation is not the main driver behind the increased likelihood of divorce, but rather the issues that coincide with those who choose to cohabitate (see Booth & Johnson, 1988). Of note, this only pertains to partners pre-engagement.

When asked why they divorced, women cited infidelity (25%), incompatibility (19%), and drinking/drug abuse (14%) as their top reasons whereas men cited incompatibility (20%), infidelity (16%), and lack of communication (13%) as their top three (Amato & Previti, 2003). This research also revealed that women were more likely than men to initiate dissolution even if they were not the least involved partner. One explanation is that women are more aware of relationship problems and more willing to take initiative.

The Process of Divorce

Breaking up with a romantic dating partner and breaking up with a spouse are not necessarily the same process; but divorce is a distancing process just like a romantic break-up or family estrangement. This means that instead of being a one-time event, divorce unfolds over time. Dissolving dating relationships could be less stressful because there is no associated stigma with casual break-ups and individuals can typically recover and move on. Furthermore, dating couples often do not have to contend with the legal and economic ramifications associated with divorce, especially when the married couple shares children. One thing dating break-ups and divorce share, however, is that relationship dissolution is often the product of decreased positive feeling as opposed to increased negative feelings (Caughlin et al., 2000).

There are multiple ways scholars have characterized the divorce process. John Gottman (1994) offers a model that suggests distance and divorce are like a cascade which includes (1) flooding – feeling overwhelmed, (2) belief that marital problems are severe, (3) desire to work on problem individually as opposed to collectively, (4) the creation of separate lives, and (5) loneliness. Flooding occurs when spouses are surprised and overwhelmed by their partner's negative emotions. This feeling of being overwhelmed causes partners to want to escape the situation. When partners are flooded, they cannot comprehend their spouse's negativity, which can lead them to believe their problems are more severe than they really are or even are unsolvable. Based on these beliefs, partners can sometimes feel like they need to solve the problem on their own, which prompts them to start building separate lives. This **divorce cascade** ultimately leads to feelings of loneliness.

Another model suggests that unlike other types of relationship dissolution, divorce is often the result of marital disaffection (Kayser & Rao, 2006). This process includes: (1) beginning disappointments, often a result of changes in partner interaction, (2) escalating anger and hurt, often a result of anticipated or actual negative partner behavior, and finally (3) reaching apathy and indifference, often signifying a "point of no return" where couples no longer feel they can maintain the relationship.

Finally, some scholars have classified stages of divorce. Bohannon (1970) describes divorce in six stages: (1) emotional divorce, (2) legal divorce, (3) economic divorce, (4) co-parental divorce, (5) community divorce, and (6) psychic divorce. Emotional divorce is characterized by a change of feeling, withdrawal from interaction, and/or dissatisfaction. This may occur over time or quickly if spurred on by an event like infidelity. Legal divorce formalizes the process in the legal system. When partners divide their financial assets, they experience economic divorce. Co-parental divorce only applies to couples with children and might include legal components like deciding on child custody. Custody decisions often require extensive amounts of communication and coordination. Community divorce involves communicating the dissolution to other network members. Finally, psychic divorce captures the point of closure when partners no longer think of themselves as married. Taken together, all of these process models suggest that decreasing interdependence requires communicative action and negotiation to dissolve the relationship and explain the dissolution to others.

Outcomes of Divorce

Divorce is a process that not only affects emotions but also influences how people think of themselves. Specifically, divorce comes with a loss of status, loss of identity, and loss of important routines and roles. Many everyday routines provide not only a structure but also a sense of identity and purpose. Often the value of these routine events is not fully recognized until the routine can no longer be followed. This means that dissolution is not just an emotional cutoff, but a process that influences the ways individuals make sense of themselves and others. Scholars suggest that social networks play a significant role in relationship dissolution, especially in the context of divorce. For example, a national sample of married individuals revealed that 33% of the participants felt that their social network's approval or disapproval was a potential facilitator or barrier to getting a divorce (Knoester & Booth, 2000). This finding suggests that individuals care about their social network's opinion of their relationship status, which holds interesting implications for the ways in which individuals communicate their dissolution to their network.

Outcomes for children have been a popular topic of research. Often, people think that children of divorced parents have very poor outcomes, though that is not always true. Despite the fact that about 70% of the divorce research suggests that children of divorced parents scored lower on well-being measures (e.g., academic achievement, social and psychological adjustment, parent–child relations) compared to children with non-divorced parents, the differences between the children, although statistically significant, were not that different in actuality (i.e., the effect sizes were small). These effects also depend on the age of the children. For example, researchers find more negative outcomes for children who are primary through high-school aged than children who are pre-school or college-aged (Amato & Keith, 1991). Furthermore, these negative outcomes are getting smaller in more recently conducted research.

Did You Know?

When asked what helped them through their divorce, four out of the five things divorced people list are related to communication (Greeff & van der Merwe, 2004).

1. Intra-family support (support from other family members)
2. Extended family support
3. Support from friends
4. Open communication between family members

For more details about supportive communication, see Chapter 17.

Did You Know?

Children who have divorced parents are more likely to get divorced themselves (Amato & Booth, 2001). One reason for this intergenerational transmission of divorce might be that children of divorced parents learn poor marital communication skills by observing and modeling their behaviors after their parents. This corresponds to Chapter 8, when you learned about modeling in social cognitive theory.

INTERESTING RESEARCH FINDINGS

Communication matters not only in everyday interactions between married partners but also with regard to how those partners discuss the marriage itself. Narrative studies suggest that couples are more likely to get divorced within the next three to five years if they tell stories about their relationship that illustrate (1) very little fondness for their partner, (2) a lack of "we" as opposed to "I" language, (3) a failure to account for glorified struggle, (4) a strong sense of marital disappointment, and (5) chaos (Buehlmann, Gottman, & Katz, 1992; Carrere, Buehlmann, Gottman, Coan, & Ruckstuhl, 2000). See Chapter 7 for more on narrative theories. These results suggest that it is not problematic for couples to acknowledge tough times so long as they can talk about those times as a catalyst for growing stronger as a couple. Couples who tell stories with these negative markers are more likely to experience emotional flooding and are more likely to feel lonely.

PRACTICAL APPLICATIONS AND THINGS TO CONSIDER

John Gottman, founder of the Gottman Institute, and his colleagues have conducted research over the decades about the factors that influence whether a couple stays together or divorces. As a result, he encourages communicative behaviors that strengthen relationships and help prevent divorce. For example, Gottman and his colleagues (2006) encourage (1) a softened start-up, (2) turning toward one's partner, (3) repairing the conversation, and (4) accepting influence. A softened start-up includes the ability of people to discuss a problem or issue a complaint without criticizing their partners. When people focus on behaviors (as opposed to characteristics of the other person), partners are more willing to listen and engage in constructive communication behaviors. Turning toward one's partner requires people to meet their partner's bid for connection with a positive communication behavior such as asking a question, providing positive nonverbal feedback, or giving their partner a hug. This shows people's partners that they are open and willing to listen as opposed to ignoring the bid for connection or meeting that bid with anger or hostility. Repairing a conversation requires people to withdraw from negative feelings during a difficult interaction to help relieve tension and express willingness. Finally, accepting influence encourages people to be mutually influenced by each other. The opposite of this behavior is stubbornness. Even though Gottman is a psychologist, there is no doubt communication plays an essential role in what helps couples stay together in happy marriages. For more on positive partner communication, see Chapter 28.

KEY TERMS

Bohannon's stages of divorce

Divorce cascade

THOUGHT ACTIVITY

About 50% of marriages end in divorce. In light of this statistic, do you think people are meant to commit to a single person for their whole life? What has changed in our culture that made getting a divorce more acceptable? What are the conditions under which divorce might be a better option than remaining married?

IN-CLASS DISCUSSION

With a partner, describe the ideal co-parent relationship. Once you have discussed what this relationship might look like, consider the following questions:

1. How should two people who share children, but are no longer in a romantic relationship with one another, communicate?

2. What kinds of rules might they discuss to keep their communication in a positive and productive place?

3. Reflecting on Chapter 4, what privacy boundaries should be in place and how should information about the children and about themselves be shared or co-owned between parents?

4. Read these 10 co-parenting tips from Holly B. Tiret at Michigan State University Extension and assess whether they line up with the relationship you described earlier. Think about what you might add to this list based on what you have learned in this class or what you might add to your description of the ideal co-parent relationship based on Tiret's list. https://www.canr.msu.edu/news/ten_tips_for_successful_co-parenting

REFERENCES

Amato, P. R. (2010). Research on divorce: Continuing trends and new developments. *Journal of Marriage and Family, 72*, 650–666. doi:10.111 1/j.1741-3737.2010.00723

Amato, P. R., & Booth, A. (2001). The legacy of parents' marital discord: Consequences for children's marital quality. *Journal of Personality and Social Psychology, 81*, 627–638. doi:10.1037/0022-3514.81.4.627

Amato, P. R., & Keith, B. (1991). Parental divorce and well-being in children: A meta-analysis. *Psychological Bulletin, 110*, 26–46. doi:10.2307/2580068

Amato, P. R., & Previti, D. (2003). People's reason for divorcing: Gender, social class, the life course, and adjustment. *Journal of Family Issues, 24*, 602–628. doi:10.1177/0192513X03254507

Bohannon, P. (1970). *Divorce and after.* New York, NY: Doubleday.

Booth, A., & Johnson, D. (1988). Premarital cohabitation and marital success. *Journal of Family Issues, 9*, 255–272. doi:10.1177/019251388009002007

Buehlmann, K. T., Gottman, J. M., & Katz, L. F. (1992). How a couple views their past predicts their future: Predicting divorce from an oral history interview. *Journal of Family Psychology, 5*, 295–318. doi:10.1037/0893-3200.5.3-4.295

Carrere, S., Buehlmann, K. T., Gottman, J. M., Coan, J. A., & Ruckstuhl, L. (2000). Predicting marital stability and divorce in newlywed couples. *Journal of Family Psychology, 14*, 42–58. doi:10.1037//0893-3200.14.1.42

Caughlin, J. P., Huston, T. L., & Houts, R. M. (2000). How does personality matter in marriage? An examination of trait anxiety, interpersonal negativity, and marital satisfaction. *Journal of Personality and Social Psychology, 78*, 326–336. doi:10.1037/0022-3514.78.2.326

Cohen, P. N. (2018, November 14). *The coming divorce decline*. Retrieved from
https://osf.io/bk4mh/download

Gottman, J. M. (1994). *What predicts divorce? The relationship between marital
processes and marital outcomes*. Hillsdale, NJ: Lawrence Erlbaum Associates.

Gottman, J., Gottman, S., & DeClaire, J. (2006). *10 lessons to transform your
marriage*. New York, NY: Three Rivers Press.

Greeff, A. P., & van der Merwe, S. (2004). Variables associated with resilience
in divorced families. *Social Indicators Research, 68*, 59–75. doi:10.1023/
B:SOCI.0000025569.95499.b5

Kayser, K., & Rao, S. S. (2006). Process of disaffection in relationship breakdown. In
M. A. Fine & J. H. Harvey (Eds.), *Handbook of divorce and relationship dissolution*
(pp. 201–222). New York, NY: Routledge.

Knoester, C., & Booth, A. (2000). Barriers to divorce: When are they effective?
When are they not? *Journal of Family Issues, 21*, 78–99. doi:10.1177/
019251300021001004

RELATED READINGS

Habibi, M., Hajieydari, Z., & Darharaj, M. (2015). Causes of divorce in the marriage
phase from the viewpoints of couples referred to Iran's family courts. *Journal of
Divorce & Remarriage, 56*, 43–56. doi:10.1080/10502556.2014.972195

Leustek, J., & Theiss, J. A. (2019). Family communication patterns that predict
perceptions of upheaval and psychological well-being for emerging adult children following late-life divorce. *Journal of Family Studies*. Advanced Online
Publication. doi:10.1080/13229400.2017.1352531

Punyanunt-Carter, N. M., Shimkowski, J. R., Colwell, M. J., & Norman, M. S. (2018).
College students' perceptions of media portrayals of divorce. *Journal of Divorce
& Remarriage, 59*, 574–589. doi:10.1080/10502556.2018.1466252

Chapter 22

Remarriage and Stepfamily Formation

Joining families after remarriage is an increasingly common way to "be" a family. In fact, about 75% of people get remarried after divorce, especially if the divorce occurred before the age of 60. When remarriage includes the presence of children, a new family form often is the result: a stepfamily. Estimates suggest that 42% of adults identify at least one step-relative and 30% report that they have a step- or half-sibling (Cherlin, 2010; Sweeney, 2010). These percentages are even higher for people under 30. Yet, despite the prevalence reported by the census, these percentages are still likely too low because nonresidential parents are not considered a member of a step-family by the government. Furthermore, children (18 years of age or older) are also not accounted for by the census because they are considered to be adults. Overall, stepfamilies are a common type of discourse-dependent family that requires communication and coordination (see Chapter 14 on Discourse Dependence).

KEY CONCEPTS

Remarriage

Research suggests that despite getting a divorce, people do not remarry with more caution the second or even third time. Indeed, the divorce rate for second marriages is even higher than first marriages (Teachman, 2008). There are multiple

Communication in Family Contexts: Theories and Processes, First Edition.
Elizabeth Dorrance Hall and Kristina M. Scharp.
© 2020 John Wiley & Sons, Inc. Published 2020 by John Wiley & Sons, Inc.
Companion website: www.wiley.com/go/dorrance_hall/communication-in-family-contexts

hypotheses about why it seems people are not learning from their mistakes: (1) divorce-prone personality hypothesis, (2) dysfunctional beliefs hypothesis, (3) remarriage market hypothesis, (4) training school hypothesis, and (5) willingness to leave marriage hypothesis (Ganong & Coleman, 1994). The **divorce-prone personality hypothesis** suggests that some people have characteristics that make them likely candidates for divorce. The **dysfunctional beliefs hypothesis** suggests that some people might believe they have learned from their mistakes and subsequently start their new marriage with unrealistic expectations. The **remarriage market hypothesis** speaks to the possibility that there are not as many desirable partners the second or third time. The **training school hypothesis** states that people develop problematic behaviors and patterns of interacting in their first marriage that they then bring into their next marriage. Finally, the **willingness to leave marriage hypothesis** suggests that because people were willing to leave a marriage once, they see divorce as a viable option in subsequent marriages.

Remarriage is not only something romantic partners must negotiate, but also something that influences both of the partners' families, especially if there are children involved. Leslie Baxter and her colleagues (2009) set out to explore the rituals around remarriage and the perceptions of the ceremony from the perspective of the stepchildren. Based on 80 interviews, the research team identified six types of remarriage ceremonies: (1) the white wedding, (2) the modified white wedding (i.e., smaller and/or more casual), (3) the civil ceremony, (4) casual event, (5) elopement, and (6) family-centered ceremony (i.e., whole family got married, not just partners). What is most interesting about this study is that the authors also looked to see what made the ceremony meaningful. Young-adult stepchildren identified three meaningful factors: (1) the type of ritual enactment, (2) the legitimation granted to the "sacred object," and (3) the degree of involvement stepchildren had in the ceremony. Specifically, young-adult stepchildren conveyed that not all of the remarriage ceremonies were equally appropriate. Most described wanting some elements of a traditional wedding but not too many. They were particularly critical of the white wedding. Legitimation had to do with the extent to which the stepchildren found the remarriage meaningful. Some stepchildren described feeling totally indifferent, some thought it was too abrupt or that the stepparent did not like them, and other stepchildren felt critical about whether their parent could sustain a new marriage. This theme generally conveyed the sadness and discontent of the stepchildren. Finally, young-adult stepchildren had a lot to say about their involvement. Although most really enjoyed being involved, many expressed wanting more involvement. The only exceptions were stepchildren who identified as being estranged from the parent who was remarrying. Ultimately, the researchers concluded that for many stepchildren, remarriage is an empty ritual.

Stepfamily Development

Despite early family clinicians who suggested that stepfamily cohesion formed in the same step-by-step fashion, communication researchers Leslie A. Baxter, Dawn O. Braithwaite, and John Nicholson (1999) conducted a turning point study that illustrates that stepfamilies form in all different ways (see Chapter 29 for more on turning point studies). They found five different stepfamily trajectories. To classify the families into the five categories, the researchers asked stepfamily members what events and experiences made them feel more or less like a family. Some of these factors included changes to the household, conflict episodes, holiday/special events, quality time, and family crises. The combinations of these events determined whether a family developed in one of the following ways: (1) accelerated, (2) prolonged, (3) stagnating, (4) declining, and (5) high-amplitude turbulent. Specifically, *accelerated* development includes a rapid integration through the establishment of rituals, roles, boundaries, and expectations. Even though in *prolonged* development members do not begin feeling like a family, eventually they progress toward family cohesion unlike members in stagnating development who report never feeling like a family over the first four years. For those who experience *declining* development, stepfamily members report immediately feeling like a family only to have that feeling dissipate over the first four years. Finally, *high-amplitude turbulent* development is marked by fluctuations over time. Taken together, their study illustrates that different patterns of communicating can influence the extent to which people can construct a new family identity. Families who were particularly successful did not expect an instant connection or feelings of immediate love. Instead, they built their identity over time.

Stepfamily Types

Given that there are different development trajectories, it might come as no surprise that there are also different types of stepfamilies. Communication scholar Paul Schrodt (2006) surveyed 586 stepchildren about their stepfamilies to develop a system for categorizing stepfamilies into five different types: (1) bonded, (2) functional, (3) ambivalent, (4) evasive, and (5) conflictual (Figure 22.1). **Bonded** stepfamilies feel very close, do not have much conflict, and communicate openly. In these stepfamilies, stepparents have authority and stepchildren like their stepparents. **Functional** stepfamilies are similar to those who are bonded but are less cohesive and stepparents have less authority. Ambivalence occurs when people have both positive and negative feelings toward something. In **ambivalent** stepfamilies, stepchildren have both positive and negative feelings for their stepparents and moderate levels of cohesion. In **evasive** families, stepchildren do not feel very close to their stepparents and these families are prone to conflict, avoidance, and a lack of open communication. Finally, **conflictual** types have extremely high levels of conflict, avoidance, and disagreement accompanied with low levels of involvement, open communication, and regard for the stepparents. What is particularly interesting about Schrodt's research is that the different types of stepfamilies differed in both their communication competence and their mental health symptoms. For example, bonded and functional stepfamilies thought of both themselves and the other stepfamily members as competent communicators and reported fewer mental health issues than the other types of stepfamilies.

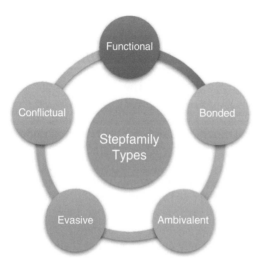

Figure 22.1 Stepfamily types.

Co-parental Communication and Contradictions

After a stepfamily forms, members often have to negotiate co-parenting. Co-parenting is a process where at least two people take responsibility for a child's well-being either through mutual agreement or because societal norms dictate the expectation for care. Because of the necessity of parental coordination, co-parenting is an inherently communicative process. Although there has not been much research about co-parenting, Braithwaite (2003), Schrodt (2006), and their colleagues began to explore this area when they conducted a series of qualitative studies. They found that coparents often behaved in a business-like way and were highly focused on the children. They also found the issues of trust, fairness, and good faith were instrumental in the co-parenting process. Together in 2010, Schrodt and Braithwaite conducted research that found that remarried co-parenting couples (i.e., the residential parent and the residential stepparent) who are supportive and cooperative are more likely to be satisfied in their romantic relationships and report fewer mental health issues. They make note, however, that stepparents still might feel stress when the residential parent relies too heavily on them for child-rearing help. They explain that because of role ambiguity, stepparents might struggle with trying to create a warm relationship and exercise parental authority. These findings point to a defining characteristic of stepfamilies: **(dys)functional ambivalence**. This means that stepfamilies have simultaneously positive and negative experiences and find their experiences to be contradictory. For example, from the perspective of stepchildren, Baxter and her colleagues (2004) found that they experienced three contradictions: (1) a desire for emotional closeness and distance, (2) a desire for open communication and privacy, and (3) a desire for parenting from the stepparent and a desire to be free of stepparent authority. Stepchildren also felt the pull and push of information and parenting with their nonresidential parent. Furthermore, even though communication between a stepparent and nonresidential parent could be difficult or awkward, a study by Schrodt (2011) revealed the more these two groups work together, the less stress and anxiety they both feel. In sum, this body of research encourages supportive and cooperative communication despite past conflict and in the face of the inherent difficulties associated with raising a child.

Communicative Challenges

In addition to the challenges of co-parenting, there are specific communicative challenges stepfamilies face. Based on interviews with 90 stepfamily members from 30 different stepfamilies, Tamara Golish (2003) found that regardless of stepfamily strength, stepfamilies encountered similar communicative challenges such as (1) feeling caught, (2) regulating boundaries with the noncustodial parent, (3) ambiguity of parenting roles, (4) traumatic bonding, (5) vying for resources, (6) discrepancies in conflict management styles, and (7) building solidarity as a family unit. To follow up on these findings, Afifi (formerly Golish; 2003) used a communication privacy management framework (see Chapter 4) to explore the communicative conditions and experience of feeling caught between two families. She found that enmeshed privacy boundaries (i.e., revealing too much information, using family members as a messenger, and inappropriate disclosures) often lead to feeling of being caught. Stepfamily members also discussed the difficulty negotiating competing loyalties (e.g., taking sides) and the uncertainties surrounding what information they should reveal or conceal.

Communicative Strengths

Despite the research that depicts stepfamily communication as stressful and less cohesive, many stepfamilies communicate in positive ways that facilitate adaptation and resilience. As we discuss in our chapter about conflict (see Chapter 11), conflict can be an opportunity for positive change. Indeed, a study by Coleman and colleagues (2001) found that conflict was often a way for stepfamilies to improve their relationships, especially when they were able to discuss their problems and find mutually satisfying resolutions. Conflict within stepfamilies was more problematic, however, when it went undiscussed and unresolved. Golish (2003) also contends that it takes time to develop a close relationship and to establish new boundaries. Communication also plays an important role in family resilience. Stepfamilies adjust better when there is open and positive communication.

INTERESTING RESEARCH FINDINGS

Everyday talk such as gossip, small talk, joking around, and reminiscing is the glue that holds most relationships together. To better understand everyday talk in stepfamily systems, Schrodt and his colleagues (2007) surveyed 342 family members from 114 stepfamilies about their everyday talking behaviors. Results suggest that regardless of the relationship (parent, stepparent, or stepchild), catching up, joking around, and recapping the day's events were the most frequent types of everyday talk. Both parents and stepparents reported engaging in love talk and reminiscing more than other types of talk whereas stepchildren preferred serious conversations, talking about problems, and reminiscing more. For all three groups (i.e., parents, stepparents, and stepchildren), interrogation was the least common. When compared, stepchildren engaged in more of almost all types of everyday talk with their parents than their stepparents or nonresidential parents. They did, however, engage in more small talk with their stepparents than their nonresidential parents as well as more love talk with their nonresidential parent than their stepparent. Otherwise, there was no difference between stepparents and nonresidential parents. For parents, they engaged in more small talk with their children than their coparent or their ex-spouse. Finally, for stepparents, they reported more small talk with their current spouse compared to their stepchildren or the nonresidential parent. What is most interesting about this research, perhaps, is that it illustrates that there are not large differences between stepparent–stepchild everyday communication and nonresidential parent–child communication. In other words, (step)children engage in all types of talk in both relationships.

Did You Know?

In Abetz and Wang's (2017) recent study, interviews from 19 adult children of divorced parents revealed four primary sources for their uncertainty:

- Uncertainty surrounding the length of parental unhappiness
- Uncertainty surrounding new roles
- Uncertainty surrounding holidays and family events
- Uncertainty surrounding being caught in the middle

PRACTICAL APPLICATIONS AND THINGS TO CONSIDER

One of the most challenging aspects of forming a stepfamily pertains to the roles each member plays. Stepparents often have to carefully balance the extent of their involvement. They must also strike a balance between playing the role of parent and playing the role of friend. Research by Fine and his colleagues (1998) suggests that the balance is complicated by the fact that children prefer stepparents to act more as a friend whereas the other adults in the relationship prefer a stronger parent role. Other research suggests, however, that the parent and friend roles might be too limiting. Indeed, research indicates that it matters more that stepparents genuinely take an interest in establishing and maintaining a close relationship with their stepchildren continuously, not just in the beginning of the relationship. This is important because the more stepchildren think of their stepparent as warm and the more satisfied they are with the relationship, the less they will avoid communicating with them.

KEY TERMS

Ambivalent stepfamilies
Bonded stepfamilies
Conflictual stepfamilies
Co-parenting
Divorce-prone personality hypothesis

(Dys)functional ambivalence
Dysfunctional beliefs hypothesis
Evasive stepfamilies
Functional stepfamilies

Remarriage market hypothesis
Stepfamily development trajectories
Training school hypothesis
Willingness to leave marriage hypothesis

REFERENCES

Abetz, J., & Wang, T. R. (2017). "Were they ever really happy the way that I remember?": Exploring sources of uncertainty for adult children of divorce. *Journal of Divorce and Remarriage, 58*, 194–211. doi:10.1080/10502556.2017.1301158

Afifi, T. D. (2003). "Feeling caught" in stepfamilies: Managing boundary turbulence through appropriate communication. *Journal of Social and Personal Relationships, 20*, 729–755. doi:10.1177/0265407503206002

Baxter, L. A., Braithwaite, D. O., Bryant, L., & Wagner, A. (2004). Stepchildren's perceptions of the contradictions in communication with stepparents. *Journal of Social and Personal Relationships, 21*, 447–467. doi:10.1177/0265407504044841

Baxter, L. A., Braithwaite, D. O., Koenig Kellas, J., LeClair-Underberg, C., Norman, E. L., Routsoung, T., & Thatcher, M. (2009). Empty ritual: Young-adult stepchildren's perceptions of the remarriage ceremony. *Journal of Social and Personal Relationships, 26*, 467–497. doi:10.1177/0265407509350872

Baxter, L. A., Braithwaite, D. O., & Nicholson, J. H. (1999). Turning points in the development of blended families. *Journal of Social and Personal Relationships, 16*, 291–314. doi:10.1177/0265407599163002

Braithwaite, D. O., McBride, M. C., & Schrodt, P. (2003). "Parent teams" and the everyday interactions of co-parenting in stepfamilies. *Communication Reports, 16*, 93–111. doi:10.1080/08934210309384493

Cherlin, A. J. (2010). Demographic trends in the United States: A review of the research in the 2000s. *Journal of Marriage and Family, 72*, 403–419. doi:10.1111/j.1741-3737.2010.00710.x

Coleman, M., Fine, M. A., Ganong, L. H., Downs, K., & Paul, N. (2001). When you're not the Brady Bunch: Identifying perceived conflicts and resolution strategies in stepfamilies. *Personal Relationships, 8*, 55–73. doi:10.1111/j.1475-6811.2001.tb00028.x

Fine, M. A., Coleman, M., & Ganong, L. H. (1998). Consistency in perceptions of the step-parent role among step-parents, parents, and stepchildren. *Journal of Social and Personal Relationships, 15*, 811–829. doi:10.1177/0265407598156006

Ganong, L. H., & Coleman, M. (1994). *Remarried family relationships*. Thousand Oaks, CA: Sage.

Golish, T. D. (2003). Stepfamily communication strengths: Understanding the ties that bind. *Human Communication Research, 29*, 41–80. doi:10.1111/j.1468-2958.2003.tb00831.x

Schrodt, P. (2006). A typological examination of communication competence and mental health in stepchildren. *Communication Monographs, 73*, 309–333. doi:10.1080/03637750600873728.

Schrodt, P. (2011). Stepparents' and nonresidential parents' relational satisfaction as a function of coparental communication in stepfamilies. *Journal of Social Personal Relationships, 28*, 983–1004. doi:10.1177/0265407510397990

Schrodt, P., & Braithwaite, D. O. (2010). Coparental communication, relational satisfaction, and mental health in stepfamilies. *Personal Relationships, 18*, 352–369. doi:10.1111/j.1475-6911.2010.01295

Schrodt, P., Braithwaite, D. O., Soliz, J., Tye-Williams, S., Miller, A., Normand, E. L., & Harrigan, M. M. (2007). An examination of everyday talk in stepfamily systems. *Western Journal of Communication, 71*, 216–234. doi:10.1080/10570310701510077

Sweeney, M. M. (2010). Remarriage and stepfamilies: Strategic sites for family scholarship in the 21st century. *Journal of Marriage and Family, 72*, 667–684. doi:10.1111/j.1741-2727.2010.00724.x

Teachman, J. (2008). Complex life course patterns and the risk of divorce in second marriages. *Journal of Marriage and Family, 70*, 294–305. doi:10.1111/j.1741-3737.2008.00482.x

RELATED READINGS

Cloete, M., & Greeff, A. P. (2015). Family resilience factors in remarried families in South Africa and Belgium. *The Social Work Practitioner-Researcher, 27*, 187–203.

Metts, S. M., Schrodt, P., & Braithwaite, D. O. (2017). Stepchildren's communicative and emotional journey from divorce to remarriage: Predictors of stepfamily satisfaction. *Journal of Divorce & Remarriage, 58*, 29–43. doi:10.1080/10502556.2016.1257904

Schrodt, P., Baxter, L. A., McBride, M. C., Braithwaite, D. O., & Fine, M. (2007). The divorce decree, communication, and the structuration of co-parenting relationships in stepfamilies. *Journal of Social and Personal Relationships, 23*, 741–759. doi:10.1177/0265407506068261

PART III

Communicating in Family Relationships

Family and Relationship Types

Chapter 23

Communication and Adoptive Families

There are approximately 2.1 million adoptees living in the United States and almost half of the American population has been touched by adoption in one way or another. Despite their prevalence and their legal ties, adoptive families are still considered a type of family that is highly discourse dependent. Discourse-dependent families are those often marginalized because of their lack of biological connections (see Chapter 14). In this chapter, we discuss the major findings related to communication and adoption in its many forms.

KEY CONCEPTS

Entrance Narratives

Communication researchers have added a lot to what we know about adoption. For example, research suggests that the stories parents tell their children about how they joined the family (i.e., entrance narratives) are particularly important for how adoptees see themselves, their adoptive families, and birth families. These stories differ depending on who is telling the story and in what context the story is told. Parents typically tell stories to their adoptive children with the themes of (1) dialectical tensions, (2) destiny, (3) compelling connection, (4) rescue, and

Communication in Family Contexts: Theories and Processes, First Edition.
Elizabeth Dorrance Hall and Kristina M. Scharp.
© 2020 John Wiley & Sons, Inc. Published 2020 by John Wiley & Sons, Inc.
Companion website: www.wiley.com/go/dorrance_hall/communication-in-family-contexts

(5) legitimacy (Krusiewicz & Wood, 2001). Adoptees, on the other hand, tell stories that feature themes of (1) openness, (2) deception, (3) chosen child, (4) fate, (5) difference, (6) rescue, and (7) reconnection. Specifically, the third, fifth, and seventh themes from adoptees' stories predict differences in adoptees' self-concept (Kranstuber & Koenig Kellas, 2011).

As research on entrance narratives has expanded, scholars have tied the content of entrance narratives to particular outcomes. For example, a study by Alexie Hays and her colleagues (2016) found that six themes emerged from 165 adoptive parents' entrance narratives about their children's open adoption: (1) birth parents as family, (2) chosen parents, (3) forever, (4) rescue, (5) fate, and (6) adoption makes us family. Based on these themes, the authors found that adoptive parents' satisfaction with the birth parents related to the stories birth parents tell, which ultimately relates to closeness between the adoptee and birth parent.

These entrance stories also matter in the foster care context. Foster entrance narratives are often marked by the following themes: (1) birth parent conse-quences, (2) deep connection, (3) special, (4) untold, (5) birth parent learning, (6) temporary, (7) pragmatic, (8) forever, and (9) better off (Nelson & Kranstuber Horstman, 2017). Their analysis suggests that there is a significant relationship bet-ween these themes, perceptions of foster child adjustment, and foster parent–child closeness. What is most important to understand from this body of literature is that narratives reflect and construct people's realities in ways that have implications for who they think they are and for happiness (i.e., satisfaction and closeness) of their relationships with others.

mohamed_hassan/pixabay

Domestic Adoption

Every year approximately 50,000 children are adopted into families living in the United States. When adoptions are domestic, there is a greater possibility that they are open. **Open adoption** means that adoptive families will have some knowledge of and interaction with birth families. Research suggests that there are numerous benefits to open adoptions such as increased closure for birth mothers, information about children's background (e.g., family health history), and identity clarity for adoptees. Yet, open adoptions can be challenging in light of ongoing negotiations about birth parent involvement. Given these complexities, communication becomes essential to facilitating openness.

Adoption is an experience that varies for each member of the **adoption triad**. This triad consists of the adoptee, adoptive parents, and birth parents. When compared, adoptive parents are the most likely to tell coherent stories about the adoption (see Chapter 7). Specifically, they are more likely to tell stories that follow along chronologically, have detail about the setting and actors in the story, as well as provide the best accounts for why things happened (Baxter, Norwood, Asbury, Jannusch, & Scharp, 2012). Birth mothers score highest, however, on congruence of affect. That means birth mothers are most likely to share their story with appropriate emotion. Indeed, birth mothers often find the adoption process extremely emotional given the experience of placing their children for adoption and the cultural pressures surrounding the meaning of motherhood. To resist the cultural notions that imply birth mothers are bad mothers (i.e., the discourse of intensive mothering), birth mothers discuss all the ways in which they were good mothers or discuss the ways in which they are not a mother at all (e.g., biological carrier rather than a mother; Baxter, Scharp, Asbury, Jannusch, & Norwood, 2012).

International Adoption

Although there are similarities between domestic and international adoption processes, there are also additional considerations and challenges in the context of transnational adoption. For example, international adoptees often look physically different from their adoptive parents and report a variety of intrusive interactions experienced by both adoptees and their adoptive parents. Sara Docan-Morgan (2010) found that Korean adoptees reported the following types of interactions as intrusive: (1) comments and questions about family relatedness, (2) compliments, (3) stares, (4) mistaken identities, and (5) adoptee-only interactions – those that happened in the absence of their adoptive families. Her research suggests that adoptees experience a range of derogatory messages including attacks about appearance and ethnicity as well as physical attacks (Docan-Morgan, 2011). Unfortunately, adoptees also expressed not wanting to discuss these attacks with their adoptive parents due to how they thought their parents would react (i.e., perceived unresponsiveness) and/or self-protection. Some adoptees, however, reported directly talking to their parents who were open and supportive. Adoptive parents also receive a variety of comments that challenged their family identity. A study of 245 parents with an adopted child from China reported that parents found three topics very challenging: (1) questions about China's history or culture, (2) stereotypes of Asians, and (3) expressions about being "wonderful for saving" (Suter, 2008). In response, adoptive parents produce identity-affirming responses based on a variety of criteria including (1) the identity of the commenter/questioner, (2) the question itself, (3) factors related to the child, (4) the timing/setting of the interaction, and (5) the disposition of the adoptive parent (Suter & Ballard, 2009). Despite these criteria, there were some questions that parents reported they would not answer no matter what, including questions about the cost of the child, the adoptees' China story, the adoption decision, and related visibility. Not all communication about the adoption process was negative. Parents also reported being proud to answer questions about or receive compliments about their child, affirmations of family relations, questions about the adoption process, comments on similarities, and compliments about parenting.

Foster Adoption

Approximately 400,000 children reside in the foster care system at any given moment in the United States and around 100,000 of those children are actively awaiting adoption. Children who spend time in the foster care system often have more chronic health issues compared to their non-fostered peers, such as depression and attachment disorders, as well as often falling behind their peers in cognitive function, language, and memory (Shin, 2005). Yet, not all former foster children report having a negative experience as some are able to overcome their experience by constructing themselves as survivors or even victors over their situation (Thomas, 2014). Nevertheless, foster adoption is still heavily stigmatized in US culture.

In response to cultural notions that adoption is a second-best way to parent, foster adoptive parents give voice to an alternative discourse of redemptive care, whereby adoption gets reframed as a way to provide care for children who needed help to overcome early life adversity (Baxter, Suter, Thomas, & Seurer, 2015). Foster adoptive parents also emphasize that the most important factors in being a family are care, love, and permanency as opposed to merely biological ties (Suter, Baxter, Seurer, & Thomas, 2014). Former foster children echo this sentiment by discussing the importance of roles, tolerance, and unconditional love as markers of family (Thomas, Jackl, & Crowley, 2017).

Adoption Reunion

When adoptees feel uncertainty about their adoption, they often seek out a member of their biological family (Powell & Afifi, 2005). Reconnecting with a person's birth family can be complicated and beneficial for a variety of reasons. For example, adoptive parent relationships were either not affected or even improved after adoptees reunited with a member of their biological family (Sachdev, 1992).

Challenges around information also exist for adoptees seeking to reconnect. We now discuss experiences pre- and post-reconnection.

Kristina Scharp and Keli Steuber (2014) collected stories from 60 adopted adult children who never reunited with their birth mothers to better understand what kinds of information adoptees would want if they were to reconnect. Based on a thematic analysis, adoptees discussed wanting to know the following types of information: (1) health information, (2) birth parent information (e.g., location of the birth family), (3) extended family information (e.g., whether they had siblings), (4) adoptee identity (e.g., nationality), (5) birth mother circumstances at the time of birth, and (6) adoption circumstances such as the process of the adoption. These findings suggest that there could be expectation violations if birth parents and adoptees are not clear on information boundaries.

The majority of research on reunion occurs in the context of domestic adoption. When domestic adoptees reconnect, they describe experiencing two different experiences of reconnection: romanticized and pragmatic (Scharp, 2013). Notions of **romantic reconnection** include desires for physical resemblance and immediate connection. Alternatively, adoptees also experience their birth families as strangers, only want to reconnect for health information, and articulate that a connection is not guaranteed. These reasons represent a more **pragmatic reconnection** approach. These competing ideas emphasize the multiple possibilities for the meanings of love and family.

Docan-Morgan has provided accounts of international reconnection in the context of Korean adoptees' reunions. In a qualitative study of 19 Korean adoptees, Docan-Morgan (2014) found that adoptees had one main message for their birth families: do not feel guilty. Adoptees also wanted to relate positive stories about their lives post-adoption. Birth families, on the other hand, were more likely to share stories about the circumstances of the adoption. During the reunion, adoptees also discussed the rituals they enacted during their reconnection. These included (1) extended touch, (2) exchanging gifts, (3) outings, (4) exchanging culture, and (5) symbolic family activities. Building off this study, Docan-Morgan (2016) found four overarching themes that illuminate the cultural differences the adoptees perceive: (1) family roles and expectations, (2) standards for beauty and femininity, (3) expectations for interactions, and (4) past and present circumstances. As a result, some adoptees felt closer to their biological families, some felt like they did not belong, and others expressed feeling a combination of something in between.

INTERESTING RESEARCH FINDINGS

Haley Kranstuber Horstman, Colleen Colaner, and Christine Rittenour (2016) used family communication patterns theory (see Chapter 5) to explore how adoptees' family communication environments predicted their identity and self-esteem. Results, based on a sample of 143 adult adoptees, suggest that conversation orientation, but not conformity orientation, significantly predicted the extent to which they perceived their adoptive parents to be open, honest, and approachable about adoption issues (i.e., adoption openness). They also found that the more adoptees perceived their environment to be open, the less likely they were to be preoccupied with thinking about their adoption. In sum, results from their study support the recommendation that having open dialogue about the adoption process can be important for both adoptees and their adoptive families.

PRACTICAL APPLICATIONS AND THINGS TO CONSIDER

The majority of adoption research in Communication Studies comes from the perspective of those in the adoption triad. Colleen Colaner and one of your text-book authors talked, however, to adoption practitioners (n = 17) about their views on open adoption relationships, including the opportunities and challenges they saw for adoptive families (Colaner & Scharp, 2016). Based in family systems theory (see Chapter 6), a thematic analysis revealed that practitioners saw many productive ways to have a positive open adoption relationship (equifinality), discussed how levels of openness between adoptive and birth families might vary, and recognized the communicative complexities between different members of both families.

Practitioners advised practicing the adoption entrance story, seeking education and counseling, and setting clear boundaries. Challenges included letting birth parents have the opportunity to grieve before working toward building a relationship and explaining the birth mothers' challenges to the adoptive children. Finally, practitioners recommend that families should consider online information privacy management as something that could both facilitate and hinder growing open relationships.

KEY TERMS

Adoption triad	Open adoption	Romantic reconnection
Entrance narrative	Pragmatic reconnection	

IN-CLASS DISCUSSION

A lot of families adopt a pet who they consider to be family. Get in groups and discuss whether our pets count as family. What are the factors that make (or don't make) your pet your family? How are they similar or different to the other people in your family?

From the Moment we Laid Eyes on You…

CASE STUDY BY LESLIE R. NELSON

Piper was startled awake by the smell of bacon. She looked around her room, admiring each of her perfectly lined up stuffed animals on her blue and gold dresser. Just then it hit Piper – today was her "Gotcha Day" – eight years of being a Sullivan! She scrambled out of bed and ran into the kitchen in a frenzy.

"Mom, it's my 'Gotcha Day!' It's July 27th!" Piper exclaimed.

Piper's mom, Kim, replied: "Of course it is, silly, that's why we are making your favorite breakfast!" Piper smiled her wide, toothy smile and sat down at the kitchen table.

"Happy 'Gotcha Day,' Pipes! I can hardly believe it's already been eight years," Piper's dad, Jack, announced as he snuck a piece of bacon from the skillet.

"Tell me the story! Tell me the story!" Piper said excitedly.

Piper was referring to her adoption story, which her parents had told her each year on her "Gotcha Day" since before she could remember. Although Piper asked to hear bits and pieces of this story on days other than her "Gotcha Day," it was one of her favorite traditions on this very day. Her favorite, of course, was getting to plan the day's activities. This year she had decided she wanted to get chocolate ice cream at the local ice cream shop, Sparky's. Afterward, they would all go to Peony Park so she could demonstrate her latest achievement: two simultaneous back flips on the bars.

"Do you want to tell it this year, dear?" Kim asked Jack, as she began cracking eggs into a small bowl. Scrambled eggs were Piper's favorite. Piper glanced toward her dad.

Jack began, "It was seemingly just like any other Monday. Your mom and I had just woken up. The phone rang. We looked at each other and wondered who could possibly be calling us at this hour! I hesitantly picked up the phone and said 'Hello?' On the other end was Jill from the adoption agency. She said she had some very exciting news. Our adoption profile had been selected by a woman who had just unexpectedly given birth to a healthy baby girl at Oakfield Hospital. I shouted for your mother, who scurried into the living room to meet me. After telling her the news, we jumped into our blue Toyota and rushed to the hospital. I was so excited I could hardly go the speed limit! We illegally parked the car – something I'm still not proud of, by the way – and ran into the hospital. We were greeted by a smiling Jill. She told us to check in at the front desk so that we could follow her back and meet you. We followed Jill down a hallway that was painted the prettiest powder blue color, just like your dresser. Then, we saw you. You were so teeny-tiny, and you hadn't yet opened your eyes. But from the moment we laid eyes on you, we knew that you were destined to be our daughter. I looked at your mom and saw tears streaming from her eyes. We had only just met you, but we already loved you. We touched each of your tiny fingers and toes, your soft brown hair, and your warm little cheeks. You were our special little girl. And that's the day you became a Sullivan. A Sullivan at first sight!" Jack beamed. Kim set Piper's plate down in front of her and ruffled her curly brown hair.

Piper looked up adoringly at her parents: "Again, again! This time I want Mommy to tell it!"

CASE STUDY DISCUSSION QUESTIONS

1. What themes can you identify in the entrance narrative Piper's father told?
2. Imagine you are Piper's parent. In what ways might you have told the story differently? Why?
3. What might be some pros and cons of celebrating "Gotcha Day?" What unique considerations might impact adoptive parents' decision to celebrate "Gotcha Day" with their adopted child?
4. Beyond narrating, what other internal boundary management strategies can you identify in this passage?
5. What potentially challenging remarks might Piper encounter from her peers at school about being adopted? What are some tips you would give Piper for managing these remarks?

REFERENCES

Baxter, L. A., Norwood, K. M., Asbury, B., Jannusch, A., & Scharp, K. M. (2012). Narrative coherence in online stories told by members of the adoption triad. *Journal of Family Communication, 12*, 265–283. doi:10.1080/15267431.2012.686944

Baxter, L. A., Scharp, K. M., Asbury, B., Jannusch, A., & Norwood, K. M. (2012). "Birthmothers are not bad people": A dialogic perspective of online birth mother narratives. *Qualitative Communication Research, 1*, 53–82. doi:101525/qcr.2012.1.1.53

Baxter, L. A., Suter, E. A., Thomas, L. J., & Seurer, L. M. (2015). The dialogic construction of "adoption" in online foster adoption narratives. *Journal of Family Communication, 15*, 193–213. doi:10.1080/15267431.2015.1043431

Colaner, C. W., & Scharp, K. M. (2016). Maintaining open adoption relationships: Practitioner insights on adoptive parents' regulation of adoption kinship networks. *Communication Studies, 67*, 359–378. doi:10.1080/10510974.2016.1164208

Docan-Morgan, S. (2010). Korean adoptees' retrospective reports of intrusive interactions: Exploring boundary management in adoptive families. *Journal of Family Communication, 10*, 137–157. doi:1080/15267431003699603

Docan-Morgan, S. (2011). "They don't know what it's like to be in my shoes": Topic avoidance about race in transracially adoptive families. *Journal of Social and Personal Relationships, 28*, 226–255.

Docan-Morgan, S. (2014). "They were strangers who loved me": Discussion, narratives, and rituals during Korean adoptees' initial reunions with birth families. *Journal of Family Communication, 14*, 352–373. doi:10.1080/15267431.2014.946033

Docan-Morgan, S. (2016). Cultural differences and perceived belonging during Korean adoptees' reunions with birth families. *Adoption Quarterly, 19*, 99–118. doi:10.1080.10926755.2015.1088109

Hays, A. H., Horstman, H. K., Colaner, C., & Nelson, L. R. (2016). "She chose us to be your parents": Exploring the content and process of adoption entrance narratives told in families formed through open adoption. *Journal of Social and Personal Relationships, 33*, 917–937. doi:10.1177/0265407515611494

Horstman, H. K., Colaner, C. W., & Rittenour, C. E. (2016). Contributing factors of adult adoptees' identity work and self-esteem: Family communication patterns and adoption-specific communication. *Journal of Family Communication, 16*, 263–276. doi:10.1080/15267431.2016.1181069

Kranstuber, H. A., & Koenig Kellas, J. (2011). The relationship between adoption entrance narratives and adoptees' self-concept. *Communication Quarterly, 59*, 179–199. doi:10.1080/01463373.2011.563440

Krusiewicz, E. S., & Wood, J. T. (2001). "He was our child from the moment we walked in that room": Entrance stories of adoptive parents. *Journal of Social and Personal Relationships, 18*, 785–803. doi:10.1177/0265407501186003

Nelson, L. R., & Kranstuber Horstman, H. K. (2017). Communicated meaning-making in foster families: Relationships between foster parents' entrance narratives and foster child well-being. *Communication Quarterly, 65*, 144–166. doi:10.1080/01463373.2016.1215337

Powell, K. A., & Afifi, T. D. (2005). Uncertainty management and adoptees' ambiguous loss of their birth parents. *Journal of Social and Personal Relationships, 22*, 129–151. doi:10.1177/0265407505049325

Sachdev, P. (1992). Adoption reunion and after: A study of the search process and the experience of adoptees. *Child Welfare, 71*, 53–70.

Scharp, K. M. (2013). Making meaning of domestic adoption reunion in online narratives: A dialogic perspective. *Departures in Critical Qualitative Research, 2*, 301–325. doi:101525/qcr.2013.2.3.301

Scharp, K. M., & Steuber, K. R. (2014). Perceived information ownership and control: Negotiating communication preferences in potential adoption reunions. *Personal Relationships, 21*, 515–529. doi:10.1111/pere.12046

Shin, S. H. (2005). Need for and actual use of mental health service by adolescents in the child welfare system. *Children and Youth Services Review, 27*, 1071–1083. doi:10.1016/j.childyouth.2004.12.027

Suter, E. A. (2008). Discursive negotiations of family identity: A study of families with adopted children from China. *Journal of Family Communication, 8*, 126–147. doi:10.1080/15267430701857406

Suter, E. A., & Ballard, R. L. (2009). "How much did you pay for her": Decision-making criteria underlying adoptive parents' responses to inappropriate remarks. *Journal of Family Communication, 9*, 107–125. doi:10.1080/15267430902773253

Suter, E. A., Baxter, L. A., Seurer, L., & Thomas, L. J. (2014). Discursive constructions of the meaning of "family" in online narratives of foster adoptive parents. *Communication Monographs, 81*, 59–78. doi:10.1080/03637751.2014.880791

Thomas, L. J. (2014). "Once a foster child …": Identity construction in former foster children's narratives. *Qualitative Research Reports in Communication, 15*, 84–91. doi:10.1080/17459435.2014.955596

Thomas, L. J., Jackl, J. A., & Crowley, J. L. (2017). "Family? … Not just blood": Discursive construction of "family" in adult, former foster children's narratives. *Journal of Family Communication, 17*, 238–253. doi:10.1080/15267431.2017.1310728

RELATED READINGS

Baxter, L. A., Norwood, K. M., Asbury, B., & Scharp, K. M. (2014). Narrating adoption: Resisting adoption as "second best" in online stories of domestic adoption told by adoptive parents. *Journal of Family Communication, 14*, 253–269. doi:10.1080/15267431.2014.908199

Colaner, C. W., Halliwell, D., & Guignon, P. (2014). "What do you say to your mother when your mother's standing beside you?" Birth and adoptive family contribution to adoptive identity via relational identity and relational-relational identity gaps. *Communication Monographs, 81*, 469–494. doi:10.1080/03637751.2014.955808

Colaner, C. W., & Horstman, H. (2010). "Forever kind of wondering": Communicatively managing uncertainty in adoptive families. *Journal of Family Communication, 10*, 236–255. doi:10.1080/15267431003682435

Nelson, L. R., & Colaner, C. W. (2018). Becoming a transracial family: Communicatively negotiating divergent identities in families formed through transracial adoption. *Journal of Family Communication, 18*, 51–67. doi:10.1080/15267431.2017.1396987

Thomas, L. J., & Scharp, K. M. (2017). "A family for every child": Discursive constructions of "ideal" adoptive families in online foster-adoption photolistings that promote adoption of children from foster care. *Adoption Quarterly, 20*, 44–64. doi:10.1080/10926755.2016.1263261

Chapter 24

In-Law Relationships

BACKGROUND

In-law relationships tend to have a bad reputation, yet in-laws serve an important function in families, linking two or more families together. In-law relationships are extremely common and can be described as "nonvoluntary" and "triadic" rather than dyadic (Morr Serewicz, 2013). Nonvoluntary relationships are not chosen by either in-law party and the costs associated with ending the relationship are high (for example, having less contact with an adult child/parent). In-law relationships are considered triadic because they tend to involve the marriage partner as well as the two in-laws (for example, husband, wife, and mother-in-law, or a set of partners and a sister-in-law). In-laws belong to a category of triads called the "triangulator as linchpin" because a third party, the linchpin (spouse), holds two parties (the parent- and child-in-law) together. In fact, Mary Claire Morr Serewicz claims that across cultures, the nature of the in-law relationship (as nonvoluntary and triadic) tends to lead to difficulty communicating and maintaining a positive relationship. Establishing and maintaining close and satisfactory in-law relationships is challenging (Merrill, 2007). **In reality, in-law relationships range from satisfying and beneficial to negative and detrimental.**

IN-LAW FAMILY SOCIALIZATION

In-law relationships are created through law and ritual, typically by a marriage ceremony. In-laws are brought together by a third party (the child/partner) and

Communication in Family Contexts: Theories and Processes, First Edition.
Elizabeth Dorrance Hall and Kristina M. Scharp.
© 2020 John Wiley & Sons, Inc. Published 2020 by John Wiley & Sons, Inc.
Companion website: www.wiley.com/go/dorrance_hall/communication-in-family-contexts

have little choice in the relationship. Like any new member of an organization or social group, new in-laws are socialized into the norms of the family. Being the "new" family member can be very intimidating as an entire family is sizing one person up for fit with the group and with the member they are marrying while teaching them the family culture. In the United States, couples tend to be fairly independent of their parents-in-law, spending less time with them and feeling less obligation to them than in more collectivist cultures. This socialization process is important as many in-laws report that feeling ambivalent about their place in the family is one of the primary struggles in their in-law relationships (Turner, Young, & Black, 2006). The socialization process might include negotiating which family the partners will spend holidays with and a meeting of each partner's families.

Like the grandparent role, the in-law role is fairly ambiguous. As a result, the way people enact or perform the in-law role varies greatly family to family. For example, some sister-in-laws are closer than sisters while others are constantly in conflict. Still others are hardly a part of each other's lives. Despite the ambiguity of the in-law role, some expectations do exist such as the obligation to form some sort of bond with a partner's family, see each other occasionally to frequently, assist one another, avoid conflict, and communicate with one another. Some people overcome these ambiguities by likening the role to that of a non-in-law relationship (e.g., treat the father-in-law like a father, act like a good brother to be a good brother-in-law).

SIBLINGS-IN-LAW

Like other in-law relationships, sibling in-law relationships are nonvoluntary and triadic. Unlike other in-law relationships, they are also peer-like because the parties are likely similar in age without much power difference. Also unique to siblings-in-law, siblings-in-law are gained when one marries, or when one's sibling marries. Communication in sibling-in-law relationships influences sibling-in-law relationship quality, which in turn may influence the well-being of all parties and play a role in other relationships like aunt/uncle and niece/nephew contact and closeness. Research on these important relationships is relatively rare, though researchers are beginning to explore light and dark sides of sibling-in-law connections including envy and affectionate communication.

Christina Yoshimura (2010) examined the experience and communication of envy in the sibling-in-law relationship. Envy occurs when one party desires or begrudges another for his or her possessions or attributes. Envy is different from jealousy because jealousy requires a threat to a valued relationship (see Chapter 28). For example, you can be envious of your sister's wit without experiencing a threat to the relationship. Yoshimura found that siblings experienced more envy of the other members than did the siblings-in-law or spouses. Based on her findings, it is likely true that I might experience more envy of my sister and her husband's relationship or the financial assistance my parent provides them than my sister or her husband would report. Spouses, however, were most likely to communicate an envious response than siblings or siblings-in-law. Possible responses include actively distancing oneself from a sibling/in-law, expressing negative emotion, avoiding, denying, communicating threats, or manipulating the sibling/in-law, among others. The relational closeness and satisfaction of all three parties were related so that the closer two parts of the triad were, the closer the other two were.

Kory Floyd and Marie Claire Morr (2003) explored a topic in the sibling-in-law relationship quite different from envy: affectionate communication exchange (see Chapter 3). Unsurprisingly, Floyd and Morr found that siblings provide more affectionate communication to one another than siblings-in-law do. They also found that when siblings provide more affectionate communication to one another, they tend to provide more affectionate communication to their siblings-in-law (in other words, exchanges of affection with each party were correlated). The more affectionate communication siblings-in-law exchanged, the better (more satisfactory and close) their relationship.

PARENTS-IN-LAW AND CHILDREN-IN-LAW

Parents-in-law are gained through marriage and are typically terminated through divorce. Parents-in-law can cause stress but can also provide support to a couple. According to Morr Serewicz (2013), "for both the parent-in-law and child-in-law, the relationship with [their spouse or child] is likely to be more salient and more rewarding than their relationship with one another" (p. 104). The third party (child/spouse) holds a lot of power in the in-law relationship and can either facilitate a positive relationship between in-laws or be a source of negativity and interference in building a strong relationship. Marital satisfaction plays a role in the health of in-law relationships. As marital satisfaction decreases, people tend to have lower quality in-law relationships (and vice versa; Morr Serewicz, 2013). In addition, a negative in-law relationship lowers the child-in-law's intentions to give care to parents-in-law later in life (Rittenour & Soliz, 2009).

An infamous issue in the **mother-in-law and daughter-in-law** relationship is the mother-in-law's criticism of the daughter-in-law's child-rearing methods. While some mother-in-law/daughter-in-law relationships are close and marked by affection and understanding, others experience hurtful communication or do not communicate at all. Keera Allendorf (2017) stresses the importance of the context surrounding the mother-in-law/daughter-in-law relationship: that of the larger family which she calls the "joint family system." The joint family system sets the stage for the in-law relationship including shaping the expectations and experiences of mother-in-law/daughter-in-law (and other in-law) relationships. A study led by Karen Fingerman (2012) found that when soon-to-be daughters-in-law had positive feelings about and spent alone time with their soon-to-be mothers-in-law before the wedding, they had a stronger relationship after the marriage. If they expressed concern that they would not be close to their mothers-in-law before the wedding, daughters-in-law reported lower relationship quality after the wedding. Rittenour and Soliz (2009) found that mothers-in-law can change their communication to benefit the mother-in-law/daughter-in-law relationship. These changes include communicating support, self-disclosing (when appropriate), showing respect for differing values, and communicating family acceptance and inclusion to the daughter-in-law.

Research on **father-in-law and son-in-law** relationships is very rare. Recently, Geoffrey Greif and Michael Woolley (2018) set out to understand how negative and positive father-in-law and son-in-law relationships differ. Based on a small sample, the researchers found that fathers in positive father-in-law/son-in-law relationships treat their sons-in-law like they were their own son, attempting to include them as much as possible and even thinking of them as friends. The fathers with strained son-in-law relationships tend to think their son-in-law and daughter do not make a good team. They also view their son-in-law negatively, describing their son-in-law's use of alcohol and drugs, viewing him as lazy, and showing a lack of respect.

INTERESTING RESEARCH FINDINGS

Relational Uncertainty in In-Law Relationships

Sylvia Mikucki-Enyart, John Caughlin, and Christine Rittenour (2015) explored the influence of children-in-law's relational uncertainty during their transition or socialization phase into the family (for a review of relationship uncertainty, see Chapter 18). The researchers conducted two studies to (1) discover concerns children-in-law have about the family, their partners, and themselves, and (2) test the relationship between these uncertainties and relationship satisfaction with their in-laws and their partners. Children-in-law report concerns about (1) their parents-in-law's approval, (2) expectation and interpretation of communication, (3) differences, (4) relational quality, (5) balancing family membership of two families, (6) meddling, (7) family obligations, (8) how the extended family will get along, (9) grandparenting and parenting input, (10) proximity to in-laws, (11) relationship support, (12) triadic influence, (13) gossip, and (14) the in-law's well-being. Uncertainty within the in-law dyad was related to lower satisfaction for the marital and in-law relationship. Because the in-law role is uncertain and ambiguous, in-laws tend to avoid rather than engage in communication. This avoidance is associated with poor relationship outcomes like lower satisfaction.

Triangular Theory of the Communication and Relationships of In-Laws

Morr Serewicz (2008) proposed and tested a triangular theory of communication and relationships of in-laws. She claims that crisis is likely if one (or more) ties between members of an in-law triad are negative. For example, if my partner and my parent do not get along, I may be expected to mediate or negotiate between the two, causing stress and conflict for all parties. The triangular theory states much of what was discussed above, including that the nonvoluntary and triadic nature of the in-law relationship define this relationship type. It also states that the in-law relationship in the in-law triad is the weakest of the three relationship links, and that the in-law triangle is always changing in regard to tensions, conflict, and feelings of closeness. Along the lines of systems theory (see Chapter 6), communication between any of the triad members has implications for the entire triad. The theory then makes predictions about how the triad interacts to influence relationship quality for all members. Morr Serewicz recruited newlywed couples and a parent of one spouse to test the theory. Each member of the triad reported on their relationship satisfaction with all other members. She found that the more the parent-in-law disclosed (about acceptance, relational trouble, and historical identity), the more satisfied the parent was with the triad relationships.

PRACTICAL APPLICATIONS AND THINGS TO CONSIDER

Carolyn Prentice (2009) found that people attempt to mediate interactions between their families and their partner when first introducing them by making sure their partner is not left alone with their (future) in-laws. If you have navigated an introduction like this, how did you handle it? If you have not experienced this first hand, chances are that you will end up meeting in-laws at some point (either your own parent in-laws or a sibling in-law). Consider how you might handle an introduction like this in the future and how you might make an introduction like this more comfortable for newcomers to your family. What are some communication strategies you could use in this situation?

DISCUSSION QUESTIONS

What nonvoluntary relationships are you a part of? How is your communication different with nonvoluntary family members than with people you choose to spend time and communicate with?

IN-CLASS ACTIVITY

Watch *Meet the Parents* (2000), a movie about a future son-in-law meeting his future parents-in-law for the first time, as a class. Take note of how the "introduction" of Greg Focker (played by Ben Stiller) to his future wife's family unfolds. What miscommunications do you notice? Can you tell that Greg is experiencing uncertainty about his future wife's family and their relationship? Be sure to watch for topic avoidance on the parts of the new husband and the father-in-law.

KEY TERMS

Envy
Family socialization
Joint family system

Nonvoluntary
relationships
Triadic relationships

The Trouble with In-Laws

CASE STUDY BY SYLVIA L. MIKUCKI-ENYART

Rich and Sophie just had their first child, a daughter named Rudy. Rich's mother (Sophie's mother-in-law), Elizabeth, is thrilled to be a grandmother for the first time.

When she visits the new family in the hospital she brings a christening gown for Rudy.

"All the children on my side of the family, including Rich, have worn this when they were baptized," she tells Rich and Sophie.

Sophie bursts into tears. "Why do you always try to make us do things your way?" she shouts. She and Rich are atheists and have no plans to christen Rudy. Elizabeth is crushed.

As she leaves the hospital, she calls her sister Lydia to vent.

"I don't know what the problem is," she says. "I was just trying to include her in a family tradition."

"Are you sure they plan on christening the baby?" Lydia asks.

"I don't see why not. Rich was baptized and Sophie always comes to Christmas Eve mass with us. But, I guess we've never really talked about her religious beliefs or whether or not they were going to baptize their children," Elizabeth responds.

Rich, Sophie, and Elizabeth never talk about the hospital incident.

A few months later, during a visit to see Rudy, Elizabeth and Sophie are getting ready to go to story time at the library. Elizabeth asks Sophie, "Aren't you going to bring a bottle in case she gets hungry?"

"Oh no, I'll just nurse her while we're out," Sophie replies.

"In my day, that's not something you did outside of the house," Elizabeth notes.

Sophie is hurt. She's not sure if Elizabeth was criticizing her or complimenting her. However, she doesn't say anything because she isn't sure if she and Elizabeth are close enough to talk about their feelings.

Later that night, when it's time to put Rudy to bed, Sophie says goodnight to Rich and her mother-in-law.

"Where are you going?" Elizabeth asks.

"To bed with Rudy. We co-sleep these days. It's the only way she'll stay asleep. And it's so much easier to nurse her through the night when she's right next to me," Sophie explains.

Elizabeth shakes her head and states, "No, no. You can't be doing that."

Without saying a word, Sophie turns around and takes Rudy to the bedroom. Rich follows her.

Once in their bedroom, Sophie tells Rich, "I cannot tolerate your mother always judging my parenting! She doesn't like me and she doesn't like how I parent. And you never stick up for me! You are going to have to talk to her. Otherwise, I'm not sure how much longer I can do this."

CASE STUDY DISCUSSION QUESTIONS

1. How is Elizabeth trying to socialize Sophie into the family?
2. What are some sources of tension in Elizabeth and Sophie's relationship?
3. How does this tension affect their relationship? How does it affect Sophie's marriage?
4. What are some suggestions for helping Sophie and Elizabeth mend their relationship?

REFERENCES

Allendorf, K. (2017). Like her own: Ideals and experiences of the mother-in-law/daughter-in-law relationship. *Journal of Family Issues*, *38*, 2102–2127. doi:10.1177/0192513X15590685

Fingerman, K. L., Gilligan, M., VanderDrift, L., & Pitzer, L. (2012). In-law relationships before and after marriage: Husbands, wives, and their mothers-in-law. *Research in Human Development*, *9*, 106–125. doi:10.1080/15427609.2012.680843

Floyd, K., & Morr, M. C. (2003). Human affection exchange: VII. Affectionate communication in the sibling/spouse/sibling-in-law triad. *Communication Quarterly*, *51*, 247–261. doi:10.1080/01463370309370155

Greif, G. L., & Woolley, M. E. (2018). The father-in-law's relationship with his son-in-law: A preliminary understanding. *Smith College Studies in Social Work*, *88*, 152–173. doi:10.1080/00377317.2018.1438243

Merrill, D. M. (2007). *Mothers-in-law and daughters-in-law: Understanding the relationship and what makes them friends or foe*. Westport, CT: Greenwood.

Mikucki-Enyart, S. L., Caughlin, J. P., & Rittenour, C. E. (2015). Content and relational implications of children-in-law's relational uncertainty within the in-law dyad during the transition to extended family. *Communication Quarterly*, *63*, 286–309. doi:10.1080/01463373.2015.1039714

Morr Serewicz, M. C. (2008). Toward a triangular theory of the communication and relationships of in-laws: Theoretical proposal and social relations analysis of relational satisfaction and private disclosure in in-law triads. *Journal of Family Communication*, *8*, 264–292.

Morr Serewicz, M. C. M. (2013). The difficulties of in-law relationships. In D. C. Kirkpatrick, S. Duck, & M. K. Foley (Eds.), *Relating difficulty* (pp. 117–134). New York, NY: Routledge.

Prentice, C. (2009). Relational dialectics among in-laws. *Journal of Family Communication*, *9*, 67–89. doi:10.1080/15267430802561667

Rittenour, C., & Soliz, J. (2009). Communicative and relational dimensions of shared family identity and relational intentions in mother-in-law/daughter-in-law relationships: Developing a conceptual model for mother-in-law/daughter-in-law research. *Western Journal of Communication*, *73*, 67–90. doi:10.1080/10570310802636334

Turner, M., Young, C. R., & Black, K. I. (2006). Daughters-in-law and mothers-in-law seeking their place within the family: A qualitative study of differing viewpoints. *Family Relations*, *55*, 588–600. doi:10.1111/j.1741-3729.2006.00428.x

Yoshimura, C. G. (2010). The experience and communication of envy among siblings, siblings-in-law, and spouses. *Journal of Social and Personal Relationships*, *27*, 1075–1088. doi:10.1177/0265407510382244

RELATED READINGS

Mikucki-Enyart, S. L. (2018). In-laws' perceptions of topic avoidance, goal inferences, and relational outcomes. *Journal of Family Communication*. Advanced Online Publication. doi:10.1080/15267431.2018.1492411

Mikucki-Enyart, S. L., & Caughlin, J. P. (2018). Integrating the relational turbulence model and a multiple goals approach to understand topic avoidance during the transition to extended family. *Communication Research*, *45*, 267–296. doi:10.1177/0093650215595075

Chapter 25
Intergenerational Relationships

BACKGROUND

Today, many grandparents are playing an important role in the lives of their grand-children. Longer lifespans are making this more possible than ever before and are increasing the length of time adults can expect to be in the grandparent role (i.e., today's grandparents will experience this role for 30 or more years). Children born today are more likely to have living grandparents than any generation before. Researchers refer to this phenomenon as the "vertical expansion" of the family. When grandparent–grandchild relationships are close, both grandparents and grandchildren benefit from spending time with one another. Grandchildren can make grandparents "feel young" and grandparents can share a lifetime's worth of wisdom and social support with grandchildren. At the same time, because people are delaying childbirth or not having children, the number of people who will never be grandparents or meet their grandchildren is also on the rise. Increased geographical distance between generations of the same family is making face-to-face contact between grandparents and grandchildren less common for some.

In general, adults tend to find the grandparenting role very satisfying (Thiele & Whelan, 2006). Grandmothers express enjoyment and many grandparents experience closeness with their grandchildren. The grandparenting role carries expectations and provides age-appropriate development experiences for older adults to bring generations of their family together and learn new things. Many older adults relish the opportunity to take on a new role later in life, contributing to their ability to feel productive and continue to grow and experience

Communication in Family Contexts: Theories and Processes, First Edition.
Elizabeth Dorrance Hall and Kristina M. Scharp.
© 2020 John Wiley & Sons, Inc. Published 2020 by John Wiley & Sons, Inc.
Companion website: www.wiley.com/go/dorrance_hall/communication-in-family-contexts

new things. Grandchildren also benefit from the grandparent–grandchild relationship, experiencing emotional gratification and learning about family history and traditions.

Multigenerational living is becoming more common in the United States. Multigenerational living refers to multiple generations of the same family living under the same roof, for example, a couple who have recently become new parents living with their parents so that grandparents, parents, and grandchildren are living in the same home. There are major advantages to living together, and these are well known in collectivist cultures where multigenerational living is the norm. Immigrants from collectivist cultures have contributed to the rise of this phenomenon in the United States along with economic downturn and the increasing cost of home prices.

THE GRANDPARENT ROLE

According to Hurme (1991) the grandparent role has at least four dimensions: attitudes and expectations, behaviors, symbolic meanings, and affective outcomes like satisfaction. As people enter older adulthood, their **attitudes** about career and roles outside of the family change as they engage less, making their roles within the family more important. Despite this, **behaviors** expected in the grandparent role can vary greatly (see the types of grandparents listed below). In general, grandparents expect to see their grandchildren often and grandchildren expect their grandparents to tell them stories of family history and traditions. Grandparents might engage in educating, socializing, and supporting (emotionally and financially) their grandchildren. Symbolic **meanings** of grandparenting are based on normative meanings like meeting society's needs for educating younger generations and personal meanings like experiencing love and closeness with grandchildren. **Satisfaction** with the grandparenting role has been associated with levels of involvement with grandchildren (not too much and not too little; Bowers & Myers, 1999).

Grandparent Types

(Developed by Cherlin & Furstenberg, 1985, 1986; Mueller, Wilhelm, & Elder, 2002; Segrin & Flora, 2011)

- **Influential** grandparents are available and involved in their grandchildren's lives. These grandparent–grandchild relationships can be described as intimate and close, yet the grandparents remain authority figures. Influential grandparents play a role in helping grandchildren make decisions about their future.

- **Supportive** grandparents see their grandchildren often, encourage their interests and passions, and have a close relationship with their grandchildren. Unlike influential grandparents, they do not engage in much rule setting or discipline.

- **Passive** grandparents are moderately involved in the lives of their grandchildren. They do not attend many activities or offer much advice or discipline. Passive grandparents are likely to live far away from their grandchildren.

- **Authority-oriented** grandparents enforce rules, discipline, and direct their grandchildren through advice and storytelling.

- **Detached** grandparents have little interaction with their grandchildren and do not play a large role in their lives. Although these grandparents are not psychologically close to their grandchildren, they might provide them with financial support.

COMMUNICATION IN THE GRANDPARENT–GRANDCHILD RELATIONSHIP

Communication varies from grandparent–grandchild relationship to grandparent–grandchild relationship. The grandparent role is not highly scripted or structured in terms of there not being a clear set of norms grandparents "should" follow. There is a wide range of appropriate grandparenting behaviors and ways of communicating and these behaviors change as grandchildren age into adulthood (Stelle et al., 2010). That said, research has identified a variety of factors that influence grandparent–grandchildren communication:

- The **age** of the grandparent and the age of the grandchild (e.g., younger grandparents who tend to be more active with their grandchildren).

- Geographical **distance** makes communication challenging, but technology makes this easier. Grandparents who live near their grandchildren have more opportunities to interact with them, though they do not always take up this opportunity. Because of technology and ease of travel, grandparents who live far from their grandchildren can still maintain close relationships.

- Whether the parents are **divorced**.

- Quality of the **parent–grandparent relationship**. Parents are important gatekeepers in the grandparent–grandchild relationship. Parents who are not close with their parents might impede or restrict the grandparent–grandchild relationship. Parents who are close to their own parents might place a large emphasis on close ties between grandparents and grandchildren.

- Strength of **family identity** (see identity section below).

Grandparents and grandchildren tend to discuss family, education, leisure activities, and friends (Lin, Harwood, & Bonnesen, 2002). For example, grandparents might tell their grandchildren stories about their time in college or talk about shared interests such as fishing, baseball, or books they have enjoyed.

mohamed_hassan/pixabay

The role of storytelling in the grandparent–grandchild relationship is important as grandparents are family history-keepers (Harwood, 2004; see Chapter 7). In the United States and beyond, we have cultural narratives of grandparents as storytellers who pass on stories that contain family culture, memories, identity, and sense-making tools. Bud Goodall (2006) calls receiving these stories from grandparents "narrative inheritance." Goodall claims people can make sense of their own identities through the stories their grandparents tell. People can compare the way they see the world with the way their grandparents do/did and notice the ways culture has changed (or stayed the same) throughout the years.

Grandmothers and mothers as kinkeepers. Older women in the family tend to take on the role of "kinkeeper." Women tend to feel higher levels of obligation for keeping the family together and maintaining family relationships than men do. Kinkeepers maintain family relationships by sharing information and planning events and get-togethers such as family reunions. Indeed, ties on the maternal side of families tend to be closer (maternal grandparents tend to be closer to their grandchildren than paternal grandparents).

IDENTITY AND THE GRANDPARENT–GRANDCHILD RELATIONSHIP

Much communication research on the grandparent–grandchild relationship has focused on identity: shared family identity, family identification, identity gaps, intergroup identities, and communication.

Jordan Soliz and his colleagues have used **social identity theory** to examine shared social identities between grandparents and grandchildren such as their family identity, and separate social identities they hold such as their age-cohort identities. Social identity theory explains that individuals who identify with a social group such as the Michigan State Spartans, their family, or Republicans (just to name a few) also adopt the goals of the group, experience the successes and failures of the group, and define their place in the social world based on their connection to the group (Ashforth & Mael, 1989). Groups are socially constructed categories people use as tools to order society and influence an individual's sense of self by defining where they belong. Individuals identify to feel part of an in-group and to fulfill the need for self-enhancement through attachment to an organization or group.

The family is an in-group that is shared by its members (Soliz & Rittenour, 2012) and is a group with which people often feel a sense of identification. **Family identification** is a sense of oneness or belonging a person feels with their family which defines, in part, who they are and how they interact with others. Family identification encompasses feelings (e.g., reactions to insults about other family members or pride in other member's accomplishments), motivations (e.g., desire to learn what others think of family or to express family identification to others), language use (e.g., using "we" language versus "they" when speaking about family), and refers to a sense of interdependence with one's family (e.g., recognizing family histories and fates are linked).

Grandparents and grandchildren share a family identity, but also each have social identities associated with different age cohorts. Jordan Soliz and Jake Harwood (2006) investigated the importance of these age-group memberships or social identities in the grandparent–grandchild relationship. They found that perceptions of a shared family identity were associated with family identification, parental encouragement of the relationship, social support, and mutual self-disclosure. They claim that young adult grandchildren might be more conscious of the age differences in their relationship with their grandparent, especially when grandparent health is impaired and they engage in a lot of intergroup communication (for example, talking about things that bring up their different group memberships such as popular culture or new technology).

Intergroup contact theory (Harwood, Hewstone, Paolini, & Voci, 2005) states that a specific interaction with an outgroup member shapes how a person thinks about other members of that outgroup. In this case, interaction with their grandparent shapes how many younger people view older people. Younger people make sense of all older people through specific interactions with their own grandparents.

Communication accommodation theory explains that people **accommodate**, or adjust and adapt their speech in response to features of other people. For example, grandchildren might adapt to the hearing loss of their grandparents by speaking louder when around them. The ability to adapt one's communication can be good for intergenerational relationships as adaptions likely make it easier for grandchildren and grandparents to communicate. When these efforts to adapt or accommodate are unnecessary or taken too far, they can also produce negative results. This phenomenon is called **overaccommodation**, and occurs when people simplify, clarify, use a demeaning tone, or presume a person has limited communication abilities simply because they are older or part of a stereotyped or misunderstood outgroup.

Jennifer Kam and Michael Hecht draw from the **communication theory of identity** to examine identity gaps in the grandparent–grandchild relationship (Kam & Hecht, 2009). **Identity gaps** in the grandparent–grandchild relationship might occur if a grandchild perceives their authentic self is different from the self their grandparents would prefer or be most proud of. These identity gaps, then, influence how grandchildren communicate with their grandparents. There are four frames that represent different aspects of identity: personal, relational, enacted, and communal (Hecht, 1993):

- Personal frames are the way individuals see themselves.

- Relational frames are ascribed by others *and* are how people see themselves as part of a larger unit (e.g., part of a couple or a family).

- Enacted frames are individual identities communicated to others.

- Communal frames are collective identities ascribed by society.

These frames can create identity gaps when there are inconsistencies between frames. Identity gaps can take many forms including these three:

- Personal–relational: when the way a person sees themselves is different than the way they think the other person sees them (for example, a young artist might be proud of their creativity but think their grandparent is not pleased with their life choice to be an artist).

- Personal–enacted: when a person behaves in ways that are inconsistent with how they see themselves.

- Relational–enacted: grandchildren not behaving in ways they think their grandparents expect them to.

Identity gaps are hard to manage and have been associated with lower satisfaction and less competent communication between people. The researchers found that the personal–enacted identity gap was related to topic avoidance (e.g., not talking about certain topics such as the grandchild's love life with the grandparent), communication, and relationship satisfaction so that grandchildren who experienced more of an identity gap engaged in less communication and experienced lower grandparent–grandchild relationship satisfaction. In 2016, Pusateri, Roaché, and Kam found that grandparent–grandchild identity gaps were associated with lower communication satisfaction in the grandparent–grandchild relationship (see references).

GRANDPARENT AS PRIMARY CAREGIVER

Increasingly, grandparents are acting as primary caregivers for their grandchildren. This happens for a variety of reasons, but is often because the parents are unable or unavailable to give primary care due to death, incarceration, teen pregnancy, unemployment, drug addiction, poor mental health, or child abuse (Aleman, 2014; Gladstone, Brown, & Fitzgerald, 2009). Families where the grandparents are the primary caregivers are sometimes called "grandfamilies" (Edwards, 2001). Children raised by their grandparents feel affection and loyalty toward their grandparents, but might struggle with making sense of where their parents fit into their family narrative. Indeed, grandfamilies are discourse dependent, often having to explain and justify to others their family situation (see Chapter 14). Grandparents face similar struggles as they enter into the child-rearing stage of life for a second time and experience physical, psychological, and resource stress.

Grandparents who are primary caregivers communicate differently with grandchildren than grandparents who play more of a supportive or passive role because they are not the primary caregivers. Because grandparents often become primary caregivers due to major family disruptions like the death of a parent, the family is already dealing with trauma that might impact the relationship.

Grandparents often need care themselves when they reach a certain age and their health begins to decline. The **intergenerational stake hypothesis** explains that people are more invested in their children than their parents because their children are their future. Though both grandparents and children might need care from the "sandwich generation" (adults positioned between two generations that are both dependent upon them for care; Brody, 2003), parents view children as continuations of themselves.

INTERESTING RESEARCH FINDINGS

Diversity in the Grandparent–Grandchild Relationship

Stelle and his team examined literature focused on three forms of diversity in the grandparent–grandchild relationship: (1) gender, (2) sexual orientation, and (3) physical and/or cognitive limitations.

- In regard to **gender**, less research has been conducted on grandfathers compared to grandmothers. The research that has been conducted has been mixed, finding either less satisfaction for grandfathers or little to no difference in satisfaction between the two grandparent genders.

- **Sexual orientation** of grandparents is also understudied, but one study found that lesbian and bisexual grandmothers who had strong relationships with their adult children (especially when those adult children accepted their parents' sexual orientation) were more likely to have close relationships with their grandchildren.

- Grandparents' physical and cognitive limitations might influence the lives of their grandchildren through their effect on family caregivers, often the grandparents' adult children. Many adult caregivers have young children themselves and others are the grandchildren of the older adult (about 8%). Established feelings of closeness between grandchildren and their grandparents can aid in keeping the relationship positive during the caregiving stage.

Relationship Maintenance in the Grandparent–Grandchild Relationship

Daniel Mansson, Scott Myers, and Lynn Turner (2010) conducted a study to examine the relationship maintenance behaviors used in the grandparent–grandchild relationship. Relationship maintenance is detailed in Chapters 28 and 29. They note that for a grandparent–grandchild relationship to be sustainable, both grandparents and grandchildren must engage in relational maintenance. The researchers surveyed undergraduate students and asked about their most recent interaction with a grandparent. In order of most to least frequent, grandchildren reported using positivity, conflict management, tasks, assurances, networks, advice, and openness with their grandparents. Grandchildren used more relational maintenance behaviors when they were satisfied with the communication in their grandparent–grandchild relationship and when they felt their grandparent supported them emotionally (by caring about their problems and giving them advice).

PRACTICAL APPLICATIONS AND THINGS TO CONSIDER

How, if at all, does your "authentic self" differ from the self you present to your grandparents? If you were to show them your authentic self, what do you think would change? If you do see a gap between your authentic self and the self you show your grandparents (or parents), how has managing this identity gap impacted your relationships? Are there certain topics you avoid bringing up around your grandparents? Are there any topics or types of news your parents advise you to keep from your grandparents?

Review the grandparent types listed above. Which type of grandparents do you have? If you have two (or more) sets of grandparents, how do they compare? What are the pros and cons of each type that you have?

KEY TERMS

Accommodation
Communication accommodation theory
Communication identity theory
Family identification

Grandfamilies
Grandparent types
Identity gaps
Intergenerational stake hypothesis
Kinkeeper

Multigenerational living
Narrative inheritance
Overaccommodation
Shared family identity
Social identity theory

IN-CLASS ACTIVITY

1. Together, watch the following *Buzzfeed* video, titled *Generations Throughout History*, about the living generations in America (e.g., Greatest Generation, Silent Generation, Baby Boomers, Gen X, Millennials [Gen Y], Gen Z, and Gen Alpha): https://youtu.be/IfYjGxI6AJ8.

2. As you watch, write down the name of each generation, the dates they were born, and something you find interesting about each generation and what shaped them as they grew up.
3. Discuss as a class any contradictions you noticed, for example, Gen X represents the largest group of startup founders yet are described as unmotivated, lazy, and overly interested in popular culture.
4. How do you think changing diversity has shaped these generations? Did you notice any facts or statistics that showed this?
5. Using the terms and theories you learned in this reading, how do you think people who are part of Gen X, Millennials, Gen Z, and Gen Alpha will differ as grandparents and older Americans compared to Baby Boomers and the Silent Generation? How will their expectations of younger people and their communication differ, if at all?

OUT-OF-CLASS ACTIVITY

Check out Harvard's Project Implicit (https://implicit.harvard.edu/implicit/selectatest.html). This project was designed to help people recognize the implicit biases they hold. We encourage you take a couple of these tests but start with the test on age. These tests let you know if you have an unconscious preference for younger people or older people. Come to class and discuss your results!

REFERENCES

Aleman, M. (2014). "I'm the parent and the grandparent": Constructing the grandfamily. In L. A. Baxter (Ed.), *Remaking family communicatively* (pp. 85–102). New York, NY: Peter Lang.

Ashforth, B. E., & Mael, F. (1989). Social identity theory and the organization. *Academy of Management Review, 14,* 20–39.

Bowers, B. F., & Myers, B. J. (1999). Grandmothers providing care for grandchildren: Consequences of various levels of caregiving. *Family Relations, 48,* 303–311. doi:10.2307/585641

Brody, E. M. (2003). *Women in the middle: Their parent-care years.* New York, NY: Springer.

Cherlin, A., & Furstenberg Jr., F. F. (1985). Styles and strategies of grandparenting. In V. L. Bengtson & J. F. Robertson (Eds.), *Sage focus editions* (Vol. 74): *Grandparenthood* (pp. 97–116). Thousand Oaks, CA: Sage.

Cherlin, A., & Furstenberg, F. F. (1986). Grandparents and family crisis. *Generations: Journal of the American Society on Aging, 10,* 26–28.

Edwards, O. W. (2001). Grandparents raising grandchildren. In M. J. Fine & S. W. Lee (Eds.), *Handbook of diversity in parent education: The changing face of parenting and parent education* (pp. 199–213). San Diego, CA: Academic Press.

Gladstone, J. W., Brown, R. A., & Fitzgerald, K. A. J. (2009). Grandparents raising their grandchildren: Tensions, service needs and involvement with child welfare agencies. *International Journal of Aging and Human Development, 69,* 55–78. doi:10.2190/AG.69.1.d

Goodall, H. L. (2006). *A need to know: The clandestine history of a CIA family.* Walnut Creek, CA: Left Coast Press.

Harwood, J. (2004). Relational, role, and social identity as expressed in grandparents' personal web sites. *Communication Studies, 55,* 300–318. doi:10.1080/10510970409388621

Harwood, J., Hewstone, M., Paolini, S., & Voci, A. (2005). Grandparent-grandchild contact and attitudes toward older adults: Moderator and mediator effects. *Personality and Social Psychology Bulletin, 31,* 393–406. doi:10.1177/0146167204271577

Hecht, M. L. (1993). 2002 – A research odyssey: Toward the development of a communication theory of identity. *Communications Monographs, 60,* 76–82. doi:10.1080/03637759309376297

Hurme, H. (1991). Dimensions of the grandparent role in Finland. In P. K. Smith (Ed.), *The psychology of grandparenthood* (pp. 19–31). London, UK: Routledge.

Kam, J. A., & Hecht, M. L. (2009). Investigating the role of identity gaps among communicative and relational outcomes within the grandparent–grandchild relationship: The young-adult grandchildren's perspective. *Western Journal of Communication, 73,* 456–480. doi:10.1080/10570310903279067

Lin, M. C., Harwood, J., & Bonnesen, J. L. (2002). Conversation topics and communication satisfaction in grandparent–grandchild relationships. *Journal of Language and Social Psychology, 21,* 302–323. doi:10.1177/0261927X02021003005

Mansson, D. H., Myers, S. A., & Turner, L. H. (2010). Relational maintenance behaviors in the grandchild–grandparent relationship. *Communication Research Reports, 27,* 68–79. doi:10.1080/08824090903526521

Mueller, M. M., Wilhelm, B., & Elder Jr., G. H. (2002). Variations in grandparenting. *Research on Aging, 24,* 360–388. doi:10.1177/0164027502243004

Pusateri, K. B., Roaché, D. J., & Kam, J. A. (2016). Grandparents' and young adult grandchildren's identity gaps and perceived caregiving intentions: An actor–partner interdependence model. *Journal of Social and Personal Relationships, 33,* 191–216. doi:10.1177/0265407514568750

Segrin, C., & Flora, J. (2011). *Family communication* (2nd ed.). New York, NY: Routledge.

Soliz, J., & Harwood, J. (2006). Shared family identity, age salience, and intergroup contact: Investigation of the grandparent–grandchild relationship. *Communication Monographs, 73,* 87–107. doi:10.1080/03637750500534388

Soliz, J., & Rittenour, C. E. (2012). Family as an intergroup arena. In J. Giles (Ed.), *The handbook of intergroup communication* (pp. 331–343). New York, NY: Routledge.

Stelle, C., Fruhauf, C. A., Orel, N., & Landry-Meyer, L. (2010). Grandparenting in the 21st century: Issues of diversity in grandparent–grandchild relationships. *Journal of Gerontological Social Work, 53,* 682–701. doi:10.1080/01634372.2010.516804

Thiele, D. M., & Whelan, T. A. (2006). The nature and dimensions of the grandparent role. *Marriage & Family Review, 40,* 93–108. doi:10.1300/J002v40n01_06

RELATED READINGS

Anderson, K., Harwood, J., & Lee Hummert, M. (2005). The grandparent–grandchild relationship: Implications for models of intergenerational communication. *Human Communication Research, 31,* 268–294. doi:10.1111/j.1468-2958.2005.tb00872.x

Miller-Day, M. A. (2004). *Communication among grandmothers, mothers, and adult daughters: A qualitative study of maternal relationships.* New York, NY: Routledge. doi:10.4324/9781410612120

Phillips, K. E., Ledbetter, A. M., Soliz, J., & Bergquist, G. (2018). Investigating the interplay between identity gaps and communication patterns in predicting relational intentions in families in the United States. *Journal of Communication, 68,* 590–611. doi:10.1093/joc/jqy016

Chapter 26
LGBTQ Families

LGBTQ families (i.e., families with at least one member who is lesbian, gay, bisexual, transgender, and/or queer) are on the rise in the United States. According to a 2017 Gallup poll, about 10 million Americans are LGBT. Furthermore, approximately 2 million children are growing up with gay or lesbian parents (Movement Advancement Project, 2011). Despite the increasing prevalence of these families, LGBTQ family members still face social stigma and are considered to be discourse dependent (see Chapter 14). Changing legislation that pertains to LGBTQ populations also creates conditions that require communication both within and outside of the family.

KEY CONCEPTS

Gay and Lesbian Families

Communicative Challenges

Research suggests that gay and lesbian parents face a variety of challenges ranging from difficult conversations about their relationship with their children to misconceptions based on expectations that people are in heterosexual relationships (Galvin, Turner, Patrick, & West, 2007). Gay men, due to their gender, for example, must contend with assumptions about whether they will be good parents and/or their trustworthiness considering people often connect child-rearing with mothers (Wells, 2011). Alternatively, lesbian mothers report being compared to mixed-sex families, disdained for their choices, nonverbally rebuked, and challenged based on failures to adhere to religious or political norms (Koenig Kellas & Suter, 2012). In response, lesbian mothers engaged in at least one of the following five strategies: (1) refusals, (2) justifications, (3) concessions, (4) preemptive responses, and (5) leading by example. Refusals took the form of challenging

Communication in Family Contexts: Theories and Processes, First Edition.
Elizabeth Dorrance Hall and Kristina M. Scharp.
© 2020 John Wiley & Sons, Inc. Published 2020 by John Wiley & Sons, Inc.
Companion website: www.wiley.com/go/dorrance_hall/communication-in-family-contexts

others back, being purposeful, being ambiguous, proving legitimacy, and exiting the conversation. They also justified their family ties or made appeals to love and normalcy. Some lesbians answered questions directly whereas others anticipated judgments. Finally, some lesbians discussed educating others by performing their family identity and meeting others where they were.

Communicative Strengths

Despite the varied communicative challenges gay and lesbian families face, they also can be extremely resilient. Research suggests that social workers consider gay and lesbian parents to be particularly resourceful and well networked, often placing the most challenging foster care children with lesbian and gay parents (Brooks & Goldberg, 2001). When lesbian and gay parents talk about their sexuality, children learn about tolerance and to celebrate people's differences. Children also learn to talk about their own sexuality with their parents, a topic which is considered extremely difficult for children of heterosexual parents (see Suter, 2015). Furthermore, children of gay and lesbian parents have to learn to communicatively navigate homophobic comments from others, which helps them overcome a variety of types of bullying and discrimination and build family identity (Breshears, 2011). Wells' (2011) research on gay parents suggests that men are transformed by parenthood and are helping to change what it means to be a father. Research does not support the speculation that children raised by gay and lesbian parents will have adjustment problems. Instead, research suggests that children of gay and lesbian parents do just as well as those raised by heterosexual parents.

Gender Dysphoria/Transgender

According to the Diagnostic and Statistical Manual of mental disorders (i.e., DSM V), **gender dysphoria** describes a condition in which people are intensely uncomfortable with their "birth gender" and strongly identify with another gender. Indeed, the technical definition focuses on the distress resulting from a gender mismatch instead of an identity disorder in need of treatment. Often, the label for a person with gender dysphoria is **transgender**. The term transgender actually refers to a broad spectrum of people who transiently or persistently identify with a different gender from their birth gender. A transgender person is different from a **cisgender** person whose gender identity aligns with the sex assigned to them at birth. A transgender person can also be distinct from a **transsexual** person who has undergone a social transformation and sometimes a physical transition.

Research suggests that transgender and transsexual people experience an extreme amount of stigma that often has implications for their family communication. Scholars have found that family members rarely have neutral reactions to transgender disclosures and transgender people require extensive communication to explain their situation to people both inside and outside the family (Norwood, 2012). Based on online postings, Norwood (2012) found that family members of transgender people expressed a variety of competing feelings and ideas. Specifically, they struggled with presence versus absence, sameness versus difference, and self versus other. For example, some parents described losing a son (i.e., absence) only to gain a daughter (i.e., presence). Furthermore, transgender people often described trying to explain how they both were the same person but also different. Finally, partners also described struggling to negotiate their own needs (i.e., the self) versus the needs of their transgender partner (i.e., the other). Ultimately, Norwood's research helped shed light on the communicative challenges for all members of the family.

INTERESTING RESEARCH FINDINGS

When faced with stigma, lesbian mothers often rely on a series of symbols and rituals to help construct their family identities. Based on 16 interviews with two lesbian mothers (with at least one child), Elizabeth Suter and her colleagues (2008) found that these mothers used the symbols of *last name* and *donor choice* as well as the rituals of attending a same-sex parenting group and doing family to help create a cohesive identity. Put a different way, mothers emphasized the importance of sharing a last name. They also selected donors who had similar physical attributes to the nonbiological mother. Parents discussed giving their children the opportunity to see other same-sex families in a same-sex parenting group. Finally, lesbian mothers emphasized "doing family" through the everyday patterned interactions that helped them stay close. These interactions might revolve around going to church, displaying family photos, or even going shopping.

Did You Know?

Legislation that pertains to LGBTQ communities is constantly changing. Based on a research study by Pamela Lannutti (2018), there are four motivations LGBTQ people gave for getting married after the 2016 US presidential election.

- Personal – love for partner; commitment to relationships; desire to share one's life with partner.
- Fearful – concern that material benefits of marriage would no longer be available.
- Political – political state for equality; against Trump/Pence administration and in tribute to Obama administration.
- Hopeful – wanted something positive to come out of a negative political environment.

PRACTICAL APPLICATIONS AND THINGS TO CONSIDER

Despite an influx of communication research about gay and lesbian families, we still know hardly anything about people who identify as bisexual. Even the research on gay men and transgender people is extremely sparse. One very notable exception to the lack of research on bisexuality is a study by Pamela Lannutti (2008) who conducted qualitative research to understand more about same-sex marriages between 26 bisexual–lesbian couples. She argues that people who identify as bisexual are often challenged by both the heterosexual and LGBTQ communities. This challenge, or what we might call **biphobia**, is based on two sets of beliefs; **explanatory beliefs** are those that call into question whether bisexuality is a true sexual orientation and **depoliticizing beliefs** suggest bisexual women are dangerous to the lesbian community because their preferences appear to be disloyal (Rust, 1995).

Based on the complications of being in a bisexual–lesbian relationship, participants discussed four interrelated themes that reflect their experiences. The themes include (1) self-image, (2) romantic relationships, (3) relationships with social network members, and (4) relationships with the LGBTQ community. Specifically, the theme of self-image refers to affirming bisexual identity and reflecting on the experience of being and having a wife within the context of same-sex marriage. Participants also discussed the ways being in a same-sex marriage challenge their romantic relationship while simultaneously strengthening it. For example, couples discussed the way the law strengthened their ties but also the stress that came from planning a wedding. Social networks also played a large part in the experience of same-sex marriage for these couples. As it happens, people experience support and/or resistance from their network. Resistance sometimes even took the form of being pressured by network members to marry. Finally, couples discussed how getting married helped them feel more connected to the LGBTQ community even though others felt more invisible. These contradictions suggest that same-sex bisexual–lesbian families might be particularly discourse dependent. The lack of communication research on people who identify as bisexual also warrants further attention.

KEY TERMS

Biphobia	Explanatory beliefs	Transgender
Cisgender	Gender dysphoria	Transsexual
Depoliticizing beliefs		

IN-CLASS ACTIVITY

1. Watch this *New York Times* video series clip titled "When your parents don't accept your marriage": https://nyti.ms/2CKSC6I

2. Ask the class to discuss:
   a. What challenges did this couple face in communicating with their parents? How were their family reactions similar or different?
   b. What challenges might gay, biracial dads face in making parenting decisions? Why?

    c. What challenges might they face when communicating with others outside the family, including meeting other parents at school? How is this family discourse dependent?

    d. How might this couple explain their unique (yet increasingly common) situation to their children?

    e. If you were in their shoes, how would you share and communicate about your culture with your children?

REFERENCES

Breshears, D. (2011). Understanding communication between lesbian parents and their children regarding outsider discourse about family identity. *Journal of GLBT Family Studies*, *7*, 264–284. doi:10.1080/1550428X.2011.564946

Brooks, D., & Goldberg, S. (2001). Gay and lesbian adoptive and foster care placements: Can they meet the needs of waiting children? *Social Work*, *46*, 147–157. doi:10.1093/sw/46.2.147

Gallup. (2017). In U.S., more adults identifying as LGBT. Retrieved from https://news.gallup.com/poll/201731/lgbt-identification-rises.aspx

Galvin, K. M., Turner, L. H., Patrick, D. G., & West, R. (2007, November). *Difficult conversations: The experiences of same-sex parents*. Paper presented at the annual meeting of the National Communication Association, Chicago, IL.

Koenig Kellas, J., & Suter, E. A. (2012). Accounting for lesbian-headed families: Lesbian mothers' responses to discursive challenges. *Communication Monographs*, *79*, 475–498. doi:10.1080/03637751.2012.723812

Lannutti, P. J. (2008). "This is not a lesbian wedding": Examining same-sex marriage and bisexual–lesbian couples. *Journal of Bisexuality*, *7*, 237–260. doi:10.1080/15299710802171316

Lannutti, P. J. (2018). GLBTQ people who decided to marry after the 2016 U.S. election: Reasons for and meanings of marriage. *Journal of GLBT Family Studies*, *14*, 85–100. doi:10.1080/1550428X.2017.1420846

Movement Advancement Project. (2011). All children matter: How legal and social inequalities hurt LGBT families. Retrieved from https://www.lgbtmap.org/file/all-children-matter-full-report.pdf

Norwood, K. (2012). Transitioning meanings? Family members' communicative struggles surrounding transgender identity. *Journal of Family Communication*, *12*, 75–92. doi:10.1080/15267431.2010.509283

Rust, P. C. (1995). *Bisexuality and the challenge to lesbian politics: Sex, loyalty, and revolution*. New York, NY: NYU Press.

Suter, E. A. (2015). Communication in lesbian and gay families. In L. Turner & R. West (Eds.), *The Sage handbook of family communication* (pp. 235–247). Thousand Oaks, CA: Sage.

Suter, E. A., Daas, K. L., & Bergen, K. M. (2008). Negotiating lesbian family identity via symbols and rituals. *Journal of Family Issues*, *29*, 26–47. doi:10.1177/0192513X07305752

Wells, G. (2011). Making room for daddies: Male couples creating families through adoption. *Journal of GLBT Family Studies*, *7*, 155–181. doi:10.1080/15504 28X.2011.537242

RELATED READINGS

Cheverette, R. (2013). Outing heteronormativity in interpersonal and family communication: Feminist applications of Queer Theory "Beyond the Sexy Streets." *Communication Theory*, *23*, 170–190. doi:10.1111.comt.12009

Dixon, J., & Dougherty, D. S. (2014). A language convergence/meaning divergence analysis exploring how LGBTQ and single employees manage traditional family expectations in the workplace. *Journal of Applied of Communication Research*, *42*, 1–19. doi:10.1080/00909882.2013.847275

Haines, K. M., Boyer, C. R., Giovanazzi, C., & Paz Galupo, M. (2018). "Not a real family": Microaggressions directed toward LGBTQ families. *Journal of Homosexuality*, *65*, 1138–1151. doi:10.1080/00918369.2017.1406217

Chapter 27

Parent–Child Relationships

BACKGROUND

Parents and children often have some of the strongest family bonds. Parents play an important role in socializing children by communicating their values and beliefs/culture to the next generation. Parents are responsible for teaching their children about how to behave and how to communicate with others. In later life, children might take on more responsibilities in caring for their parents in which communication, again, becomes important in everyday life but also in decision-making processes about health and living arrangements. In this chapter we discuss some primary theories and developmental phases of parent–child communication.

KEY CONCEPTS

Attachment Theory

Attachment theory was developed by John Bowlby who wanted to explain how the relationship between infants and their caregivers influenced a child's personality development in later years (see Ainsworth & Bowlby, 1991). When children are **securely attached**, they feel free to explore their environment but still use their mother as a base; when they are separated, they show some distress but eventually calm down. Children who are **anxious ambivalent** cry when left alone and do not feel comfortable exploring their environment; when reunited with their mother, these children appear relieved but angry. Finally, **avoidant** children

Communication in Family Contexts: Theories and Processes, First Edition.
Elizabeth Dorrance Hall and Kristina M. Scharp.
© 2020 John Wiley & Sons, Inc. Published 2020 by John Wiley & Sons, Inc.
Companion website: www.wiley.com/go/dorrance_hall/communication-in-family-contexts

explore their environment without paying attention to their mother and do not notice or care when they are together or apart. Of interest to communication scholars is the idea that these attachment styles form as a result of parent–child communication even during infancy. Consistent and responsive care leads to secure attachment whereas inconsistent care leads to insecurity.

Research suggests that these attachment styles persist into adulthood. When thinking about adult attachment styles, however, Bartholomew and Horowitz (1991) reconceptualized the styles to reflect our views of ourselves (attachment anxiety) contrasted with our views of others (attachment avoidance). For example, when people have a positive view of themselves and others, they are secure. When they have a positive view of themselves but a negative view of others, they are dismissive. People with dismissive attachment styles are not dependent on others to the extent they distance themselves from others to pursue their own goals. Alternatively, when people have a negative view of themselves and a positive view of others they can be preoccupied. Preoccupied types crave intimacy often to the point of pushing others away. People with fearful attachments have a negative view of themselves and of others. These individuals want close relationships but are afraid of rejection. They often give off mixed messages, "Come here – go away!" Consequently, these styles influence how we communicate, especially in romantic relationships.

In addition to serving as a cause and consequence, communication plays two other important roles in the attachment process. First, communication helps explain why attachment is related to a variety of family characteristics such as cohesion, expressiveness, and adaptability (Mikulincer & Florian, 1999). For example, people who have secure attachment styles tend to communicate with more positivity and in more constructive ways. Because of this positivity, people with secure attachment styles tend to engage in conflict in more constructive ways (Feeney, 1994). Connecting this finding to the chapter about different methodologies (Chapter 2), in this study, communication is a mediating variable between attachment and family characteristics.

Finally, communication might also work to reinforce attachment styles. Imagine Jim who has a fearful attachment style. Jim makes a great first impression but as time goes by, he becomes afraid that others will hurt or reject him so he stops disclosing and decides to hang out less and less. Jim's friends can't understand what has happened so eventually they assume Jim does not want to be friends any longer so they stop inviting him out. When his friends stop inviting him out, it just reaffirms to Jim that others cannot be trusted. This pattern of behavior is sometimes called a self-fulfilling prophecy. Reinforcement might also happen when attachment styles are transmitted to children via social learning (see Chapter 8). **Thus, communication plays an important role in attachment and family relationships**.

Family Communication Patterns Theory

Much research on parent–child communication in the field of family communication has been conducted utilizing family communication patterns theory (FCP; Chapter 5). Based on the theory, scholars argue that communication environments develop over time yet are fairly consistent across childhood. Communication environments tend to change when there are major changes to the family such as divorce or when children "leave the nest" for work or to attend college. Each of the four family types described in Chapter 5 communicates differently with their children. Children can play a role in directing communication patterns in the family. This occurs when parents and children engage in "reciprocal communication" where each party's communication influences the other. Communication environments often have lasting effects on the way people communicate within and outside of the family. For example, a person's FCP as a child can be used to predict the success of their future interpersonal relationships. Another example of this aligns with the chapter on affection exchange theory (Chapter 3). Floyd and Morman (2000) found that affection from fathers predicts men's affections with their own sons.

Baumrind's Parenting Styles

Diana Baumrind (1991) developed four parenting styles based on the demandingness and responsiveness of the parents. Demandingness refers to how controlling a parent is of their child's behaviors. Parents who are high in responsiveness express warmth and acceptance. Responsive parents are sensitive to their children's emotional and developmental needs. These parenting styles influence how parents communicate with their children.

- Authoritative (high demand, high warmth/acceptance) – parents communicate clear rules and high expectations coupled with warmth and acceptance, kids tend to have better social skills and higher self-esteem.

- Authoritarian (high demand, low warmth/acceptance) – communication is cold, strict rules are given with high expectations but without kindness and warmth, kids tend to have lower self-esteem and poorer social skills, may engage in risky behaviors like drugs/alcohol.

- Permissive (low demand, high warmth/acceptance) – kids have poorer social skills and are more impulsive, few rules are communicated along with warmth and acceptance no matter what.

- Neglectful (low demand, low warmth/acceptance) – no rules communicated along with cold communication, kids more likely to do risky things like consume alcohol, drugs, delinquent behavior.

In brief: parenting behaviors can be understood by how they vary on demandingness and responsiveness. Children who are raised with various combinations of demand and warmth/acceptance tend to have different outcomes as children and as adults.

PARENT–CHILD COMMUNICATION CHANGES AS CHILDREN DEVELOP

Communication with Young Children

Communication with children is limited by the developmental stage of the child. Very young children do not respond well to reason and logic when parents discipline them. John Gottman, Lynn Katz, and Carole Hooven (1997) suggest an emotion coaching approach to communicating with younger children that balances warmth and control. Their method recommends that parents provide statements of warmth and understanding *before* they suggest or demand different behavior from their children. The emotion coaching technique unfolds over five steps:

1. Notice low-intensity emotions *before* they develop into full-fledged tantrums.

2. See the negative emotion as an opportunity for teaching the child and making a connection.

3. Listen, empathize, and validate the child's emotions (much like the concept of acceptance in confirmation theory).

4. Help the child label the emotion.

5. Set limits and help the child explore problem-solving strategies (much like the concept of challenge in confirmation theory).

Communication with Adolescents

Adolescence is another important time when parent–child communication can make a big difference in whether or not adolescents engage in risky behaviors. For example, research suggests that parents who talk to their children in adolescence about reproductive health have children who engage in less risky sexual behavior (Gavin et al., 2015). Quality communication also matters. Poor parent–child communication is related to increased problematic internet use (e.g., addiction)

mohamed_hassan/pixabay

and increased reports of being (cyber)bullied (Boniel-Nissim & Sasson, 2018). The opposite is also true; positive parent–child communication also helps to reduce reports of (cyber)bullying victimization and problematic internet use. Although much of the research on communication with adolescents is conducted outside of the field of communication studies, family communication scholar Michelle Miller-Day has done extensive research related to family communication and substance use. Miller-Day (2002) found that adolescents tend to prefer talking about alcohol, tobacco, and drug use with their mothers compared to other family members. These talks were also a part of their everyday family talk instead of being reserved for specific "drug talk." She (2008) went on to explore the strategies parents used to create expectations around alcohol and other drug use. The strategies included:

- Parents telling their children to use their best judgment.
- Hinting that children should not use drugs.
- Parents creating a no tolerance rule.
- Parents providing their children with information.
- Rewarding their children for nonuse.
- Never addressing the issue.

Of these strategies, the no tolerance policy appeared to be the most effective regardless of whether your family was high/low in conversation openness or high/low in desiring conformity (see Chapter 5). All of these studies taken together, however, illustrate that parents who communicate with their adolescents tend to have adolescents who have fewer problems with substance abuse, (cyber)bullying, and risky sexual behaviors.

Communication with Adult Children

Emerging adulthood is the beginning of adulthood and marks a time when young adults strike out on their own, establish their independence, and (re)negotiate their relationship with their parents (Aquilino, 2006; Arnett & Tanner, 2016). Emerging adulthood tends to be a tumultuous time in the life course marked by change and identity exploration. Emerging adults experience a multitude of life events in rapid succession, making 18–30 years old a uniquely self-focused life stage where identity exploration takes place in terms of options for love, career, and worldview (Arnett, 2000).

Aquilino stresses the interdependence of the parent–child relationship during emerging adulthood as life events and changing roles affect both the child and the parent during this time. Parent–child communication often changes during emerging adulthood due to the developmental nature of the life stage. For example, emerging adults are able to relate to their parents in more complex ways during this life stage including the ability to understand motivations behind relationship choices such as divorce (Arnett, 2006). In a study on parent–child communication about adult status, Jablonski and Martino (2013) found that emerging adults and their parents discussed a range of topics including the changes in their relationship, the emerging adults' financial and decision-making abilities, and family obligations. Despite the self-focus of this stage, parents are often an important source of support during this unsettled time.

Support is essential to adjustment to adult life, and parents are often a strong provider of support, even after children leave their home (see Chapter 17 on Supportive Communication in Families). Taking the transition to college as an example, parental support is linked to higher confidence in students' academic abilities, persistence, better personal adjustment, lower loneliness, depression, and academic stress (Demaray & Malecki, 2003; Dorrance Hall et al., 2017).

Parental support can easily be taken too far. **Overparenting**, or helicopter parenting, refers to over-involved and developmentally inappropriate parenting that is typically well intentioned by parents but not appreciated by their adult children. Parents who engage in helicopter parenting tend to be overprotective, make decisions for their children, and engage in controlling behaviors like micromanaging. Too much involvement violates basic needs like autonomy, competence, and relatedness. Emerging adult children who experience overparenting tend to be more stressed, have higher anxiety, lower self-confidence, and not adapt as well to new situations (like the transition to college; Dorrance Hall et al., 2018; Odenweller et al., 2014; Padilla-Walker & Nelson, 2012; Rousseau & Scharf, 2015).

A Note on Parent–Child Communication in Later Years

Despite the importance of parent–child communication, family communication scholars still have many opportunities to conduct research about this relationship in later years. One thing we do know is that communication might become more strained when adult children begin to have children. Indeed, adult children often argue with their parents over parenting styles and caretaking roles such as babysitting (Segrin & Flora, 2011). Such family conflict, mismanaged when aggression and hostility enter into the equation, can strain even the strongest adult child–parent relationships. Some adult children also engage in caregiving for their aging parents (see Chapter 10).

INTERESTING RESEARCH FINDINGS

Hurtful Parent–Child Interactions

Rachel McLaren and Alan Sillars (2014) recognize that some interactions between parents and their adolescent children are hurtful. Indeed, bickering increases in the parent–child relationship during this life stage. The researchers had 95 pairs of parents and children come into the laboratory (made to look like a living room) and interact. The participants wrote down recent times their parent or child did or said something hurtful. The parent–child pairs were then shown what the other person wrote down and were asked to discuss the events including why the event occurred and why it was hurtful. The researchers found that parents and children differ in regard to the types of events they find hurtful.

Types of hurtful events include (1) discipline such as children being yelled at by parents, (2) disparagement/disregard including sibling favoritism, criticism, and broken promises, and (3) misconduct including misbehaving. In general, children were less affected by hurtful episodes overall than their parents.

PRACTICAL APPLICATIONS AND THINGS TO CONSIDER

Memorable messages, defined as "verbal messages which might be remembered for extremely long periods of time" (Knapp, Stohl, & Reardon, 1981), continue to influence children's beliefs, attitudes, and behaviors long after they have left home. Elizabeth Dorrance Hall (one of your textbook authors) along with a team of researchers (2016) conducted a study to understand the memorable messages about diet and exercise received from parents throughout adolescence. She conducted focus groups with 77 adult women and asked them about messages from parents that stood out to them from their childhood. Based on these messages, three parenting styles emerged: the parental critic, parental professor, and the parental protector. Parental critics provided memorable messages to their children that primarily disapproved of their diet and exercise behaviors (e.g., "maybe you shouldn't have that cookie"). Parental professors emphasized learning and teaching children about healthy diets and exercise. Memorable messages from parental professors centered on reading food labels and exercising as a family. Parental protectors spoke about diet and exercise in accepting ways, encouraging self-love and "beauty at any size."

> What memorable messages stand out to you from your childhood about food? Diet? Exercise? Write them down and compare with a neighbor. Which type of parent (based on the three types described above) do you think you had growing up?

> Can you think of memorable messages you received about college? What about career? Where did these messages come from? (They do not need to come only from parents.)

DISCUSSION QUESTIONS

How has your communication with your parent changed over the past 15 years? Can you identify conversations that were especially important or meaningful? What was memorable about those conversations?

KEY TERMS

Attachment (secure, anxious ambivalent, avoidant)
Authoritative parenting
Authoritarian parenting

Demandingness
Emerging adulthood
Emotion coaching
Permissive parenting

Neglectful parenting
Overparenting
Responsiveness

The New Neighbors

CASE STUDY BY KELLY G. ODENWELLER

In a quiet, well-kept suburban neighborhood, the Millers sat down at their dining room table to eat dinner. Mr. Miller picked up a platter of chicken and passed it to his oldest son, Jimmy. Jimmy placed a piece of chicken on his plate and then passed the platter to his younger sister, Jessica, who took a piece and passed it to her younger brother, Joey. Mrs. Miller joined the family at the table with a bowl of mashed potatoes.

"How was everyone's day?" Mr. Miller asked as the family started to take their first bites of food.

"Good," Jimmy and Jessica said in unison.

"Really good!" Joey exclaimed. "I played with the new neighbor after school today."

"New neighbor?" Mr. Miller asked cautiously, peering over at Mrs. Miller with a concerned look on his face.

"Yeah, the boy who moved in down the street a few weeks ago. We played football and rode our bikes and then we went to his house and played video games. He has the new PlayStation and a ton of cool games!" Joey explained excitedly.

"The blue house on the corner?" Mr. Miller asked as he scrunched his face up in disgust.

"Yeah, the family with really dark skin," Jessica explained. "I saw them out there playing."

"Hmm...did your mother know you were over there?" Mr. Miller stared at Mrs. Miller now.

"Well, she didn't know I was in his house," Joey said quietly, suddenly feeling guilty. "He asked me to come inside and I forgot to – "

"You can't be going into people's houses without us knowing about it," Mr. Miller interrupted. His voice got louder as he started to reprimand Joey. "Especially that house. I don't think that's a boy you should be playing with."

"Yeah," Jimmy chimed in. "Those people are weird. I saw his brother just sitting on his front porch the other day with his Dad's car radio blaring from the driveway. He was wearing, like, baggy clothes and a backwards hat."

"They just aren't our kind of people," Mr. Miller said sternly.

"Yeah, I saw his mother at the grocery store today and she did not look very friendly," Mrs. Miller added. "And she let her daughter scream and run around the whole time she was shopping. I don't think they have very good discipline over there."

"Yeah, Joey, we don't really like this family," Mr. Miller concluded.

"But Dad, Ray's a really nice – " Joey tried to defend his new friend.

"Excuse me, Joey," Mr. Miller scolded. He put his hand up like a crossing guard to signal Joey to stop talking. "You know we don't interrupt adults in this family."

"I'm sorry," Joey mumbled as he looked down into his lap.

The family sat in silence for a few minutes while they ate.

Finally, Joey asked, "Can Ray play at our house where Mom can see us?"

"No, you can play with the other kids in the neighborhood," Mr. Miller instructed. "We know they come from good families."

"But Dad – " Joey started.

"That's enough, Joey. We're not going to argue about this any longer." Mr. Miller ended the conversation.

Across the street, the Smiths had also just sat down for dinner. Mrs. Smith served herself a spoonful of pasta and passed the bowl to her daughter, Rebecca. Rebecca scooped some pasta onto her plate and passed the bowl to her younger brother, Jonathan. After Jonathan served himself, he passed the food to his father.

"How was everyone's day?" Mrs. Smith asked as she took a sip from her water glass.

"Good," Rebecca and Jonathan said as they took their first bites of pasta.

"Busy, busy," Mr. Smith said, shoveling a large bite of pasta into his mouth.

"How was your day, Mom?" Rebecca asked.

"Oh, it was nice." Mrs. Smith started. "I ran into the new neighbors in the grocery store."

"New neighbors?" Mr. Smith asked inquisitively. "The blue house on the corner?"

"Yeah, the mother and her daughter were shopping today." Mrs. Smith said cheerfully. "Her name is Rochelle and her daughter, who is probably two years old, is named Bailey. I think she said she has two older boys, too."

"How nice to finally run into them," Mr. Smith said. "I have been meaning to walk down there and introduce myself."

"They were so friendly!" Mrs. Smith continued. "She said she is still unpacking. You know how difficult it is to move with kids!"

"Oh, definitely," Mr. Smith agreed.

"Yeah, they seem really nice," Rebecca said. "They smiled and waved when I rode my bike past their house the other day."

"The boy is in my class at school. He's really nice. His name is Ray. We play basketball on the playground together," Jonathan said.

"Oh, I didn't know he was in your class. Well, how nice!" Mrs. Smith exclaimed.

"Some people at school make fun of his skin color, but I think it's really cool," Jonathan explained.

"Why do the other kids make fun of his skin?" Mr. Smith asked.

"I don't know. Some people are just mean to him," Jonathan explained.

"I think they're mean because he's different from them and they don't take the time to get to know him," Rebecca offered.

"Really?" Mrs. Smith asked, astonished.

"People in my class can be like that, too," Rebecca added. "Sometimes the people who have different skin or different hair get left out."

"That is so sad," Mrs. Smith said, listening intently to her children's words.

"How does that make you feel when kids are teased or excluded?" Mr. Smith asked.

"I don't like it. One time I saw one of the girls, Atong, crying on the playground. I went over and asked her to play tag with me and my friends. I think that made her feel a little better."

"That was a very nice thing to do, Rebecca. I'm very impressed," Mrs. Smith praised.

"I would be very upset if the other kids made fun of how I looked," Jonathan added. "I wonder if that's how Ray feels."

Mrs. Smith sat quietly for a few minutes while she ate her dinner. Then she had an idea. "Do you think we should invite Ray and Bailey, and even their older brother, over to play this weekend? Maybe that would help Rochelle finish her unpacking and help the kids make some new friends."

"Yes!" Jonathan and Rebecca shouted in union.

CASE STUDY DISCUSSION QUESTIONS

1. Which family communication patterns characterize the Millers' and Smiths' communication?
2. How did the Miller and Smith children conform to, resist, or influence their parents' messages?
3. In what ways are the Millers' and Smiths' communication similar to or different from your family's communication?
4. How do you think the Millers' and Smiths' communication at the dinner table shapes the children's attitudes about and communication with the new neighbors moving forward?

REFERENCES

Ainsworth, M. D. S., & Bowlby, J. (1991). An ethological approach to personality development. *American Psychologist, 46*, 333–341. doi:10.1037/0003-066X.46.4.333

Aquilino, W. S. (2006). Family relationships and support systems in emerging adulthood. In J. J. Arnett & J. L. Tanner (Eds.), *Emerging adults in America: Coming of age in the 21st century* (pp. 193–217). Washington, DC: American Psychological Association. doi:10.1037/11381-008

Arnett, J. J. (2000). Emerging adulthood: A theory of development from the late teens through the twenties. *American Psychologist, 55*, 469–480. doi:10.1037/0003-066X.55.5.469

Arnett, J. J. (2006). The psychology of emerging adulthood: What is known, and what remains to be known? In J. J. Arnett & J. L. Tanner (Eds.), *Emerging adults in America: Coming of age in the 21st century* (pp. 303–330). Washington, DC: American Psychological Association.

Arnett, J. J., & Tanner, J. L. (2016). The emergence of emerging adulthood: The new life stage between adolescence and young adulthood. In A. Furlong (Ed.), *Routledge handbook of youth and young adulthood* (pp. 50–56). New York, NY: Routledge.

Bartholomew, K., & Horowitz, L. M. (1991). Attachment styles among young adults: A test of a four-category model. *Journal of Personality and Social Psychology, 61,* 226–244. doi:10.1037/0022-3514.61.2.226

Baumrind, D. (1991). The influence of parenting style on adolescent competence and substance use. *Journal of Early Adolescence, 11,* 56–95. doi:10.1177/0272431691111004

Boniel-Nissim, M., & Sasson, H. (2018). Bullying victimization and poor relationships with parents as risk factors of problematic internet use in adolescents. *Computers in Human Behavior, 88,* 176–183. doi:10.1016/j.chb.2018.05.041

Demaray, M. K., & Malecki, C. K. (2003). Perceptions of the frequency and importance of social support by students classified as victims, bullies, and bully/victims in an urban middle school. *School Psychology Review, 32,* 471–490.

Dorrance Hall, E., Billott-Verhoff, C., Yue, C., McNallie, J., & Wilson, S. R. (2018, May). *The effect of over-parenting on college adjustment: Family support and protective buffering for U.S. domestic and Chinese international students.* Paper presented at the annual meeting of the International Communication Association Conference, Prague, Czech Republic.

Dorrance Hall, E., McNallie, J., Custers, K., Timmermans, E., Wilson, S., & Van den Bulck, J. (2017). A cross-cultural examination of the mediating role of family support and parental advice quality on the relationship between family communication patterns and first-year college student adjustment in the United States and Belgium. *Communication Research, 44,* 638–667. doi:10.1177/0093650216657755

Dorrance Hall, E., Ruth-McSwain, A., & Ferrara, M. H. (2016). Models of health: Exploring memorable messages received from parents about diet and exercise. *Journal of Communication in Healthcare, 9,* 247–255. doi:10.1080/17538068.2016.1187892

Feeney, J. A. (1994). Attachment style, communication patterns, and satisfaction across the life cycle of marriage. *Personal Relationships, 1,* 333–348. doi:10.1111/j.1475-6811.1994.tb00069.x

Floyd, K., & Morman, M. T. (2000). Affection received from fathers as a predictor of men's affection with their own sons: Tests of the modeling and compensation hypotheses. *Communications Monographs, 67,* 347–361. doi:10.1080/03637750009376516

Gavin, L. E., Williams, J. R., Rivera, M., & Lachance, C. R. (2015). Programs to strengthen parent–adolescent communication about reproductive health. *American Journal of Preventative Medicine, 49,* S65–S72. doi:10.1016/j.amepre.2015.03.022

Gottman, J. M., Katz, L. F., & Hooven, C. (1997). *Meta-emotion: How families communicate emotionally.* Mahwah, NJ: Lawrence Erlbaum Associates.

Jablonski, J. F., & Martino, S. D. (2013). A qualitative exploration of emerging adults' and parents' perspectives on communicating adulthood status. *The Qualitative Report, 18,* 1–12.

Knapp, M. L., Stohl, C., & Reardon, K. K. (1981). "Memorable" messages. *Journal of Communication, 31,* 27–41. doi:10.1111/j.1460-2466.1981.tb00448.x

McLaren, R. M., & Sillars, A. (2014). Hurtful episodes in parent–adolescent relationships: How accounts and attributions contribute to the difficulty of talking about hurt. *Communication Monographs, 81,* 359–385. doi:10.1080/03637751.2014.933244

Mikulincer, M., & Florian, V. (1999). The association between parental reports of attachment styles and family dynamics, and offspring's reports of adult attachment style. *Family Process, 38,* 243–257. doi:10.1111/j.1545-5300.1999.00243

Miller-Day, M. A. (2002). Parent–adolescent communication about alcohol, tobacco, and other drug use. *Journal of Adolescent Research, 17,* 604–616. doi:10.1177/074355802237466

Miller-Day, M. (2008). Talking to youth about drugs: What do youth say about parental strategies? *Family Relations, 57,* 1–12. doi:10.1111/j.1741-3729.2007.00478.x

Odenweller, K. G., Booth-Butterfield, M., & Weber, K. (2014). Investigating helicopter parenting, family environments, and relational outcomes for millennials. *Communication Studies, 65,* 407–425. doi:10.1080/10510974.2013.811434

Padilla-Walker, L. M., & Nelson, L. J. (2012). Black hawk down? Establishing helicopter parenting as a distinct construct from other forms of parental control during emerging adulthood. *Journal of Adolescence, 35,* 1177–1190. doi:10.1016/j.adolescence.2012.03.007

Rousseau, S., & Scharf, M. (2015). "I will guide you": The indirect link between overparenting and young adults' adjustment. *Psychiatry Research, 228,* 826–834. doi:10.1016/j.psychres.2015.05.016

Segrin, C., & Flora, J. (2011). *Family communication* (2nd ed.). New York, NY: Routledge.

RELATED READINGS

Bowlby, J. (1951). *Maternal care and mental health.* Geneva, Switzerland: World Health Organization.

Reed, K., Duncan, J. M., Lucier-Greer, M., Fixelle, C., & Ferraro, A. J. (2016). Helicopter parenting and emerging adult self-efficacy: Implications for mental and physical health. *Journal of Child Family Studies, 25,* 3136–3149. doi:10.1007/s10826-016-0466-x

Rossetto, K. R. (2015). Bereaved parents' strategies and reactions when supporting their surviving children. *Western Journal of Communication, 79,* 533–554. doi:10.1080/10570314.2015.1079332

Schiffrin, H. H., & Liss, M. (2017). The effects of helicopter parenting on academic motivation. *Journal of Child and Family Studies, 26,* 1472–1480. doi:10.1007/s10826-017-0658-z

Chapter 28
Partner Relationships

BACKGROUND

Decades of research have shown that quality of communication predicts marital and long-term committed romantic relationship satisfaction. This chapter asks you to consider how the context of a committed relationship could change the way two people communicate. What is unique about long-term committed romantic relationships?

MAINTAINING PARTNER RELATIONSHIPS

Relationship maintenance strategies are important for sustaining long-term committed relationships. The small things couples do for one another often can add up and contribute to marital success. Many maintenance strategies have been identified by research, some of which can be found in Chapter 29 as they pertain to sibling relationships. According to Laura Stafford and Daniel Canary (1991), partners use **positivity**, **openness**, **assurances**, **social networks**, and **sharing tasks** (all described in Chapter 29). More recent research by Stafford (2011) expands openness to include **self-disclosure** and **relational talk** as important elements of relationship maintenance. **Understanding** is included in addition to positivity. Assurances (e.g., communicating commitment), networks (e.g., sharing friends), and tasks (e.g., sharing housework responsibilities) remain important relationship maintenance behaviors. These maintenance behaviors are linked to marital satisfaction, commitment, liking, and love. In fact, both mixed-and

Communication in Family Contexts: Theories and Processes, First Edition.
Elizabeth Dorrance Hall and Kristina M. Scharp.
© 2020 John Wiley & Sons, Inc. Published 2020 by John Wiley & Sons, Inc.
Companion website: www.wiley.com/go/dorrance_hall/communication-in-family-contexts

mohamed_hassan/pixabay

same-sex couples report sharing tasks as the most commonly used maintenance behavior (Haas & Stafford, 2005). **In brief: consistent relational maintenance work is linked to positive outcomes for relationships including feeling more satisfied in the relationship.**

There are also negative behaviors that are used to maintain relationships such as allowing control, destructive conflict, spying, jealousy induction, avoidance, and infidelity (Dainton & Gross, 2008). These behaviors can be considered the "dark side" of maintenance and they are associated with lower relationship satisfaction. They are still classified as maintenance behaviors because partners do them to keep their relationship in a desired state. For example, if one partner feels the other is not attentive enough, they might engage in negative maintenance behaviors to get them to pay more attention. Deception might be used to keep the relationship in a positive state if the truth would cause conflict. We explain more about the "dark side" of marital communication near the end of this chapter.

INVESTMENT AND EQUITY

Rusbult created the **investment model** to understand why some relationships survive and thrive whereas other relationships that seem like they have a good chance end up withering and ending (Rusbult et al., 1994). The investment model includes four important factors that can help predict whether or not a couple will stay together: satisfaction, size of investment, quality of alternatives, and commitment to the relationship. **Satisfaction** refers to how couples feel about the relationship, either positive or negative. **Investment size** includes the resources attached to the relationship, for example, material things like a partner's good job and income, but also emotional attachments like the affection a partner gives and feelings of stability associated with having a long-term partner. **Quality of alternatives** refers to a person's other options. For example, are there other people they could imagine being with (for example, a co-worker they've been getting closer to) where these other people could meet their needs? Finally, **commitment** is the intent to continue the relationship long term. The model says satisfaction, investment, and quality of alternatives predict a person's commitment levels. If any one of the first three factors is low, or all three are low, commitment to the relationship will drop.

Another factor that can play a role in commitment is whether the partners are investing equally, or fairly, in the relationship. When a couple invests equally in the relationship, the relationship is considered equitable. Studies have shown that when the relationship is unfair (either the person is giving more than he or she is getting or vice versa), the use of maintenance strategies decreases (Canary & Stafford, 1992). However, a couple's investment or commitment in the relationship does not always match. These couples are called **asymmetrically committed**. In an asymmetrically committed relationship, one partner is the "weak link" or less committed partner and the other is the "strong link" or more committed partner. Weak link partners tend to have difficulty depending on others, difficulty with closeness and intimacy, and have many alternative partners available to them (Stanley et al., 2017). Stanley and his team followed asymmetrical couples for two years and found that the majority stay together (65%) but 35% had broken up. The couples who stayed together tended to have made joint investments in the relationship including buying a house or leasing an apartment together or getting a pet. His team also found that a couple is more likely to break up if the woman is the weak link the relationship.

Why do people stay in bad relationships? Because they are invested in them! Research has found that high investment in the relationship and few alternative partners can explain, in part, why people stay in bad relationships.

TYPES OF COUPLES

Fitzpatrick's (1988) couple types focus on communication between partners, especially when it comes to conflict. Fitzpatrick claims that marriages differ in at least three ways:

1. How couples think about partner roles (i.e., conventional or nonconventional). Conventional ways of thinking about gender roles might include beliefs about who should take care of the home and the children according to gender, or that women should take their husband's last name.

2. How couples are connected (i.e., interdependent or independent). Couples vary in the extent to which each person wants to be their own person or be interdependent with their partner.

3. How couples engage in conflict (i.e., engage or avoid) and how willing they are to engage in conflict.

Each of her couple types can be described using these three factors. The three couple types are:

- **Traditional couples** subscribe to traditional gender roles, have conventional values, are interdependent, share information and intimacy, and engage in conflict when it is serious and necessary.

- **Independent couples** have nontraditional values and ways of thinking about gender roles (for example, housework might be split equally between the partners), are close companions, share openly with one another, and embrace conflict. Independent couples are psychologically close but spend time apart for some leisure activities.

- **Separate couples** avoid conflict at all costs, especially in public, and spend a lot of time apart. Although they hold traditional values and ways of thinking about gender roles, they do not have a traditionally warm and close marriage. They are not very open in their communication. These couples maintain psychological and physical space from one another.

The majority of couples are made up of people with matching types (60%), that is, both partners are the same type. This is not always the case. A common mismatched yet functional combination is the separate/traditional type. This type has medium levels of interdependence, hold conventional values, and do not avoid conflict but also do not openly embrace it.

Gottman's (1994) couple types capture three different ways couples create positive and stable relationship climates. Each type varies on how they influence one another, resolve conflict, and communicate about emotions.

- **Volatile couples** are emotionally expressive, value openness, express their emotions, and are honest with one another. Volatile couples have strong disagreements but often passionately make up afterward (hence the name volatile – they are extreme in their conflicts in both the fighting and the making up). Notably, they do not typically use contempt in their conflict episodes (for more about contempt, see the section on the Four Horsemen in Chapter 11 on conflict).

- **Validating couples** view themselves as a team. They are moderately expressive, but become more expressive during important conflicts. They attempt to solve conflicts in ways that benefit both members of the couple. These couples emphasize understanding and taking their partner's point of view.

- **Conflict-avoiding couples** minimize and avoid conflict at great costs. These couples tend to agree to disagree, yet they are empathetic and accept each other as they are. They see each other as separate people with individual interests.

Since the 1990s, Gottman (2014) has described two additional couple types he describes as "unhappy couple types":

- **Hostile couples** are similar to validating couples but their interactions are marked by defensiveness on the part of both people in the couple. Hostile couples spend a lot of their energy in conflict deflecting their responsibility for the problem and reiterating their own perspectives without showing perspective-taking or understanding for the other person's point of view.

- **Hostile-detached couples** experience standoffs in conflict with neither side willing to back down. Their fights are rife with sniping comments and emotional detachment from their issues and relationship. They may feel resigned to fail with no compromise or collaboration in sight.

Like Fitzpatrick's types above, it is possible for the two partners of a couple to have a different type. Gottman calls these couples "mismatched," indicating their unique communication styles will be difficult to manage. **In brief, there are different ways couples can engage in conflict and interaction and have a happy marriage. Gottman describes these couples as volatile, validating, or conflict-avoiding. Gottman categorizes unhappy couples as hostile or hostile-detached.**

EMOTION REGULATION IN COMMITTED RELATIONSHIPS

Emotion regulation is used to manage affect, or emotion, during conflict. Emotion regulation happens in many different types of relationships, but especially in close relationships with people we see daily. Emotion regulation is critical to achieving our interpersonal goals because without it, we would scream every time we are mad and cry whenever we feel sad. This would be a strange way to interact with others in today's society and would make achieving our goals difficult. There are three main emotion regulation strategies.

1. Disengagement – expressive suppression, avoid, shift focus.
2. Aversive cognitive preservation – rumination, exaggerated emotions, over-engagement with negative emotions/thoughts. Fixating on a problem that might stop the person from focusing instead on how to solve the problem.
3. Adaptive engagement – reappraisal, constructive and collaborative problem solving, changing the way they think about an issue, thinking about the problem in a way that helped them stay calm.

Emotional suppression is one way to regulate emotions and it has short- and long-term negative effects on marital satisfaction (Crockett, Neff, & Gleason, 2018). Actually, engaging in conflict instead of suppressing emotion has short-term negative effects but long-term positive effects. Over a longer period of time, actually engaging in conflict is good for the relationship even if it does not feel good when it is happening. Emotional suppression tends to just create more problems.

MYRIAD PREDICTORS OF MARITAL SATISFACTION

Before we can discuss the predictors of marital satisfaction, we should recognize that satisfaction means different things to different people. We can think about success in terms of stability and length of the marriage, perceived satisfaction, ability to adjust to married life and challenges that come up during the life course, and commitment to one another.

There are hundreds if not thousands of studies focused on predicting marital success and satisfaction from personality to similar interests and demographics like age, race/ethnicity, education levels, and length of marriage. As communication scientists, we are most interested in the communicative predictors of a successful marriage. Research has shown that dyadic coping is related to relationship and marital satisfaction across genders and cultures (Falconier, Randall, & Bodenmann, 2016). Other communication factors that predict marital success include high levels of intimacy, support of one another, self-disclosure, and the use of relational maintenance strategies as described above.

According to John Gottman, there is a "magic ratio" couples should try to meet. **The magic ratio for happy relationships consists of five positive interactions to every one negative interaction.** This establishes a culture of positivity in the relationship while allowing for some negative relational behaviors. Gottman's principles of making marriage work include taking time to nurture fondness and admiration for each other, turn toward each other instead of away when times get hard, let your partner influence you, and establish shared meaning and a shared culture in the relationship by having inside jokes, rituals you share, and places that are meaningful to you. Gottman suggests several other principles (see recommended readings and Chapter 19).

DARK SIDE OF PARTNER COMMUNICATION

On the flip side of marital success and satisfaction lies the dark side of partner communication including jealousy, deception, infidelity, and sexual coercion.

Jealousy is a reaction (thoughts, feelings, behaviors) to a perceived threat to a person's romantic relationship by a real or imagined rival. Some jealousy can be a good sign, that a relationship is meaningful and that a jealous partner would be hurt if it ended, but jealousy can quickly be taken too far and create major problems in relationships like dissatisfaction, conflict, uncertainty, and possessiveness. Jealous communication, that is, talking about the jealousy a person experiences with their partner, can strengthen or harm a relationship depending on how they communicate. According to Jennifer Bevan (2013), there are four types of communication responses to jealousy: constructive, destructive, avoidant, and rival-focused.

- **Destructive** jealousy communication like yelling, arguing, threatening, or even engaging in violence tends to make the partner feel bad and is designed to control the partner.

- **Constructive** jealousy communication attempts to maintain the relationship through disclosure and open discussion about the feelings of jealousy.

- **Avoidant** jealousy communication includes the silent treatment or denial.

- **Rival-focused** jealousy communication might include surveillance, putting down the rival, or confronting the rival.

Deception, or intentional manipulation of information or misrepresentation of information, is discussed further in Chapter 16 but can be especially harmful to long-term committed romantic relationships where trust is paramount. Partners often learn about deception indirectly. Deception is a form of relationship devaluation. Relationship devaluation is especially hurtful because one partner often realizes the other does not love or respect them as much as they thought.

Cheating on one's partner can take the form of either **emotional** or **physical infidelity**. Cheating, like deception, is a form of betrayal and is especially hurtful because it devalues the relationship. Sexual infidelity is engaging in sexual activity with someone other than a person's committed partner. The appropriateness of sexual infidelity and the consequences of it on a relationship vary greatly from culture to culture. The United States has a relatively low tolerance for cheating. Emotional infidelity occurs when strong romantic and emotional bonds or attachments are formed with a someone other than a partner's committed partner. **Take a moment and think about which you would find more hurtful**. Would you leave your partner if they cheated sexually? Emotionally? Over half of men and women (60%) say they would leave if a partner cheated on them sexually.

Sexual coercion is a type of persuasive communication that uses strategies such as guilt tripping, manipulation, or using verbal threats to get a partner to have sex (Spitzberg & Rhea, 1999). More extreme forms of sexual coercion include sexual violence and assault. Sexual coercion tends to occur when there is a discrepancy in the amount of desire each partner has for sex. Half of all couples report sexual coercion happens in their relationship. Sexual coercion leads to depression, post-traumatic stress disorder (PTSD), and decreased relationship quality.

INTERESTING RESEARCH FINDINGS

Romantic Jealousy Interactions: Face-to-Face and Over Technology

Jennifer Bevan (2013) set out to understand how jealousy messages in face-to-face communication differed from jealousy messages in technologically mediated communication, especially in how they made people feel and how they impacted relationship satisfaction and investment in the relationship. She asked over 600 people about the last time they expressed jealousy to their romantic partner. Specifically, she asked how they communicated the fact that they were jealous (e.g., face-to-face or over technology). Participants could also indicate that they started the conversation over text but it moved to face-to-face or vice versa. She found that most people use more than one mode of communication to express jealousy, and that face-to-face was the most frequently used mode followed by text message. Finally, she found that the way jealousy was communicated was related to relationship satisfaction and investment. For example, people who communicated their jealousy exclusively face-to-face were the most invested in their relationships.

Relationship Maintenance Intervention

Tamara Afifi along with her team (2018) conducted a study with couples who had a child with type I diabetes. She asked the couples about their relational maintenance over the past month. Next, she asked half of the couples to participate in a two-week intervention. The intervention involved spending 15 minutes of quality alone time with one another, hugging each other every day, talking to each other about what they like that the other person did for them to show love and appreciation, and telling their partner what they wish they did more of. The research team found that having a communal orientation, or thinking of the partnership as a team, predicted doing more relationship maintenance during this time period. Wives who were in the intervention group reported higher levels of thriving than wives in a control group who did not do the intervention activities. The wives in the intervention felt more connected to their partners and felt their husbands were more invested in helping them manage their child's diabetes. Finally, she found that husbands and wives felt less lonely over time if they were in the intervention. Afifi's work is a great example of how asking people to change their communication with their partner can have positive effects on their relationship.

PRACTICAL APPLICATIONS AND THINGS TO CONSIDER

Above, we discussed the importance of maintaining your long-term committed relationships through positivity, understanding, openness, relational talk, assurances, sharing tasks, and network strategies. If you currently have a partner, what relationship maintenance strategies do you use to invest in your relationship and maintain a positive status for your relationship? The theory of resilience and relational load (TRRL; Afifi, Merrill, & Davis, 2016) says couples need to invest in their relationship *before* stress happens. Couples can invest in their relationship by engaging in relational maintenance behaviors (e.g., verbal, nonverbal, and actions such as making coffee for your partner because you know they like it). This investment will predict how the couple adapts to stress, their individual health, and whether the stressor depletes them. If they do not do this, they might experience relationship burnout (Afifi calls this relational load). Do you ever think of the maintenance strategies you use now as an investment in the future of the relationship? If not, what would you do differently, keeping in mind that the maintenance you do now will continue to serve your relationship in the future, especially in hard times?

DISCUSSION QUESTIONS

1. If you noticed some "dark side" partner communication creeping into your relationship such as deception or jealousy, how would you feel?
    a. If you were to confront your partner, what would you say?
    b. At what point would you end the relationship? Where do you draw the line?

2. What is your personal definition of a successful marriage? What is most important to you?

KEY TERMS

Asymmetrically committed couples

Conflict-avoiding couples

Deception

Dyadic coping

Equity

Expectancy violations theory

Independent couples

Infidelity

Investment model

Jealousy

Magic ratio

Marital satisfaction

Marital tension

Micro stress

Separate couples

Sexual coercion

Traditional couples

Validating couples

Volatile couples

REFERENCES

Afifi, T., Granger, D., Ersig, A., Tsalikian, E., Shahnazi, A., Davis, S., … Scranton, A. (2018). Testing the theory of resilience and relational load (TRRL) in families with type I diabetes. *Health Communication*. doi:10.1080/10410236.2018.1461585

Afifi, T. D., Merrill, A. F., & Davis, S. (2016). The theory of resilience and relational load. *Personal Relationships, 23*, 663–683. doi:10.1111/pere.12159

Bevan, J. L. (2013). *The communication of jealousy*. New York, NY: Peter Lang.

Canary, D. J., & Stafford, L. (1992). Relational maintenance strategies and equity in marriage. *Communications Monographs, 59*, 243–267. doi:10.1080/03637759209376268

Crockett, E. E., Neff, L. A., & Gleason, M. E. (2018). *Holding your tongue is costly: The ironic consequences of using emotional suppression to avoid marital conflict.* Paper presented at the annual meeting of the International Association of Relationship Researchers, Fort Collins, CO.

Dainton, M., & Gross, J. (2008). The use of negative behaviors to maintain relationships. *Communication Research Reports, 25*, 179–191. doi:10.1080/08824090802237600

Falconier, M. K., Randall, A. K., & Bodenmann, G. (2016). *Couples coping with stress: A cross-cultural perspective*. New York, NY: Routledge.

Fitzpatrick, M. A. (1988). *Between husbands and wives:Communication in marriage*. Newbury, CA: Sage.

Gottman, J. M. (1994). *What predicts divorce? The relationship between marital processes and marital outcomes*. Hillsdale, NJ: Lawrence Erlbaum Associates.

Gottman, J. (2014, November 22). *The 5 types of couples*. Retrieved from https://www.gottman.com/blog/the-5-couple-types/

Haas, S. M., & Stafford, L. (2005). Maintenance behaviors in same-sex and marital relationships: A matched sample comparison. *Journal of Family Communication, 5*, 43–60. doi:10.1207/s15327698jfc0501_3

Rusbult, C. E., Drigotas, S. M., & Verette, J. (1994). The investment model: An interdependence analysis of commitment processes and relationship maintenance phenomena. In D. J. Canary & L. Stafford (Eds.), *Communication and relational maintenance* (pp. 115–139). San Diego, CA: Academic Press.

Spitzberg, B. H., & Rhea, J. (1999). Obsessive relational intrusion and sexual coercion victimization. *Journal of Interpersonal Violence, 14*, 3–20. doi:10.1177/088626099014001001

Stafford, L. (2011). Measuring relationship maintenance behaviors: Critique and development of the revised relationship maintenance behavior scale. *Journal of Social and Personal Relationships, 28*, 278–303. doi:10.1177/0265407510378125

Stafford, L., & Canary, D. J. (1991). Maintenance strategies and romantic relation-ship type, gender and relational characteristics. *Journal of Social and Personal Relationships, 8*, 217–242. doi:10.1177/026540759108204

Stanley, S. M., Rhoades, G. K., Scott, S. B., Kelmer, G., Markman, H. J., & Fincham, F. D. (2017). Asymmetrically committed relationships. *Journal of Social and Personal Relationships, 34*, 1241–1259. doi:10.1177/0265407516672013

RELATED READINGS

Bevan, J. L. (2008). Experiencing and communicating romantic jealousy: Questioning the investment model. *Southern Communication Journal, 73*, 42–67. doi:10.1080/10417940701815626

Butler, E. A., Lee, T. L., & Gross, J. J. (2007). Emotion regulation and culture: Are the social consequences of emotion suppression culture-specific? *Emotion, 7*, 30–48. doi:10.1037/1528-3542.7.1.30

Gottman, J. M., & Silver, N. (2015). *The seven principles for making marriage work*. Easton, PA: Harmony.

Gottman, J., Gottman, J. M., & Silver, N. (1995). *Why marriages succeed or fail: And how you can make yours last*. New York, NY: Simon & Schuster.

Hendrick, S. S. (1981). Self-disclosure and marital satisfaction. *Journal of Personality and Social Psychology, 40*, 1150–1159. doi:10.1037/0022-3514.40.6.1150

Patrick, S., Sells, J. N., Giordano, F. G., & Tollerud, T. R. (2007). Intimacy, differentiation, and personality variables as predictors of marital satisfaction. *The Family Journal, 15*, 359–367. doi:10.1177/1066480707303754

Chapter 29
Sibling Relationships

BACKGROUND

Siblings are unique among family relationships because people tend to know their siblings their entire lives. Unlike parents who likely pass away before the end-of-life and unlike partners who tend to come into one's life in adulthood, siblings are around from "cradle to grave." Siblings often share the same upbringing and have jokes and stories shared between them that no one else understands. Sibling relationships are more egalitarian (i.e., equal in power) than other family relationships, though siblings can also be a source of conflict and rivalry. Siblings are important sources of advice, support, and companionship throughout life. In fact, a study by Lynn White and Agnes Riedman (1992) reported that two-thirds of adults consider one of their siblings their closest friend. According to White, siblings are permanent but flexible members of social networks, meaning their role in each other's lives is renegotiated throughout the lifespan based on changing circumstances and obligations to others.

The amount of contact and communication between siblings varies over time. Siblings tend to communicate frequently in childhood, less in early and middle adulthood, and then a resurgence of communication can occur in late adulthood. Communication tends to decrease in early and middle adulthood because many people start a new "family or orientation" by getting married and having children. Siblings remain important during this time, but are relied on less for everyday communication and support. Moving away and starting demanding careers are other reasons for less contact. According to Paula Avioli (1989), the **principle**

Communication in Family Contexts: Theories and Processes, First Edition.
Elizabeth Dorrance Hall and Kristina M. Scharp.
© 2020 John Wiley & Sons, Inc. Published 2020 by John Wiley & Sons, Inc.
Companion website: www.wiley.com/go/dorrance_hall/communication-in-family-contexts

of substitution states that adult siblings are more likely to support each other when other key sources of support such as children and a partner/spouse are not available. In late life, siblings provide each other with companionship. They reminisce over memories that only they share and long-standing rivalries tend to fade away. Despite the change in communication over the lifespan, commitment (i.e., psychological attachment) in sibling relationships tends to remain high and steady.

TYPES OF SIBLINGS

There are several ways siblings can be categorized. The first set of types of siblings vary based on biological, legal, or commitment-based ties to one another.

- **Adoptive** siblings are legally bound.
- **Fictive** siblings are those who perform the role of a sibling but are not blood or legally related. Fictive siblings are siblings you choose.
- **Full** siblings share the same parents and have 33–66% of their genes in common.
- **Half** siblings share only one biological parent.
- **Step** siblings are linked by the marriage of one parent to one of the step-siblings' parents.

Siblings can also be categorized into types based on how close they are in age and by developmental competency.

- **Reciprocal** siblings are close in age and therefore in similar stages of development. This is especially true in childhood but can also apply in adulthood as siblings close in age tend to get married and have children around the same time. Reciprocal siblings tend to interact like peers and engage in more sibling rivalry.
- **Complementary** siblings are further apart in age, typically four or more years apart. Because of this larger age difference, they tend to be in different developmental stages. In complementary sibling relationships the older sibling often takes on the role of leader, teacher, and caregiver of the younger sibling. These sibling relationships tend to have a hierarchy that can continue into adulthood, though, as mentioned above, most sibling relationships become more egalitarian over time.

Finally, Deborah Gold's (1989) typology of sibling relationships is based on instrumental and emotional support, contact, closeness, envy, resentment, approval, and involvement between siblings.

- **Intimate** siblings are devoted to one another and share psychological closeness that goes beyond a sense of obligation to family. These siblings often confide secrets and share their feelings. They support one another and their relationship is based on love, concern, empathy, understanding, and protection. Intimate siblings communicate frequently in person (though they do not necessarily need to live near one another) and via technology.

- **Congenial** siblings are good friends but are not as close as intimate siblings. Congenial siblings communicate consistently, on a weekly or monthly basis. Congenial siblings happily support one another, but often this support must be asked for. Congenial siblings approve of one another but occasionally express disapproval.

- **Loyal** siblings have bonds based on family identity and obligation rather than personal interests. Closeness in these sibling pairs might be idealized or romanticized rather than the real, deep closeness experienced in intimate sibling relationships. Loyal siblings support one another, but less than intimate or congenial siblings. Loyal siblings might disapprove of each other's partners or life choices, they might also experience envy and resentment, but their bond exists anyway. They feel they are linked for life through their family bond.

- **Apathetic** siblings are indifferent to one another. They do not feel obligated to stay in contact or take responsibility for helping each other out. They might have never felt close, even when living in the same household. Communication is very minimal in this type of sibling relationship.

- **Hostile** sibling relationships are marked by anger, resentment, rejection, and even hatred. Siblings in this type of relationship disapprove of each other's choices and think that nothing could bring them back together. Communication is rare to nonexistent. These siblings do not support one another and indicate they would not provide support if it was requested.

SIBLING RELATIONSHIP MAINTENANCE

Like all relationships, sibling relationships require maintenance to stay in a "good" place. The relationship maintenance framework identifies five main types of maintenance people do to keep their relationships in a good place.

1. Positivity refers to being optimistic, cheerful, funny, happy, or just pleasant. People tend to enjoy being around others who are positive, which helps to maintain the relationship.

2. Openness refers to sharing what is going on in your life, including being open to discussing your relationship. Openness can be especially important in sibling relationships since siblings have likely known each other longer than anyone else in their lives.

3. Assurances refers to telling a sibling that they mean a lot and that they are cared for. This kind of communication is often unspoken, especially in family relationships.

4. Social networks refers to having overlapping circles of friends and family. Overlap in social circles tends to allow for more time spent together.

5. Sharing tasks refers to equally contributing to the relationship and the work you do together like planning family get-togethers or coordinating visits.

According to Mikkelson, Myers, and Hannawa (2011), siblings use task, positivity, and assurances the most. Myers (2011) has also done research to discover why people choose to maintain their sibling relationships. The top reasons include "because we are family," "we provide each other with support," and "we share similar/common interests and experiences."

INTERESTING RESEARCH FINDINGS

Motives for Sibling Communication (Fowler, 2009)

The interpersonal communication motives model (see related readings for more on this model) explains that people are motivated by different reasons to communicate with others. Craig Fowler set out to customize these motives to the sibling relationship, for example, taking into account the obligation many people feel to communicate with their sibling. In his study, Fowler discovered what motivates siblings to communicate with one another. The five sibling communication motives are explained in Table 29.1 and are ordered from most to least frequently reported motives for communicating with a sibling.

Fowler also found that sister–sister sibling pairs are more motivated than any other combination (sister–brother, brother–brother) to communicate for comfort and intimacy.

Sibling Affectionate Communication (Myers, 2015)

Scott Myers compared the four types of siblings outlined by Gold on how frequently they used affectionate communication. You can read more about affectionate communication in Chapter 3. He also compared how important and appropriate each type thought affectionate communication was for their sibling relationship. Myers found that people who have **intimate** type relationships with their siblings engage in more affectionate communication with their sibling and consider using affection communication with their

Table 29.1 Sibling Communication Motives

Motive (Communicating for...)	Definition	Rank
Intimacy	Show concern and appreciation, enjoyment	1
Comfort	Excitement, fun, reassurance, reduce loneliness and distress	2
Mutuality	Habit, routine, achieve mutual goals	3
Obligation	Family norms dictate talk	4
Control/Escape	Get others to agree or comply, tell them what to do, avoid other activities	5

siblings more important and appropriate than those who have sibling relationships that are classified as congenial, loyal, or apathetic/hostile. **In brief, siblings who have a relationship marked by devotion and psychological closeness exchange more affection through communication than other types of sibling relationships.**

PRACTICAL APPLICATIONS AND THINGS TO CONSIDER

The **resource dilution hypothesis** applies in large families. The more siblings who are added to the family, the fewer parenting resources there are for each child. The up side of being from a large family is that siblings have more options for family members to go to for support or friendship. "Mega families," by necessity, tend to use a managerial style of parenting. How did your parents or parent-figures distribute their time and energy to members of your family?

One of your textbook authors, Dorrance Hall, along with her colleague, Jenna McNallie, compared reports of how much maintenance people wanted from their sibling to how much maintenance they thought their sibling was actually doing (Dorrance Hall & McNallie, 2016). They found that across the board siblings tend to want more maintenance than they are currently getting. They also found that perceptions of how much maintenance a sibling is doing is linked to reports of relationship satisfaction. In other words, the more people do to maintain their sibling relationships, the better those relationships. If applicable, how do you maintain your relationship(s) with your brother(s) and/or sister(s)? Consider doing more to maintain your sibling relationship. You can gain ideas about how to do so by reviewing the list of maintenance strategies above.

KEY TERMS

Adoptive siblings	Full siblings	Reciprocal siblings
Assurances	Half siblings	Resource dilution
Complementary siblings	Networks	hypothesis
Egalitarian	Openness	Step siblings
Fictive siblings	Positivity	Tasks

DISCUSSION QUESTIONS

1. Are you from a large family? If yes, do you find that parenting resources were limited growing up? Do the resources added by having extra siblings to go to for help and advice make up for it?
2. If you are from a small family, what do you think you would gain by having more siblings? What would you lose?
3. How does your communication differ with different siblings? Are there things you talk about with your sibling that you would not share with your parents?

IN- OR OUT-OF-CLASS ACTIVITY: SIBLING TURNING POINTS

Complete a turning point analysis of a family relationship (sibling, or parent if you are an only child).

- Identify at least 5 "turning points" that changed the degree of psychological closeness in your relationship on the graph below. A turning point is "any event or occurrence that is associated with change in a relationship." For example, moving away to college might have increased or decreased the closeness you feel with your family member.
  - Notice that psychological closeness ranges from 1 (no closeness) to 5 (strong degree of closeness) on the y axis. On the x axis you will find time, which ranges from age 5 (child) to present (adult).
- Put a dot on the graph for each turning point based on how close you felt and when the change/event happened. Then, connect the dots to create your relationship trajectory.
- Write down what the turning points represent in a few sentences. What happened? Did they have anything to do with communication?
- Bonus: call your siblinga and ask them about what events they think had a big impact on how close the two of you are (or are not). You can tell them about your points if it is appropriate and compare to see how your relationship differs depending on whose point of view is represented.

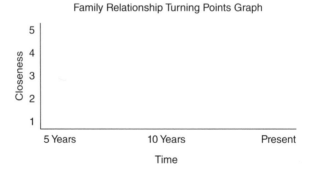

Family Relationship Turning Points Graph

Sisters are Best Friends, Until the Parents Interfere
CASE STUDY BY KAITLIN E. PHILLIPS

Lindi was counting down the days until her 18th birthday. Her parents had promised her a new car for her birthday and she couldn't wait to drive it off to college. Her older sister Cara was coming home from college for her birthday and she was looking forward to spending some time with her. Now that Cara has moved away to college, Lindi doesn't get to talk with her as often, and she feels like that might be because her sister doesn't have time for her anymore. She's hoping this weekend will give them a chance to reconnect.

Cara is excited to be going home for the weekend. Her summer class has been grueling and she's ready to spend the weekend with her family. She's been planning a surprise outing to Lindi's favorite restaurant for her birthday, and she can't wait to celebrate her birthday with her. College has occupied more of her time than she expected, and she feels like she hasn't had much time to keep in touch with Lindi.

Cara pulls in the driveway and Lindi runs out to meet her and throws her arms around her in a hug. "You're home! I've missed you so much! We have lots to catch up on."

Cara gives Lindi a hug, "I love you too, sis. Ready for your big birthday weekend?"

"Of course! We were just waiting for you to get home so we could eat birthday cake, and Dad just texted me to say that my birthday gift is almost here!"

"Here? Did Amazon get delayed or something?"

"Oh! We haven't talked in ages, I forgot to tell you, they got me a car!"

Cara takes a step back and looks at Lindi. She didn't get a car for her 18th birthday, in fact she didn't get a car until she turned 20 once she had finally saved enough to buy a used one. "Did you have to help pay for it?" she asks.

"Nope! It's the best birthday gift ever! I can't wait to see it!"

All of a sudden, Cara's Dad pulls up in a brand new red Mustang. "Happy birthday, Lindi!" her Dad shouts from the driveway. Lindi runs over to check out her new car, and doesn't realize that instead of coming with her, Cara heads inside.

CASE STUDY DISCUSSION QUESTIONS

1. Using Gold's typology, which type of sibling relationship best represents Lindi and Cara's relationship? Why?
2. Sibling relationships first develop within the context of their family and do not exist in isolation. How are Lindi and Cara's parents influential in their communication with each other? Do you think their parents intended to interfere in Lindi and Cara's relationship? Why or why not?
3. What is the initial motivation behind Lindi and Cara's communication over Lindi's birthday weekend? Is this motive consistent with Fowler's research?
4. What relational maintenance behaviors do Lindi and Cara use? Are these strategic or routine relational maintenance behaviors?

REFERENCES

Avioli, P. S. (1989). The social support functions of siblings in later life: A theoretical model. *American Behavioral Scientist, 33*, 45–57.

Dorrance Hall, E., & McNallie, J. (2016). The mediating role of sibling maintenance behavior expectations and perceptions in the relationship between family communication patterns and relationship satisfaction. *Journal of Family Communication, 16*, 386–402. doi:10.1080/15267431.2016.1215316

Fowler, C. (2009). Motives for sibling communication across the lifespan. *Communication Quarterly, 57*, 51–66. doi:10.1080/01463370802662499

Gold, D. T. (1989). Sibling relationships in old age: A typology. *International Journal of Aging and Human Development, 28*, 37–51. doi:10.2190/VGYX-BRHN-J51V-0V39

Mikkelson, A. C., Myers, S. A., & Hannawa, A. F. (2011). The differential use of relational maintenance behaviors in adult sibling relationships. *Communication Studies, 62*, 258–271. doi:10.1080/10510974.2011.555490

Myers, S. A. (2011). "I have to love her, even if sometimes I may not like her": The reasons why adults maintain their sibling relationships. *North American Journal of Psychology, 13*, 51–62.

Myers, S. A. (2015). Using Gold's typology of adult sibling relationships to explore sibling affectionate communication. *North American Journal of Psychology, 17*, 301–310.

White, L. K., & Riedman, A. (1992). When the Brady bunch grows up: Step/half- and full sibling relationships in adulthood. *Journal of Marriage & the Family, 54*, 197–208. doi:10.2307/353287

RELATED READINGS

Lamb, M. E. (2014). Sibling relationships across the lifespan: An overview and introduction. In M. E. Lamb & B. Sutton-Smith (Eds.), *Sibling relationships: Their nature and significance across the lifespan* (pp. 1–11). New York, NY: Psychology Press.

Mikkelson, A. C. (2014). Adult sibling relationships. In K. Floyd & M. T. Morman (Eds.), *Widening the family circle: New research on family communication* (pp. 19–34). Los Angeles, CA: Sage.

Myers, S. A., Byrnes, K. A., Frisby, B. N., & Mansson, D. H. (2011). Adult siblings' use of affectionate communication as a strategic and routine relational maintenance behavior. *Communication Research Reports, 28*, 151–158. doi:10.1080/08824096.2011.565276

Myers, S. A., & Goodboy, A. K. (2013). Using equity theory to explore adult siblings' use of relational maintenance behaviors and relational characteristics. *Communication Research Reports, 30*, 275–281. doi:10.1080/08824096.2013.836627

Phillips, K. E., & Schrodt, P. (2015). Sibling confirmation as a moderator of rivalries and relational outcomes in sibling relationships. *Journal of Family Communication, 15*, 58–74. doi:10.1080/15267431.2014.980825

Rubin, R. B., Perse, E. M., & Barbato, C. A. (1988). Conceptualization and measurement of interpersonal communication motives. *Human Communication Research, 14*, 602–628. doi:10.1111/j.1468-2958.1988.tb00169.x

Chapter 30
Voluntary Kin Families

As you read about in the first chapter of this book, families can be defined in a variety of ways that emphasize structure, task, or transaction. The idea of voluntary kin is rooted in a transactional definition of family where language and affection constitute a family bond. Specifically, **voluntary kin** are people who are perceived to be family, yet do not share blood or legal ties (Braithwaite et al., 2010). Voluntary kin families, just like many of the families you have read about, are inherently discourse dependent (see Chapter 14). In this chapter, we discuss the different types of voluntary kin families and why people might seek to choose their family in addition to, or instead of, counting only structural family ties.

BACKGROUND

Even though "family-like" relationships have existed throughout the ages, it has only been about 50 years since researchers have begun to study voluntary kin relationships (see Nelson, 2013). Sometimes referred to as **fictive kin**, Dawn Braithwaite and her colleagues (2010) argue that the label fictive is problematic. They argue that the word fictive suggests a deficit and contributes to stigma and beliefs that voluntary kin are not "real" relationships. As they so aptly conclude the term, "*Voluntary kin* [emphasis in the original] implies a mutuality of selection, rather than framing these relationships as asymmetrical structures of chooser and chosen" (p. 390). Nonetheless, you might hear people reference terms like ritual kin, kinkeepers, chosen-kin, self-ascribed kin, othermothers, or even urban tribes (see Nelson, 2013).

Communication in Family Contexts: Theories and Processes, First Edition.
Elizabeth Dorrance Hall and Kristina M. Scharp.
© 2020 John Wiley & Sons, Inc. Published 2020 by John Wiley & Sons, Inc.
Companion website: www.wiley.com/go/dorrance_hall/communication-in-family-contexts

KEY CONCEPTS

Despite different labels and definitions, there are two essential components that contribute to the meaning of voluntary kin: positive importance and choice. Research suggests that when people discuss their voluntary kin they are consistently speaking about people who are especially important compared to others. These people are not only important but also engage in positive communicative behaviors such as providing social support, affection, intimacy, love, and tangible resources. These relationships are typically also marked by trust, shared responsibility, and closeness (see Nelson, 2013). Nonetheless, it is important to remember that voluntary kin relationships can also be complex. Indeed, voluntary kin still engage in conflict, experience disappointment, and carry obligation.

Within the field of Communication Studies, research on voluntary kin is relatively sparse. In answer, Braithwaite and her team (2010) developed a typology of voluntary kin based on 110 interviews with voluntary kin members: (1) voluntary kin as substitute family, (2) voluntary kin as supplemental family, (3) voluntary kin as convenience family, and (4) voluntary kin as extended family (Figure 30.1). Three of these types emerged as a result of deficits in blood and legal ties whereas one type was constructed as an integration of blood and legal ties.

INTERESTING RESEARCH FINDINGS

To follow up on their original typology study, Braithwaite and a new set of colleagues (2016) sought to explore the communication structures that characterize the relationships between supplementary voluntary kin and biological/legal families. They spoke with 36 people who identified as having supplemental voluntary kin. Specifically, they found four different communication structures: (1) intertwined, (2) limited, (3) separate, and (4) hostile. **Intertwined** types discussed members being very much a part of each other's lives. In this regard, there was a complete triad of family members, tied by shared family rituals. **Limited** types discussed the voluntary kin and biological/legal family members as casual acquaintances. Thus, these people were tied but less tightly than those who were intertwined. **Separate** types were those where the primary linchpin family member maintained a separate relationship with their voluntary kin and their biological/legal family. Visually, this type might be thought of as two lines coming to a point but those lines do not connect at the base. Finally, **hostile** types were characterized by dislike, competitiveness, jealousy, and discomfort between at least one voluntary kin member and a member of the biological/legal family.

PRACTICAL APPLICATIONS AND THINGS TO CONSIDER

Different labels for voluntary kin are often tied to different marginalized groups such as African American/Black populations and members of the LGBTQ community (see Johnson, 2000; Nelson, 2014). Nelson (2014) argues that this

Substitute Family	Supplemental Family
• When people seek to replace their biological and legal family altogether, they might construct a substitute family. • The need for a substitute family typically results from either death or estrangement.	• Supplemental families were most common. • These voluntary kin play one of four roles: • (1) fulfill needs unmet by blood and legal ties, (2) meet an unmet need, (3) meet an underperformed role, (4) enact a family role for a bio/legal family member who was geographically distant • Can fill a deficit created by blood or legal relations. • Voluntary and bio/legal families often know about one another but remain largely separate.
Convenience Family	**Extended Family**
• Voluntary kin who resulted from convenience typically discussed a specific context (e.g., workplace), stage of life (e.g., undergraduate college years) or time period (e.g., support group for a 12-step program) that brought the members together. • Convenience family relationships are often time-bound but might turn into a different voluntary kin type when the members are forced to transcend the time and/or context.	• Unlike the first three types that were based on a deficit model, the extended family type integrated blood/legal and voluntary kin families. • Extended family units have both permeable and overlapping boundaries that created strong ties and sense of community. • Often transcend both time and distance.

Figure 30.1 Typology of voluntary kin.

is problematic. Based on a review of 500 articles that reference fictive kin, she found that when discussing African American communities, people emphasize the "fiction" of **fictive kin** without acknowledging real obligation. In comparison, people who write about the LGBTQ community often emphasize "choice" when they talk about **chosen families**. She contends that even the use of voluntary kin to address White populations draws distinctions about race. Ultimately, Nelson's research reinforces the importance of language and how using certain words carries both content and relational meanings. These labels often do meaningful work in reinforcing or resisting problematic ideologies such as racism, homophobia, and others depending on which label is spoken and reproduced.

KEY TERMS

Chosen families
Convenience family
Extended family

Fictive kin
Substitute family

Supplemental family
Voluntary kin

IN-CLASS DISCUSSION

Journal on your own and then share with a neighbor or the class your answers to the following questions.

1. What does it mean to be "*like* a family member?"
2. What would a person need to do to become a part of your family?
3. What is the difference between friends and your voluntary kin?
4. Is there anything at stake if we say our voluntary kin are only "like" our other family members? If this phrasing is potentially problematic, what should we say instead?

REFERENCES

Braithwaite, D. O., Bach, B. W., Baxter, L. A., DiVerniero, R., Hammonds, J. R., Hosek, A. M., … Wolf, B. M. (2010). Constructing family: A typology of voluntary kin. *Journal of Social & Personal Relationships, 27*, 388–407. doi:10.1177/0265407510361615

Braithwaite, D. O., Stephenson Abetz, J., Moore, J., & Brockhage, K. (2016). Communication structures of supplemental voluntary kin relationships. *Family Relations, 65*, 616–630. doi:10.1111/fare.12215

Johnson, C. L. (2000). Perspective on American kinship in the late 1990s. *Journal of Marriage and Family, 62*, 623–639. doi:10.1177/0265407510361615

Nelson, M. K. (2013). Fictive kin, families we choose, and voluntary kin: What does the discourse tell us? *Journal of Family Theory and Review, 5*, 259–281. doi:10.111/jftr.12019

Nelson, M. K. (2014). Whither fictive kin? Or, what's in a name? *Journal of Family Issues, 35*, 201–222. doi:10.1177/0192513X12470621

RELATED READINGS

Brooks, J. E., & Allen, K. R. (2014). The influence of fictive kin relationships and religiosity on the academic persistence of African American college students attending an HBCU. *Family Issues, 37*, 814–832. doi:10.1177/0192513X14540160

Muraco, A. (2006). Intentional families: Fictive kin ties between cross-gender, different sexual orientation friend. *Journal of Marriage and Family, 68*, 1313–1325. doi:10.1111/j.1741-3737.2006.00330.x

Family Communication in Context

Chapter 31

Family Communication in Health Contexts

Family health problems, including psychological and physical, are prevalent in the United States and deeply affect all members of the family system. This is concerning, considering approximately 48% of the population might have a diagnosable mental health condition at some point in their life (Regier et al., 1993). Research suggests that relationships also profoundly influence our physical health. Indeed, married couples tend to be more physically healthy than their single or widowed peers (Liu, 2009). In addition to the ways communication might influence health, families must also communicate about health issues. Because there are many journals and researchers devoted to the study of health communication or communication in health contexts, we focused only on general information and a selection of research that pertains to family communication and health. If this chapter piques your interest, we encourage you to take a course on health communication in interpersonal contexts to get a more in-depth picture.

KEY CONCEPTS

Mental Health

Almost 20% of adults in the United States experience mental health issues every year. In addition to being distressing on their own, these mental health issues

Communication in Family Contexts: Theories and Processes, First Edition.
Elizabeth Dorrance Hall and Kristina M. Scharp.
© 2020 John Wiley & Sons, Inc. Published 2020 by John Wiley & Sons, Inc.
Companion website: www.wiley.com/go/dorrance_hall/communication-in-family-contexts

are often stigmatized. People experience mental health stigma at a public and personal level. People who face public stigma must contend with stereotypes, prejudices, and discriminatory behaviors enacted or believed to be enacted by the public. When they internalize that public stigma, people then have to cope with personal stigma (Brohan, Slade, Clement, & Thornicroft, 2010). Feeling stigmatized can make mental health issues worse and serve as a barrier to getting help. Thus, people with a stigmatized problem often suffer on multiple levels.

Families play an important role in a person's experience of mental illness and the stigma they face. Sometimes this might mean providing support, helping younger children/siblings understand, or even creating conditions that make the mental illness worse (see Segrin, 2013). A study by Flood-Grady and Koenig Kellas (2018) revealed that young adults often hear stories of *caution* and *struggle* from family members about their mental illness. Stories of caution include warnings about the negative outcomes associated with mental illness whereas stories of struggle were simply about the difficulties their parents experienced and how hard it was to cope. Despite hearing these mostly negative stories, adult children said those stories were useful in creating awareness and understanding the importance of mental illness. Thus, their findings suggest that positive lessons about mental health might emerge from discussing the hard realities with other family members.

We now discuss three specific mental illnesses that family communication researchers have examined in their studies. It is important to note that family communication might play an important role in a variety of additional mental illness conditions we do not discuss here such as anxiety, bipolar disorder, borderline personality disorder, loneliness, narcissistic personality disorder, obsessive-compulsive disorder, and schizophrenia.

Depression

Major depressive disorder is a common mental illness that gets diagnosed after two weeks of persistent symptoms such as depressed mood, weight loss/gain, disturbed sleep, loss of interest, difficulty concentrating, suicidal ideation, thoughts of death, and/or feelings of worthlessness (American Psychiatric Association, 2013; APA). Although everyone could experience depression, some depression is particularly related to the family.

Prenatal and post-partum depression: In the United States, approximately 10–20% of women experience prenatal depression during their pregnancy (PD; Fellenzer & Cibula, 2014), and 10–20% of new mothers experience post-partum depression (PPD; O'Hara & McCabe, 2013). Although the causes are unknown, both PD and PPD are related to adverse outcomes for both the mother and her children. In addition to experiencing depression and the stigma associated with mental illness, women who have PD and PPD also must face the cultural narrative that they are not living up to the standard of being a "good mother." To understand the unique pressures associated with this mental illness, one of your textbook authors (Kristina Scharp) and Lindsey Thomas (2017) used relational dialectics theory (see Chapter 9) to explore the meaning of motherhood for women with PD or PPD. Based on online stories written by women with PD and PPD, they found that the meaning of motherhood emerged from the competition of two opposing ideologies: (1) the discourse of (self-)sacrificing blissful moms and (2) the discourse of mothers as whole people. They found that even though mothers with PD and PPD acknowledged expectations about motherhood, they also provided accounts that expanded what a mother could feel and do. They emphasized in their narratives that women were important individuals who could experience a range of emotions instead of constant joy. Women also discussed how love for a child did not have to be immediate, but rather could grow. Expanding this meaning might help decrease the stigma surrounding PD and PPD, which might help reduce suicide rates among mothers.

Eating Disorders

Eating disorders, largely classified into anorexia nervosa, bulimia nervosa, and binge eating disorder, affect millions of people as well as their families. This is problematic for many reasons, especially since those numbers are on the rise (APA, 2013). Of those diagnosed with eating disorders, approximately 90% are women. Of mental illnesses, eating disorders have the highest mortality rate. People with eating disorders generally come from families low in cohesion but are still deeply affected by communication from parents. Critical comments from mothers influence how dissatisfied young women are with their bodies. Indeed, criticism can lead to obsession, stress, and eating disorders (Wade, Gillespie, & Martin, 2007). When fathers encourage open communication and approach conflict in a collaborative or compromising way, their daughters are less likely to exhibit eating disorder symptoms (Botta & Dumlao, 2002). In sum, family communication plays an important role in body dissatisfaction and disordered eating.

Substance Use Disorders

The APA (2013) divides substance abuse disorders into two categories: substance dependence and substance abuse. Substance dependence refers to a problematic pattern of use associated with symptoms such as substance tolerance, withdrawal, and taking more of a substance than intended. Substance abuse is a problematic pattern of use associated with negative effects such as continued use despite interpersonal problems, use that creates hazards, and use that prohibits one's ability to do one's job. Alcohol dependence, commonly referred to as alcoholism, is a kind of substance dependence. Related to family communication, alcohol dependence can adversely impact marital, parent–child, and extended family relationships. For example, between couples, alcoholism is associated with physical aggression, negative communication behavior, and more negative reciprocity in their communication (see Segrin & Flora, 2011). Research suggests that communication between siblings, especially if there are mixed messages about drinking behavior, can serve to reinforce problematic drinking behavior (Glowacki, 2017). Furthermore, alcoholic families convey more negative feelings and alcoholic parents are less sensitive to their babies. This lack of attention might have severe consequences for children's emerging attachment styles (see Chapter 27). For older children of alcoholics, research suggests that they are two to four times more likely than children of non-alcoholics to see their parents get a divorce or separate, face unemployment, or die (Menees & Segrin, 2000).

In sum, there are many issues that fall under the broad category of mental health. What is important to remember is that families can make a significant difference in how a person experiences and responds to these serious, but often invisible, health struggles.

Physical Health

Just like mental illness, family communication plays an important role in understanding and coping with physical health. Family communication might influence health outcomes but health also might be the subject of conversation. In Chapter 3, we discussed affection research that has been linked to physiological outcomes. Indeed, communication scholars are increasingly becoming interested in the ways communication can serve as a catalyst for changes in biological markers such as heart rate, cortisol, and oxytocin. Research also documents that family communication about health is important in a variety of contexts such as cancer (Krieger, 2014) and inherited genetic conditions (Wilson et al., 2004), especially considering people report that their mothers are the best source of supportive communication (see Chapter 17). We now discuss how families can play an important role in treatment decisions for physical health problems.

Decision Making

When it comes to treating health issues, families play an important role in the decision-making process and the support process. According to the Family Determinant of Clinical Decisions Typology (DECIDE; Krieger, 2014), both patients and their families should be involved in serious treatment decisions. According to this model, the primary goals (either interdependence or autonomy) of both the patient and family are taken into consideration. These considerations create four types: (1) independent, (2) isolated, (3) collaborative, and (4) demanding. For independent types, patients want to make decisions for themselves and their families support them in doing so. For isolated types, patients look to family members for help but are met with resistance. The collaborative type emphasizes the patients' desire for family input and the family's desire to help. Finally, the demanding type reflects a situation where family members want to be included in the decision-making process but patients want to make their own decisions. This way of categorizing patients and their families can help medical professionals provide the best care and understand patient decisions surrounding treatment. **Taken together, our physical health can be both a product of communication and the subject of conversation in the family.**

Did You Know?

- With regard to genetic inheritance, Wilson and her colleagues (2004) found that biological families communicated about four factors when discussing genetic risk: (1) disease factors such as patterns of inheritance, (2) individual factors such as risk perceptions, (3) family factors such as family myths, and (4) socio-cultural factors such as concerns about discrimination.

- As we discussed in Chapter 13 (Difficult Family Conversations) and Chapter 16 (Information Management and Disclosure in Families), sex is one of the most taboo topics for family members to discuss. Research from Heather Powell and Chris Segrin (2004) found, however, that the more families communicate in general, the more they talk about sex and communication about HIV/AIDS with dating partners.

INTERESTING RESEARCH FINDINGS

When Might Communication Be Harmful for Your Health?

Not all communication is good communication. Sometimes, critical words and disapproving messages can have negative consequences for families. To better understand how family interaction influenced young women's body image, Analisa Arroyo and Chris Segrin (2013) explored how social competence and psychological distress mediated the relationship between family interaction (i.e., conflict, control, and expressed emotion) and disordered eating attitudes. Based on the responses of 858 young adult women, these communication researchers found that family-expressed emotion (emotional involvement and perceived criticism) was related to low social competence. Social competence was related to low psychological distress. Psychological distress was then related to high disordered eating attitudes. Put simply, when young adults perceive they are being criticized by their parents it affects their competence and well-being, which in turn affects their attitudes about eating. Overall, these authors recommend that parents help their children develop social competence skills and communicate messages of acceptance.

PRACTICAL APPLICATIONS AND THINGS TO CONSIDER

Health issues influence not only the people who must cope with the illness but everyone in the family. A study by Elaine Wittenberg-Lyles and her colleagues (2014) found that family members who provide care for a terminally sick loved one experience social support burden for a variety of reasons, including (1) perceived relationship barriers, (2) desire to remain in control, and (3) recognition of the loss of support from the patient. This perceived loss surrounded not being able to turn to the patient for help making decisions, providing emotional support, and the change that resulted from new patterns of communicating. Based on this research, the authors recommend that hospice workers provide support for not only the patient but also family members that is tailored to their specific needs.

KEY TERMS

Collaborative decision-making type

Demanding decision-making type

Independent decision-making type

Isolated decision-making type

Mental health

Physical health

Post-partum depression

Prenatal depression

Stigma

THOUGHT ACTIVITY

Mental health issues are a serious problem on college campuses across the nation. Do you know where you can go if you are suffering from mental health issues? If you do not know, spend a few minutes looking up that information online now. Would you know how to talk to a friend about the struggles they were facing? How could you reassure someone that it was okay to ask for help?

Skipping Class: Mental Health In the Family

CASE STUDY BY LEAH M. SEURER

Anna stared across the room at the pile of books next to her laptop, heaved a tired sigh, and unlocked her phone. If she got up now, she could still make her 10:00 a.m. class. But she also didn't *have* to go today. Opening her messages, she sent a text to her roommate.

"Going to bio today?"

"Sure am! Want me to sign you in again?" Natalie responded.

"That would be amazing. I just cannot today. Thanks, friend!"

Anna clicked off her phone and rolled back into her pillow. She wondered if their third roommate, her brother Ben, was on his way back from his 8:00 a.m. class. Maybe he could grab a coffee for her, but then he'd know that she hadn't gone to her class. That might start another conversation that she was honestly too tired to have.

She looked at her phone. 10:02 a.m. Dr. Swents would be firing up her Powerpoint. Staring up at the ceiling, she tried to remember when it had started. Was it before her knee surgery this summer? Or maybe over midterms when she'd decided to break it off with Jake? Did she break up with him because of it? When had she stopped attending class? Thank God parents couldn't see grades. She heard the door slowly creak open. "I'm awake, Ben, don't be creepy."

Ben pounced onto the bed. "I've already been to class and worked out! Bad day again?"

"Sort of." Anna yawned. "I'm just super tired again today. Natalie is signing me into bio. I'll go to my lab tomorrow so it should be fine."

"I'm sure you know what I'm going to say next but I still need to say it." Ben waited for Anna to look at him. "I think you should go and talk to someone. You've been like this on and off for a while, and I feel like it's gotten progressively worse since Jake. Not that it's because of him. I'm just saying that we are going on almost seven weeks of it being this bad."

"Maybe. But I could also start eating better, get back to the gym with you. Get back into my pre-surgery shape, before I was this sad sack, you know?"

"That would all be great," Ben smiled. "I definitely think you should do that, but I also think that this is our thing. This is our family. This is Dad. This is Aunt Stacey after Norah was born. This is the million times they've told us to be aware of our genetics! We need to approach this from all fronts."

"But we're twins!" Anna moaned. "Where's your depression, dang it!"

"This is what happens when bio majors skip classes," Ben laughed. "You know genetics write some of the story, but not all of it. Maybe it will happen to me someday. And maybe you can come and annoy me like I'm annoying you. Now come on, get dressed and I'll take you to the counseling center. Let's use that free health insurance coverage from Dad while we still can!"

CASE STUDY DISCUSSION QUESTIONS

1. What types of reasons did Anna and Ben attribute to Anna's depression? How might these reasons affect conversations about mental health in the family?
2. How did the communication environment of Anna and Ben's family help or hinder the discussion about Anna's depression?
3. How does your family talk about mental illness? How might this shape your beliefs about it in terms of treatments?
4. If you don't talk about mental illness in your family, why not?

REFERENCES

American Psychiatric Association (APA). (2013). *Diagnostic and statistical manual of mental disorders* (5th ed.). Arlington, VA: American Psychiatric Publishing.

Arroyo, A., & Segrin, C. (2013). Family interactions and disordered eating attitudes: The mediating roles of social competence and psychological distress. *Communication Monographs, 80*, 399–424. doi:10.1080/03637751.2013.828158

Botta, R. A., & Dumlao, R. (2002). How do conflict and communication patterns between fathers and daughters contribute to or offset eating disorders? *Health Communication, 14*, 199–219. doi:10.1207/S15327027HC1402_3

Brohan, E., Slade, M., Clement, S., & Thornicroft, G. (2010). Experiences of mental illness stigma, prejudice and discrimination: A review of measures. *BMC Health Services Research, 10*. doi:10.1186/1472-6963-10-80

Fellenzer, J. L., & Cibula, D. A. (2014). Intendedness of pregnancy and other predictive factors for symptoms of prenatal depression in a population-based study. *Maternal and Child Health Journal, 18,* 2426–2436. doi:10.1007/s10995-014-1481-4

Flood-Grady, E., & Koenig Kellas, J. (2018). Sense-making, socialization, and stigma: Exploring narratives told in families about mental illness. *Health Communication.* Advanced Online Publication. doi:10.1080/10410236.2018.1431016

Glowacki, E. M. (2017). Examining sibling communication about problematic drinking: An application of inconsistent nurturing as control theory. *Journal of Family Communication, 17,* 65–87. doi:10.1080/15267431/2016.1251919

Krieger, J. L. (2014). Family communication about cancer treatment decision making: A description of the DECIDE typology. *Annals of the International Communication Association, 38,* 279–305. doi:10.1080/23808985.2014.11679165

Liu, H. (2009). Till death do us part: Marital status and U.S. mortality trends, 1986–2000. *Journal of Marriage and Family, 71,* 1158–1173. doi:10.1111/j.1741-3737.2009.00661.x

Menees, M. M., & Segrin, C. (2000). The specificity of disrupted processes in families of adult children of alcoholics. *Alcohol and Alcoholism, 35,* 361–367. doi:10.1093/alcalc/35.4.361

O'Hara, M. W., & McCabe, J. E. (2013). Postpartum depression: Current status and future directions. *Annual Review of Clinical Psychology, 9,* 379–407. doi:10.1146/annurev-clinpsy-050212-185612

Powell, H. L., & Segrin, C. (2004). The effect of family and peer communication on college students' communication with dating partners about HIV and AIDS. *Health Communication, 16,* 427–449. doi:10.1207/s15327027hc1604

Regier, D. A., Narrow, W. E., Rae, D. S., Manderscheid, R. W., Locke, B. Z., & Goodwin, F. K. (1993). The de facto US mental and addictive disorders service system: Epidemiologic catchment are prospective 1-year prevalence rates of disorders and services. *Archives of General Psychiatry, 50,* 85–94. doi:10.1001/archpsyc.1993.01820140007001

Scharp, K. M., & Thomas, L. J. (2017). "What would a loving mom do today?": Exploring the meaning of motherhood in stories of pre-natal and post-partum depression. *Journal of Family Communication, 17,* 401–414. doi:10.1080/15267431.2017.1355803

Segrin, C. (2013). Mental health. In A. Vangelisti (Ed.), *The Routledge handbook of family communication* (2nd ed., pp. 512–527). New York, NY: Routledge.

Segrin, C., & Flora, J. (2011). *Family communication.* New York, NY: Routledge.

Wade, T. D., Gillespie, N., & Martin, N. G. (2007). A comparison of early family life events amongst monozygotic twin women with lifetime anorexia nervosa, bulimia nervosa, or major depression. *International Journal of Eating Disorders, 40,* 679–686. doi:10.1002/eat.20461

Wilson, B. J., Forrest, K., van Teijlingen, E. R., McKee, L., Haites, N., Matthres, E., & Simpson, S. A. (2004). Family communication about genetic risk: The little that is known. *Community Genetics, 7,* 15–24. doi:10.1159/000080300

Wittenberg-Lyles, E., Washington, K., Demiris, G., Oliver, D. P., & Shaunfield, S. (2014). Understanding social support burden among family caregivers. *Health Communication, 29,* 901–910. doi:10.1080/10410236.2013.815111

RELATED READINGS

Hong, S. J. (2018). Gendered cultural identities: The influences of family and privacy boundaries, subjective norms, and stigma beliefs on family health history communication. *Health Communication, 33*, 927–938. doi:10.1080/10410236. 2017.1322480

Thompson, T., Seo, J., Griffith, J., Baxter, M., James, A., & Kaphingst, K. A. (2015). The context of collecting family health history: Examining definitions of family and family communication about health among African-American women. *Journal of Health Communication, 20*, 416–423. doi:10.1080/10810730 .2014.977466

Williams, T. T., Pichon, L. C., & Campbell, B. (2015). Sexual health communication within African-American families. *Health Communication, 30*, 328–338. doi:10.1080/ 10410236.2013.856743

Chapter 32

Family Communication in Organizational Contexts

BACKGROUND

What is "balance," what is "work," and what is "leisure"? These are questions each person needs to answer for themselves, as balance, work, and life or leisure look different for every person. **Work–life balance** refers to the (potentially unattainable) balance of work demands and home demands while making time for family, leisure, and play (Figure 32.1). Work can be considered career or ambition, or perhaps in your stage of life, it is your academic pursuits. Life or leisure consists of hobbies, down time, family time, or spiritual development. Balance can mean spending equal amounts of time on work and leisure or it can mean spending ideal amounts of time on each, as defined by you. Other people argue that work *is* life, and that a discussion of work–life balance is unnecessary and segments work as something we must do outside of "real living." This chapter discusses each of these issues as well as topics that contribute to work–life balance or a lack thereof such as gender gaps in pay and unpaid work.

Communication in Family Contexts: Theories and Processes, First Edition.
Elizabeth Dorrance Hall and Kristina M. Scharp.
© 2020 John Wiley & Sons, Inc. Published 2020 by John Wiley & Sons, Inc.
Companion website: www.wiley.com/go/dorrance_hall/communication-in-family-contexts

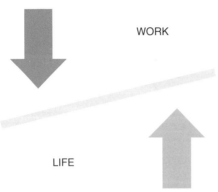

Figure 32.1 Work–life balance.

DIVISION OF HOUSEHOLD LABOR

Division of domestic labor refers to how housework is allocated between partners. Historically, the division of labor has been skewed to favor men. Women, whether employed or not, have been responsible for the majority of housework including child-rearing duties (Shelton & John, 1996), though this varies across age groups and historical periods (Lam, McHale, & Crouter, 2012). In fact, working women often have a "**second shift**" (Hochschild & Machung, 1989), or a second full-time job working to take care of the home and family. Refer to Chapter 8 for an activity asking you to recall what the division of labor was like in your home growing up. In today's society where more women are working, both partners in a couple might be overburdened by the demands of their "day jobs" and taking care of the home (Bianchi, Milkie, Sayer, & Robinson, 2000). The division of household labor is more equitable in lesbian and gay couples (Kurdek, 2007). The unequal division of labor has consequences for working toward work–life balance and avoiding work–life conflict.

WORK–FAMILY AND FAMILY–WORK CONFLICT

Work–family conflict occurs when role pressures at work influence the ability to function at home. For example, when working late several nights in a row to meet an important deadline for a time-consuming project, a partner might fail to pitch in as much at home and might not do their fair share of the housework. Constantly checking emails instead of engaging with children during dinner or playing games is another example of work–family conflict. In these cases, their role as employee is interfering with their role as partner. Work–family conflict tends to happen to people who are Type A, or overly ambitious, full of energy, competitive, and impatient, people who tend to have a negative outlook on life, people with especially demanding jobs that include a lot of pressure or require them to "fake" emotions like staying positive when dealing with rude or negative clients. Job involvement, job stress, and work hours contribute to work–family conflict although working in a supportive environment (e.g., having a supportive boss) decreases work–family conflict. Work–family conflict can lead to conflict and hostile interactions with partners, reduced marital and life satisfaction, withdrawal from family interaction, and lower-quality parent–child communication. This type of conflict is common as 38% of parents say being a working parent (i.e., having a job) has made it difficult to be a good parent (though 10% say having a job makes being a good parent easier; Pew Research Center, 2013).

Family–work conflict occurs when role pressures at home influence the ability to function at work. A sick spouse or a child who needs to be picked up from school might interfere with a person's ability to complete their work. In other words, their role as parent or partner is interfering with their role as employee. This type of conflict is also common. In fact, 53% of working mothers say they have had to take significant time off work to care for a child or another family member. Nearly one-third of parents say being a parent has made it harder to advance in their careers. Looking ahead, 62% of millennials without children expect that having children will hinder their career advancement. Family–work conflict increases when there is more family conflict and stress happening at home, while family members provide too little support.

Both types of conflict are communication challenges as employees have to negotiate with their employers to take time off and justify the time needed. Working adults also need to negotiate with their families when they need to spend extra time at work or spend time working from home. Partners might agree to take turns spending more time keeping up with housework while the other is especially busy at work. Couples who engage in dyadic or communal coping (see Chapters 12 and 28) attempt to help the other when one is feeling stressed at work or at home (or both). While stressful times can be difficult or even impossible to plan, dyadic coping works best when couples take turns feeling especially stressed. Dyadic coping tends to break down when both partners in a couple are experiencing extreme stress at the same time. Sometimes these negotiations fail, and people leave their jobs when they are not flexible enough. Other times, people reduce their work hours to spend more time with family.

An alternative to work–family and family–work conflict is that the two roles might enrich one another so that work enriches family life and family life enriches work (Greenhaus & Powell, 2006). This line of thinking argues that participating in work and family life can increase a person's energy and support resources which can lead to personal growth and fulfillment. For example, co-workers might become friends who then share parenting advice and support during playdates with their children on the weekends.

THE SPILLOVER–CROSSOVER MODEL

Both types of conflict (work–family and family–work) might lead to spillover and crossover, ideas central to the spillover–crossover model. The spillover–crossover model provides another way to look at the push and pull people experience between work and life. This model, developed by Arnold Bakker and Evangelia Demerouti (2013), explains how and why stress at work can bleed into our home life and even impact our partner's well-being.

Spillover is an individual experience that happens when work stress follows a person home and they experience more stress at home. This might take the form of working at home after putting children to bed, or being distracted at dinner due to worrying and ruminating about work at home. The basic idea is that people do not always leave work at work and instead end up focusing on work at the expense of focusing on family or social obligations when away from work. Spillover tends to have negative consequences for people's social and family lives.

Crossover is an interactive process between two people that happens when the work stress brought home by one partner starts to affect the other partner. Work stress is effectively crossing over to a completely separate person. This can happen through the transfer of negative emotions or even burnout (complete exhaustion due to overwork and job stress). Researchers have found that exposure to a burned-out partner increases one's own level of burnout.

Spillover and crossover are not always negative. Imagine a woman who has a job she loves where she is given much responsibility. Feeling empowered at work, she takes initiative at home to make a plan to pay off the family's debt. Inspired by her sense of empowerment at home, her partner starts spending more time teaching his children to read and write, a task he found overwhelming before. In this case, the woman's empowerment at work spilled over to her home life. Her empowerment had an effect on her husband (i.e., crossover) so that he also felt more empowered in working with their children. Research has found evidence of spillover–crossover of anxiety, distress, marital dissatisfaction, and burnout, but also of satisfaction, quality of life, autonomy, social support, work engagement, and vigor.

Communication patterns such as support and social undermining can explain how crossover happens. Bakker and Demerouti call these communication factors "interpersonal exchange." Social undermining can include criticizing one's partner, engaging in hostile interactions, and hindering partner's ability to reach their goals. Because stress can cause aggressive behavior, partners who are stressed might engage in more social undermining, which might then stress out the other partner. Communicating empathy can also influence crossover. When one partner is easily affected by the other's emotions, crossover is more likely to occur.

COMMUTER FAMILIES

Commuter families represent a unique kind of family that must balance work and life along with distance. In commuter families, one spouse works and lives away from the rest of the family, usually owning or renting a second home to accommodate their work. This distant spouse usually sees the family periodically instead of daily and is apart from the family at least three nights per week (Bergen, 2014). This type of family is increasingly common across the globe. These families are discourse dependent because families are commonly expected to live together, and see each other daily. Commuter families must explain and defend their situation to others, causing stress on the geographically distant parent and the rest of the family. Karla Bergen's research has found that despite identifying as a family with a single primary residence and shared concern for loved ones, others outside of the family sometimes assume the partners live apart due to marital problems.

WORK/FAMILY BORDER THEORY

Work/family border theory proposes another way of thinking about work/family balance. The theory, developed by Sue Campbell Clark (2000), focuses on how people cross, create, and manage borders between work and home. The theory claims that work and family are separate domains that are interdependent and influence each other. Work and home have different purposes and cultures, for example, different tasks are completed at work and at home. The language you use and the behaviors that are acceptable are likely different at the two locations. There are things you might say at home that you would never say at work. On the flip side, it is likely your work has jargon associated with it that your family would not understand. People vary on just how different their work and home lives are, but anyone who works outside the home has to do some level of "border-crossing" as they transition between the two settings. Border-crossing involves adapting communication styles to each domain. Clark defines balance as "satisfaction and good functioning at work and at home, with a minimum of role conflict" (p. 751). **People who are better at adapting their communication style along with their focus and goals have an easier time border-crossing each day.**

FEMINIST THEORIES AND INTERSECTIONALITY

Critical feminist theories include standpoint theories, radical feminism, social feminist theories, and poststructural/postmodern/postcolonial theories. They focus on problematizing assumptions about power, some that is reinforced institutionally (e.g., class, gender, race) and power that is reproduced as a taken-for-granted way of life (i.e., hegemony). Specifically, researchers who use standpoint theories come to their scholarship with the assumption that our social locations (e.g., gender, class, race) always influence our knowledge of social life. With this in mind, critical scholars engage in a process called **reflexivity** that asks them to constantly think about the ways their own experiences influence how they understand what they are researching. This is important because they recognize that their experiences communicate their values, which in turn helps to reproduce certain power structures. Patricia Sotirin and Laura Ellingson (2018) explain that researchers applying a radical feminist approach argue that women's difference is essential in understanding the gendered ways that influence people's enactment of family life. Some of what you just read about with regards to women who work aligns more with social feminist theories which focus on economics and critique the patriarchal exploitation of gendered labor. Indeed, these commitments speak to what critical scholars refer to as praxis. **Praxis** refers to applying theory to people's everyday lives with the goal of creating social change. Finally, although they differ in some regards, poststructural/ postmodern/postcolonial theorists take issue with the claim that representation is a reflection or mirror of a predetermined reality. Instead, they advocate that representation constructs, rather than reflects, reality. **In sum, there is no one single definition of feminism or critical feminist theory. Those who take a feminist approach, however, attend to issues of gender and sexuality as site of power, identity, and experience that is situated in and always subject to communication and culture.** In doing so, feminist theorizing is a continual process as opposed to a static representation (Sotirin & Ellingson, 2018).

In addition to critical feminist theories, Kimberlé Crenshaw (1993) argued that it is not enough to problematize gender and race separately; rather, it is important to attend to the ways that overlapping identities create unique conditions for the people who must perform them. With the lived experience of Black women in mind, Crenshaw helped to forward the concept of **intersectionality**. Intersectionality is a critical framework that acknowledges the fluidity, variability, and temporality of the interpersonal relating that occurs between, within, and among social groups/institutions/ideology/social practice (Few-Demo, Moore, & Abdi, 2018). **Put simply, intersectionality acknowledges the mutual influence of social positions such as race, class, and gender.**

INTERESTING RESEARCH FINDINGS

Readjusting Work–Life and Identity in Retirement

A recent study by Patricia Gettings (2018) explored societal discourses of retirement. Retirement marks a time when work–life balance shifts and retirees must renegotiate their identities in the face of a major source of identity loss: ending their career. Due to longer life expectancies and the recent economic downturn, today's retirees draw from the societal discourse of retirement portrayed in the media to make sense of their retirement experience and how to handle a major change in their work–life balance. Gettings claims there is an "ideal" baby-boomer retiree identity portrayed in the media (e.g., newspapers, magazines) that is likely hard to achieve for most people. Facets of this identity include staying active in retirement, being able to afford a similar lifestyle after retirement, and "doing" retirement on their own terms rather that the way it has been done by others.

Portrayals of Good Working Mothers

Like Gettings' study above, Erika Kirby and her team (2016) conducted a study to understand how a work–life issue is portrayed in the media: "good working mothers." Kirby's team analyzed the movies *One Fine Day* and *I Don't Know*

How She Does It. According to the discourses represented in these movies, "good working mothers" must meet high standards as an "ideal" worker, host/ domestic figure, and exceptional mother.

Many mothers think of work and parenting as two separate roles (i.e., a dichotomy) requiring "cognitive acrobatics" to manage (Johnston & Swanson, 2007). Kirby and her team note that "good working mothers" are constantly on the defensive about their two identities and when either one is threatened, they must communicate to shield themselves from the person or behavior threatening their identity. For example, when a mother's ability to spend enough time with her children due to work demands is questioned, she could respond defensively by saying "I am a single mother" to remind others she must work to support the family. Some consequences of the portrayals of good working mothers in the film are that others might believe that mothers who work are only good if they can handle solving problems on their own and choose family over work.

PRACTICAL APPLICATIONS AND THINGS TO CONSIDER

Sheryl Sandberg, the Chief Operating Officer of Facebook, claims that women need to Lean In (Sandberg, 2013). Leaning in means sitting at "the table," attributing success to your own abilities rather than luck or help from others. She notes that women tend to focus on pleasing others before advancing their own careers and that women do not self-promote as well as men. Sandberg says each of these issues contributes to women working more, for less money, and in lower positions in a company. Sandberg also offers advice for couples that speaks to work–life balance: if they want a 50–50 partnership, they must establish that pattern from the outset of their relationship. Sandberg also advises parents to set boundaries over their schedules since people are working longer hours than ever before, especially childfree employees. Finally, she notes that work–life balance might be more challenging for certain groups of people such as single parents, people in lower-paying jobs, and people with unsupportive and inflexible supervisors. What factors do you think contribute to these challenges? Sandberg's message of "leaning in" has garnered quite a bit of criticism. What do you think might be problematic about her message?

IN- OR OUT-OF-CLASS ACTIVITY

1. Watch the following video and take a few minutes to assess your own work–life balance: https://www.youtube.com/watch?v=MPR3o6Hnf2g. As students, life can feel pretty focused on academic work, yet many students balance jobs, family obligations, and social commitments. What is the impact of work–life balance and imbalance on your mental and physical health? What is the impact on your relationships? Imagine your life in 5 years and in 10 years. What will your ideal day look like? How do you see yourself balancing work and life at those times? What will make achieving balance difficult?

2. Organizations are making strides to facilitate work–family balance. According to Baltes, Clark, and Chakrabarti (2009), more companies are offering flextime (i.e., flexible arrival and departure times), a compressed workweek (i.e., working four 10-hour days instead of five 8-hour days), telecommuting (i.e., working from home for part/all of the week), on-site childcare, and more family-friendly climates (i.e., employees actually use the family-focused benefits). Organizations are also beginning to recognize the enrichment perspective we covered above, that both work and family roles can improve one's quality of life, a concept they call "work–family facilitation."
   a. Think of two companies you might like to work for someday. Research their work–family balance policies (flextime, maternity/paternity leave, family sick leave, childcare on site, etc.). Compare with the company your neighbor chose. Report back to the class.
   b. If you were to start your own company or run a company, what policies would you put in place? Which ones would you leave out? Why?
3. Brainstorm a list of coping strategies you could use to achieve/work toward work–life/family balance. How does your list compare to lists offered online?

KEY TERMS

Border-crossing

Care gap

Commuter family

Crossover

Division of labor

Family–work conflict

Income gap

Intersectionality

Praxis

Reflexivity

Role conflict

Role rigidity

Second shift

Social undermining

Spillover

Work–family conflict

DISCUSSION QUESTIONS

1. Is work–family balance possible?
2. What are some criticisms of promoting the idea of work–family balance?
3. How does work–family balance change throughout the life course?

Grams is Not Retiring to Watch Her Grandchildren

CASE STUDY BY PATRICIA E. GETTINGS

It was the end of an era. Kay Lakeson had been teaching at Northshore Elementary School for 35 years. She had taught hundreds of kids about fractions, state capitals, the solar system, how to write in paragraphs, and so many other things that third-grade students must master. But yesterday was her last day. Today she was retired.

Kay was still in bed as these thoughts ran through her mind. It was 4:55 a.m. and she was wide awake, as she always was at this time. She hadn't set the coffee pot last night to automatically start at 5:05 a.m. like she had been doing forever. Instead, she figured she'd get up and make it today because she had the extra time. Her husband was still asleep next to her. He'd get up in about an hour to get ready for work. He was still planning to work for another few years. But she was awake and retired. Now what?

Kay quietly slipped out of bed and walked to the kitchen. She wasn't really sure how to feel yet about being retired. She was excited, of course. People dream their whole working lives about the day they retire, right? She felt a little bit sad, too, because she knew she'd miss the kids, and the other teachers and staff who had become her work family. Kay was also feeling a bit nervous. She didn't think she'd be bored because she had lots of ideas about what she wanted to do. But she was anxious because she didn't know exactly what she should do next. Kay shook these thoughts out of her head and said to herself, "Just make the coffee. Take it one step at a time."

The next few hours passed much like they would for Kay on a Saturday. She had breakfast and coffee while watching the news. She took a walk. She weeded her garden. She emptied the dishwasher. Her phone buzzed a little before 11. It was her daughter, Amelia, who was calling from work.

"Hi Mom. Happy first day of retirement! What are you up to?" Amelia asked.

"I was just putting a few dishes into the dishwasher. Then I was going to think about having something for lunch. How are you?" Kay responded.

"Well, the YMCA just called and Henry is sick. Kevin has a ton of stuff going on at the office so he really can't help. Do you think you could pick him up from camp and watch him for a few hours until I can leave work? I have an important meeting at 3 but can probably leave after that. I can stop and get Rachel from daycare on my way. I'll have to figure out how to get Henry to the doctor tomorrow because they won't let him back at summer camp without a doctor's note…." Amelia's voice trailed off.

Kay could tell her daughter was overwhelmed but she wasn't really sure how to respond. She absolutely didn't mind helping her daughter out and loved spending time with her grandkids. That was actually one of the reasons she had decided to retire now, while she was still healthy and energetic to be active with them. But somehow she wasn't prepared for this request on her very first day of retirement. This issue had come up before when Kay had first announced she was retiring. Her last day of school was pretty close to Henry's last day of second grade so Amelia had joked about Kay hosting "Camp Grams" for the summer. Kay had bristled at the idea – she wasn't retiring to *raise* her grandchildren! Amelia must have sensed her hesitation because she had enrolled Henry in YMCA Day Camp the next day and announced that Rachel, her 3-year-old, would attend daycare all summer. But here the issue was creeping up again. Kay really needed to figure out how to set boundaries about what she was and wasn't willing to do with her time in retirement. She also didn't want to upset her daughter.

"I don't mind picking Henry up from camp today…" Kay started, "But…."

CASE STUDY DISCUSSION QUESTIONS

1. How do you think Kay should respond?
2. How is family–work conflict experienced?
3. What should be expected of retirees in terms of caring for grandchildren? Other responsibilities?
4. What do you think about Kevin's role in this situation? Should he be more involved in these discussions? Why or why not?
5. How might organizational work–life policies assist Amelia and Kevin in managing challenges like these?

REFERENCES

Bakker, A. B., & Demerouti, E. (2013). The spillover-crossover model. In J. G. Grzywacz & E. Demerouti (Eds.), *New frontiers in work and family*. New York, NY: Routledge.

Baltes, B. B., Clark, M. A., & Chakrabarti, M. (2009). Work–life balance: The roles of work–family conflict and work–family facilitation. In N. Garcea, S. Harrington, & P. A. Linley (Eds.), *Oxford handbook of positive psychology and work* (pp. 201–212). Oxford, UK: Oxford University Press. doi:10.1093/oxfor dhb/9780195335446.013.0016

Bergen, K. (2014). Discourse dependence in the commuter family. In L. A. Baxter (Ed.), *Remaking family communicatively* (pp. 211–228). New York, NY: Peter Lang.

Bianchi, S. M., Milkie, M. A., Sayer, L. C., & Robinson, J. P. (2000). Is anyone doing the housework? Trends in the gender division of household labor. *Social Forces*, *79*, 191–228. doi:10.1093/sf/79.191

Clark, S. C. (2000). Work/family border theory: A new theory of work/family balance. *Human Relations*, *53*, 747–770. doi:10.1177/0018726700536001

Crenshaw, K. (1993). Demarginalizing the interaction of race and sex: A Black feminist critique of antidiscrimination doctrine, feminist theory, and anti-racist politics. In D. Weisburg, (Ed.), *Feminist legal theory: Foundations* (pp. 383–411). Philadelphia, PA: Temple University Press.

Few-Demo, A. L., Moore, J., & Abdi, S. (2018). Intersectionality: (Re)considering family communication from within the margins. In D. O. Braithwaite, E. A. Suter, & K. Floyd (Eds.), *Engaging theories in family communication* (pp. 175–186). New York, NY: Routledge.

Gettings, P. E. (2018). Discourses of retirement in the United States. *Work, Aging and Retirement*, *4*, 315–329. doi:10.1093/workar/way008

Greenhaus, J. H., & Powell, G. N. (2006). When work and family are allies: A theory of work–family enrichment. *Academy of Management Review*, *31*, 72–92.

Hochschild, A., & Machung, A. (1989). *The second shift: Working parents and the revolution at home*. New York, NY: Avon Books.

Johnston, D. D., & Swanson, D. H. (2007). Cognitive acrobatics in the construction of worker-mother identity. *Sex Roles*, *57*, 447–459. doi:10.1007/s11199-007-9267-4

Kirby, E. L., Riforgiate, S. E., Anderson, I. K., Lahman, M. P., & Lietzenmighter, A. M. (2016). Good working mothers as jugglers: A critical look at two work–family balance films. *Journal of Family Communication, 16*, 76–93. doi:10.1080/15267431. 2015.1111216

Kurdek, L. A. (2007). The allocation of household labor by partners in gay and lesbian couples. *Journal of Family Issues, 28*, 132–148. doi:10.1177/0192 513X06292019

Lam, C. B., McHale, S. M., & Crouter, A. C. (2012). The division of household labor: Longitudinal changes and within-couple variation. *Journal of Marriage and Family, 74*, 944–952. doi:10.1111/j.1741-3737.2012.01007.x

Pew Research Center. (2013). Balancing work and family. *Pew Research Center.* Retrieved from http://www.pewsocialtrends.org/2013/12/11/chapter-5-balancing-work-and-family/

Sandberg, S. (2013). *Lean in: Women, work, and the will to lead.* New York, NY: Random House.

Shelton, B. A., & John, D. (1996). The division of household labor. *Annual Review of Sociology, 22*, 299–322.

Sotirin, P. J., & Ellingson, L. L. (2018). Critical feminist family communication theory. In D. O. Braithwaite, E. A. Suter, & K. Floyd (Eds.), *Engaging theories in family communication* (pp. 110–121). New York, NY: Routledge.

RELATED READINGS

Bodenmann, G. (2005). Dyadic coping and its significance for marital functioning. In T. Revenson, K. Kayser, & G. Bodenmann (Eds.), *Couples coping with stress: Emerging perspectives on dyadic coping* (pp. 33–50). Washington, DC: American Psychological Association.

Fondas, N. (2014). Your work–life balance should be your company's problem. *Harvard Business Review.* Retrieved from https://hbr.org/2014/06/your-work-life-balance-should-be-your-companys-problem

Frone, M. R., Russell, M., & Cooper, M. L. (1992). Antecedents and outcomes of work–family conflict: Testing a model of the work–family interface. *Journal of Applied Psychology, 77*, 65–78.

Frone, M. R., Russell, M., & Cooper, M. L. (1997). Relation of work–family conflict to health outcomes: A four-year longitudinal study of employed parents. *Journal of Occupational and Organizational Psychology, 70*, 325–335. doi:10.1111/j.2044-8325.1997.tb00652.x

Rodríguez-Muñoz, A., Sanz-Vergel, A. I., Demerouti, E., & Bakker, A. B. (2014). Engaged at work and happy at home: A spillover-crossover model. *Journal of Happiness Studies, 15*, 271–283. doi:10.1007/s10902-013-9421-3

Wright, K. B., Abendschein, B., Wombacher, K., O'Connor, M., Hoffman, M., Dempsey, M., … Shelton, A. (2014). Work-related communication technology use outside of regular work hours and work life conflict: The influence of communication technologies on perceived work life conflict, burnout, job satisfaction, and turnover intentions. *Management Communication Quarterly, 28*, 507–530. doi:10.1177/0893318914533332

Chapter 33
Family Communication in Technological Contexts

BACKGROUND

Technology is an important part of family life in the twenty-first century. Siblings can easily keep in touch with one another no matter how far apart they live. Parents can track their children's location with the click of a button. Grandparents can see pictures of their grandchildren on their phones. Technology is shaping family life and families are shaping new technological innovations. Indeed, families use technology to communicate and engage in family functions across the lifespan (Wilkes Karraker, 2015).

The way families use media has changed dramatically over the past decade. Social media has also had a substantial impact on family communication (Fife, LaCava, & Nelson, 2013; Padilla-Walker, Coyne, & Fraser, 2012). Today, when a family sits down to watch a show or movie together, it is not uncommon for members to interact with their individual screens while watching the television screen together (e.g., on their own tablet or cell phone). According to Laura Padilla-Walker, cell phone use and watching television or movies are the most commonly used technologies in families. Cell phone use affects family interactions, family dynamics, and household guidelines (Padilla-Walker et al., 2012).

Communication in Family Contexts: Theories and Processes, First Edition.
Elizabeth Dorrance Hall and Kristina M. Scharp.
© 2020 John Wiley & Sons, Inc. Published 2020 by John Wiley & Sons, Inc.
Companion website: www.wiley.com/go/dorrance_hall/communication-in-family-contexts

THE TECHNOLOGY PARADOX

Technology has the ability to both bring families together and pull families apart. When something has contradictory or inconsistent qualities, such as negative and positive outcomes, it is considered paradoxical. Paradoxes must be managed, often through communication. Sirkka L. Jarvenpaa, Karl Reiner Lang, and Virpi Kristiina Tuunainen (2005) write about eight technology paradoxes. They describe the **empowerment–enslavement paradox** which includes, for example, being able to stay on top of work even after hours, but then also feeling increased pressure to always be available. Parents may feel relieved that they can check in on their children from anywhere using GPS tracking technology, yet they may also feel the temptation or pressure to check in on them more frequently than they would like. The researchers also describe the **engaging–disengaging paradox**. In this paradox, people may struggle with wanting to be able to choose when to be involved with others, attempting to strike a balance between engagement and alone time. Other paradoxes identified include:

- Independence–dependence paradox: technology has allowed people to be more independent than ever in terms of mobility, but many people develop a strong dependence on the technology.

- Fulfills needs–creates needs paradox: technology provides solutions to problems such as access to shared family calendars for scheduling but also creates new problems such as distractions during scheduled family time.

- Competence–incompetence paradox: technology provides knowledge at our fingertips, giving us the ability to do things we could not do before. Yet, technology also allows us to not fully learn skills if there are tech workarounds and it may decrease our in-person social adaptability.

- Planning–improvisation paradox: technology has made making long-term plans with others quick and easy, but it also allows people to make plans on the spot, increasing their ability to improvise.

- Public–private paradox: because of technology, people can have private conversations in public spaces. Technology also creates digital records of information people would often like to keep private.

- Illusion–disillusion paradox: many people have a vision of what their technology can do for them that is unrealistic. Instead, conversations via video chat that are supposed to feel like "being together in person" are rife with interruptions and buffering.

Technology brings families together

Technology brings families together by closing the gap distance used to create in family relationships. Communicating via social media can bring family members closer together psychologically by providing a new space to communicate and providing new topics to communicate about. Families who co-view together also experience positive effects on their relationships. Finally, couples are using new technology to communicate more effectively and improve their relationship.

Technology literally affords families ways to contact one another when they are apart, bringing their voices or images together. Technology has greatly increased the ability of long-distance extended families to communicate. Commuter families, where one family member lives apart from the others at least three days per week (described in Chapter 32), often rely heavily on communication technology to "be present" even when they are away. Video conferencing technology allows family members to interact in similar ways as when they are together in the same place and time (Judge, Neustaedter, Harrison, & Blose, 2011). New technology has broken down distance as a major barrier of having close family relationships.

The use of technology to communicate with one another can have positive effects on family relationships. Parents and children who interact through Facebook experience less conflict and higher satisfaction with their parent–child relationship (Kanter, Afifi, & Robbins, 2012). Families might also talk about communication technology as a topic of conversation (for example, a parent asking a child if they saw a friend's inappropriate post; Child & Westermann, 2013).

Co-viewing of media is another way technology can bring families together. Co-viewing refers to watching the same program (television or other media) with others in the family. Parental co-viewing with children is important to help children understand what they are seeing and make connections to things they have learned at school or read about at home they might otherwise miss. Co-viewing television and movies and co-playing video games is connected to higher levels of family connection (Padilla-Walker et al., 2012).

mohamed_hassan/pixabay

Technology has been shown to help couples better manage conflict, communicate more effectively, and can even increase their feelings of closeness (Lenhart & Duggan, 2014; Scissors & Gergle, 2013). Fred P. Piercy and his team (2015) report that therapists are using technology to help couples improve their relationship through online assessment tools, online resources like TED talks, asking couples to connect via text, phone calls, or email throughout the day, and slow down their responses when angry with one another by asking them to email or text one another. Some therapists even suggest couples use GPS tracking or internet search history on their phones to rebuild trust after an affair.

Technology pulls families apart

Technology can pull families apart by distracting members when they are together, facilitating miscommunications between members, or offering too shallow or lean of a medium to fruitfully maintain the relationship. When family members are physically together, communication technology can distract and detract from meaningful, high-quality family time. According to Alessondra Villegas (2013), American families are living in a "media bubble." This bubble has effects on the foundation of a family. For example, eating meals together has long been an opportunity for families to communicate and connect. Today, the majority of households have a television on during meals. Television and other devices present at mealtime serve as a distraction to everyone and hinder their ability to communicate effectively (Villegas, 2013). Another distraction from high-quality family time happens when parents who are overwhelmed at work or struggling with work–life balance bring work home with them (see Chapter 32 for more on work–life balance). Adults might check email or text colleagues instead of engaging with family while at home. Partner phubbing refers to how much a person uses or is distracted by their cell phone while spending time with their romantic partner. According to James Roberts and Meredith David (2016), partner phubbing has a negative effect on relationship satisfaction and indirectly reduced life satisfaction while increasing levels of depression. In addition, many married adults engage in cyber-affairs and cyber-cheating (Millner, 2008). These negative relational behaviors are made possible, in part, by new technology.

Miscommunications are common via text and can cause conflict between members. Unanswered or ignored posts or text may also have negative repercussions for family relationships. Some forms of media are just too shallow or "lean" to facilitate meaningful relationships. Svetlana Yarosh, Denise Chew, and Gregory Abowd (2009) claim that mobile phones are good for check-ins but are not a replacement for meaningful conversations. Families who depend on these conversations to maintain their relationships may struggle to do so.

Parental monitoring of technology use and violated privacy boundaries are also technology-based sources of family conflict. Parents can now monitor where their children are at all times as well as the content on and the amount of time spent on their devices. Limiting technology use and tracking a child's location can be useful for raising children to be responsible and not overly dependent on technology.

Conflicts can arise when privacy boundaries are crossed or parents are monitoring more than a child may like (Ledbetter et al., 2010).

Finally, use barriers and nonadoption of technology might further the divide between younger and older family members. Despite the popularity of communication technology, there continue to be nonadopters, often older adults who reject new technology or lack necessary skills for productive use. Grandparents, for example, who are not technologically savvy may be missing an opportunity to connect with their grandchildren.

Misconceptions about Families and Communication Technology

Lynn Webb (2015) created a list of eight misconceptions people tend to hold about families and communication technology.

1. **Children's use of communication technology prompts family conflicts**. Instead, parents tend to provoke these conflicts through monitoring or limiting use.

2. **Technology is primarily used to stay in touch with out-of-town family members**. Although families do use technology for this purpose, they also tend to use technology to maintain their offline/face-to-face relationships.

3. **Internet use is bad for family functioning**. Instead, communication technology can have positive *or* negative effects on family functioning (as described above). Technology can distract but it can also be used to support family members in need.

4. **The use of technology decreases face-to-face family interactions**. Instead, many family members use online technology to enhance their offline interactions (see the Interesting Research Findings study below by Child and his team).

5. **Families abuse technology to avoid face-to-face interaction and to distract children**. Many parents are able to use communication technology with their children in ways that benefit them both.

6. **"Googling" is replacing the wisdom of family elders**. People who seek information on the internet typically do so because the information they need is not available to them through trusted sources like family elders or they believe the most accurate information is available online.

7. **Children are the technology experts in families**. Adults now use a wide variety of technologies at work and are often more expert than younger people.

8. **Families are formed, and then use technology**. Today, many families are being formed using technology such as online dating, adoption, or surrogacy websites.

INTERESTING RESEARCH FINDINGS

Privacy Management on Facebook with Multiple Generations of Family

Jeffrey Child and a team of researchers (2015) used communication privacy management theory (see Chapter 4) to conduct a study that explored how young adults manage private information on Facebook across different generations in their family. Many young adult Facebook users are friends with family members, and therefore must manage boundaries around their online information. The researchers asked 383 young adults about their communication with siblings, parents, and grandparents on Facebook. They found that young adults' interior family privacy orientation, or how much a family shares private information with other family members (Petronio, 2002), was related to how much they communicated with their siblings and parents about Facebook content offline. Having an open family privacy orientation was also related to how much they communicated with their parents on Facebook. The researchers also found that young adults communicate via Facebook about different things with family members of different generations.

Family Communication Patterns and Communication via Technology

Jessie Rudi, Amy Walkner, and Jodi Dworkin (2014) conducted a study to understand the role of family communication patterns (for a review of this theory, see Chapter 5) in parent–child communication via technology. The researchers surveyed 195 adolescents aged 13–18 and found that children who grew up in high conformity families used text messaging with their mothers less than children who grew up in low conformity families. High conversation orientation families reported more cell phone use with the father of the family. They also found that families with high conversation orientation and low conformity orientation tended to email one another more often. Email was the least used form of communication (compared to face-to-face, phone calls, and texting). The researchers noted that though their study was focused on technology, they found that communicating in person was the most frequent form of communication between parents and children.

PRACTICAL APPLICATIONS AND THINGS TO CONSIDER

College students who connect with their parents via technology are able to maintain positive, close relationships with parents and ultimately experience a smoother transition to college (Ramsey, Oberhauser, & Gentzler, 2016). What role did technology play in your transition to college? What do you think the transition would have been like if you did not have multiple ways to communicate with your family back home? How might you use technology to better maintain your family relationships right now? Review the relational maintenance strategies discussed in Chapters 28 and 29. Which of those strategies could you engage in via technology? Which would be challenging to perform via technology?

IN-CLASS ACTIVITY: CONSTRUCT A FAMILY TECHNOLOGY GENOGRAM*

Therapists use genograms to understand patterns of family communication, assess and treat problems, and increase understanding of family relationships (Blumer & Hertlein, 2015). A genogram should look like a well-annotated family tree.

- To create your own genogram, select family members you would like to include. You might choose siblings, parents, and grandparents, but feel free to think outside the "nuclear family" box to your family of choice. You will include each family member's gender, their occupation, role in the family, and how the members are related (married, siblings, parent–child links).

- Next, indicate the closeness of each relationship using lines. Very close relationships should be connected using three lines, close relationships get two lines, and distant (in terms of psychological closeness) should be indicated with broken or dashed lines. Conflict in a relationship is depicted using zig zag lines.

- Indicate technology use in each relationship. How do you communicate with other family members? Draw symbols on the lines to indicate cell phone, social media, and video chat usage. Do you know how others in your family communicate with one another? If yes, include that information.

- Finally, reflect on the genogram with the following questions:
  - What is the percent of communication between family members that occurs via face-to-face versus technology?
  - How has technology impacted your family relationships positively? Negatively?
  - Have you ever discussed with your family members the pros and cons of technology use for family communication? If yes, what did you discuss? If no, why might this type of conversation be useful?
  - If the family has ever encountered conflict due to technology use, how have they managed those concerns?
  - What rules or norms exist in your family concerning technology use?

*This activity is based on Blumer and Hertlein's (2015) technology-focused genogram tool.

DISCUSSION QUESTIONS

Refer to Chapter 4 on Communication Privacy Management Theory.

1. With that theory in mind, how, if at all, do you set boundaries with your parents about technology?
2. How have those boundaries changed from when you were living at home to living on your own?

KEY TERMS

Co-viewing

Cyber-affair

Genogram

Interior family privacy orientation

Lean media

Monitoring

Paradox

Partner phubbing

Unicorn_b2

CASE STUDY BY SAMUEL HARDMAN TAYLOR

Jazmine does not actually like going to her high school basketball games, but she wanted to go to the game to hang out with her friends. Because she knows that her parents will not let her go unless she has completed her daily chores, she quickly unloads the dishwasher, vacuums her room, and takes out the trash. Even after finishing her chores, Jazmine's parents were still at work, so she texts her stepmom, Claudia, to ask if she can go to the game tonight.

She texts, "Some of my friends are going to the basketball game tonight. Can I go too? I've done my chores."

"Sure, sweetie. Just come home immediately after the game is over because you leave for your debate competition early tomorrow morning. Luv you <3," was her stepmother's response. So, Jazmine gets ready for the game.

When Jazmine gets to the basketball game, she goes and sits with her friends Aaliyah, Mia, and Jordan. After talking with each other for a while, Jazmine suggests that they take a group photo for her to post to her Instagram. The group huddles together, and Jazmine snaps a photo. She spends the next few minutes editing the photo, and then she posts the photo on her Instagram. She includes the caption, "LOVE THESE GIRLS. #bff" She tags Aaliyah, Mia, and Jordan in the photo.

Within an hour, the photo has over 80 likes and 15 comments. One of the comments was from her stepmom, "Have fun!" Jazmine sees this comment and rolls her eyes.

Jazmine is embarrassed and annoyed by this comment from her stepmom because she posted the photo to connect with other people in her high school. Claudia has commented on nearly every photo Jazmine has posted on Instagram, and Jazmine is getting tired of it. Claudia commenting on all her Instagram photos makes Jazmine feel like she cannot hang out with her friends without her parents watching. Jazmine mentions to her friends that she feels embarrassed and annoyed by her stepmom's frequent Instagram comments.

Aaliyah responds, "Why don't you just create a second account for posting photos you do not want your parents to see? I have two Instagram accounts. One is public and anyone can follow it. My second one is a private account that I only allow my best friends to follow. I cannot believe you do not follow my other Instagram account, Jazmine. Like, are we even friends?"

Jazmine laughs off Aaliyah's comment, but she thinks that her idea is a good way to keep Claudia from commenting on every picture she posts on Instagram. She spends the remainder of the basketball game creating a second Instagram account underneath the username "unicorn_b2." She puts a picture of Beyoncé as her profile picture, so that no one will know that it is her. She makes her unicorn_b2 account private, and only lets Aaliyah, Mia, and Jordan follow her posts.

Jazmine deletes the group photo from the game from her original Instagram account and then reposts it to her new Instagram account with the new caption "idk what i would do without you girls."

When Jazmine gets home after the game, Claudia was sitting in the living room watching Netflix. Claudia turns off the TV, and asks Jazmine, "How was the game?"

"Good. We won the game," Jazmine replies.

"Who was this Mia girl in your photo? I do not recognize her."

This sparks a conversation between Jazmine and her stepmom about how she met Mia through the debate team.

CASE STUDY DISCUSSION QUESTIONS

1. How is the technology paradox in family communication demonstrated by Jazmine's Friday night?
2. How does Jazmine manage her privacy with her stepmom?
3. What misconceptions about families and communication technology does the communication between Jazmine and Claudia challenge?
4. How have you used social media and mobile phones to connect with your immediate family members?
5. What privacy rules and boundaries have you created for your own social media accounts? How do you communicate those rules and boundaries to others?

Podcast with Jeff Child, Kent State University: www.familycommlab.com/podcast

Jeff Child discusses the evolution of family communication and technology research and gives a behind-the-scenes look at the journal article publishing process including what it's like to edit the *Journal of Family Communication.*

JEFF CHILD PODCAST REFLECTION QUESTIONS

1. How did privacy concerns with technology change as LiveJournal (blogging), Facebook and Instagram (among others) users changed (i.e., parents and older people joined/no longer just for college students, social media channels become mainstream)?
2. What are some of the privacy rules mentioned that parents teach to their children?
3. What privacy rules do children teach to their parents and grandparents in the twenty-first century?
4. What happens when people are more vulnerable than others on social media? What are deletion motivations?
5. What are some consequences Dr. Child mentions of not monitoring your social media for how it represents your identity or creates a reputation for you?
6. What percentage of employers actively screen potential new hires based on what they find on their social media?
7. What is one piece of advice you took from Dr. Child's interview about monitoring your social media that you found useful?
8. Summarize the research article publishing process described by Dr. Child. What is a double-blind review?

REFERENCES

Blumer, M. L. C., & Hertlein, K. M. (2015). The technology-focused genogram. In C. J. Bruess (Ed.), *Family communication in the age of digital and social media* (pp. 471–489). New York, NY: Peter Lang.

Child, J. T., Duck, A. R., Andrews, L. A., Butauski, M., & Petronio, S. (2015). Young adults' management of privacy on Facebook with multiple generations of family members. *Journal of Family Communication, 15,* 349–367. doi:10.1080/15267431.2015.1076425

Child, J. T., & Westermann, D. A. (2013). Let's be Facebook friends: Exploring parental Facebook friend requests from a communication privacy management

(CPM) perspective. *Journal of Family Communication, 13*, 46–59. doi:10.1080/152 67431.2012.742089

Fife, E. M., LaCava, L., & Nelson, C. L. (2013). Family communication, privacy, and Facebook. *Journal of Social Media in Society, 2*, 106–125.

Jarvenpaa, S. L., Lang, K. R., & Tuunainen, V. K. (2005). Friend or foe? The ambivalent relationship between mobile technology and its users. In *Designing ubiquitous information environments: Socio-technical issues and challenges* (pp. 29–42). Boston, MA: Springer. doi:10.1007/0-387-28918-6_5

Judge, T. K., Neustaedter, C., Harrison, S., & Blose, A. (2011, May). Family portals: Connecting families through a multifamily media space. In *Proceedings of the SIGCHI conference on human factors in computing systems* (pp. 1205–1214). ACM.

Kanter, M., Afifi, T., & Robbins, S. (2012). The impact of parents "friending" their young adult children on Facebook on perceptions of parental privacy invasions and parent–child relationship quality. *Journal of Communication, 62*, 900–917. doi:10.1111/j.1460-2466.2012.01669

Ledbetter, A. M., Heiss, S., Sibal, K., Lev, E., Battle-Fisher, M., & Shubert, N. (2010). Parental invasive and children's defensive behaviors at home and away at college: Mediated communication and privacy boundary management. *Communication Studies, 61*, 184–204. doi:10.1080/10510971003603960

Lenhart, A., & Duggan, M. (2014). Couples, the internet, and social media. *Pew Internet and American Life Project.*

Millner, V. S. (2008). Internet infidelity: A case of intimacy with detachment. *The Family Journal, 16*, 78–82. doi:10.1177/1066480707308918

Padilla-Walker, L. M., Coyne, S. M., & Fraser, A. M. (2012). Getting a high-speed family connection: Associations between family media use and family connection. *Family Relations, 61*, 426–440. doi:10.1111/j.1741-3729.2012.00710.x

Petronio, S. (2002). *The boundaries of privacy: Dialectics of disclosure.* Albany, NY: State University of New York Press.

Piercy, F. P., Riger, D., Voskanova, C., Chang, W., Haugen, E., & Sturdivant, L. (2015). What marriage and family therapists tell us about improving couple relationships through technology. In C. J. Bruess (Ed.), *Family communication in the age of digital and social media* (pp. 207–227). New York, NY: Peter Lang.

Ramsey, M. A., Oberhauser, A. M., & Gentzler, A. L. (2016). College students' use of communication technology with parents: Influences of distance, gender, and social presence. In G. Riva, B. K. Wiederhold, & P. Cipresso (Eds.), *The psychology of social networking: Identity and relationships in online communities* (pp. 128–140). Berlin: De Gruyter Open.

Roberts, J. A., & David, M. E. (2016). My life has become a major distraction from my cell phone: Partner phubbing and relationship satisfaction among romantic partners. *Computers in Human Behavior, 54*, 134–141. doi:10.1016/j.chb.2015.07.058

Rudi, J. H., Walkner, A., & Dworkin, J. (2014). Adolescent–parent communication in a digital world: Differences by family communication patterns. *Youth & Society, 47*, 811–828. doi:10.1177/0044118X14560334

Scissors, L. E., & Gergle, D. (2013). Back and forth, back and forth: Channel switching in romantic couple conflict. In *Proceedings of the 2013 conference on computer supported cooperative work* (pp. 237–248). ACM.

Villegas, A. (2013). The influence of technology on family dynamics. *Proceedings of the New York State Communication Association, 2012*, 10.

Webb, L. (2015). Research on technology and the family. In C. J. Bruess (Ed.), *Family communication in the age of digital and social media* (pp. 3–31). New York, NY: Peter Lang.

Wilkes Karraker, M. (2015). Global families in a digital age. In C. J. Bruess (Ed.), *Family communication in the age of digital and social media* (pp. 55–75). New York, NY: Peter Lang.

Yarosh, S., Chew, Y. D., & Abowd, G. D. (2009). Supporting parent–child communication in divorced families. *International Journal of Human–Computer Studies, 67*, 192–203. doi:10.1016/j.ijhcs.2008.09.005

RELATED READINGS

Caughlin, J. P., Basinger, E. D., & Sharabi, L. L. (2016). The connections between communication technologies and relational conflict. In J. A. Samp (Ed.), *Communicating interpersonal conflict in close relationships: Contexts, challenges, and opportunities*. New York, NY: Routledge.

Caughlin, J. P., & Sharabi, L. L. (2013). A communicative interdependence perspective of close relationships: The connections between mediated and unmediated interactions matter. *Journal of Communication, 63*, 873–893. doi:10.1111/jcom.12046

Dorrance Hall, E., & Feister, M. K. (2015). Navigating emerging adulthood with communication technology. In C. J. Bruess (Ed.), *Family communication in the age of digital and social media* (pp. 161–183). New York, NY: Peter Lang.

Francisco, V. (2015). "The internet is magic": Technology, intimacy, and transnational families. *Critical Sociology, 41*, 173–190. doi:10.1177/0896920513484602

Gonzalez, C., & Katz, V. S. (2016). Transnational family communication as a driver of technology adoption. *International Journal of Communication, 10*, 2683–2703.

Wilding, R. (2006). "Virtual" intimacies? Families connecting across transnational contexts. *Global Networks, 6*, 125–142. doi:10.1111/j.1471-0374.2006.00137.x

Author Index

Page locators in *italic* type indicate illustrations.

A

B

C

D

Communication in Family Contexts: Theories and Processes, First Edition.
Elizabeth Dorrance Hall and Kristina M. Scharp.
© 2020 John Wiley & Sons, Inc. Published 2020 by John Wiley & Sons, Inc.
Companion website: www.wiley.com/go/dorrance_hall/communication-in-family-contexts

Subject Index

A

actor–partner interdependence
    model, 12, 53
addiction, 110, 132, 279
    see also substance dependence
adolescence, 244–245, 246–247, 304
adoption, 32, 205, 206, 207, 210
    case study, 211–212
    communication research, 205–206
    fostering for, 208
    international *see* international adoption
    open, 207, 210
    triad, 207
    see also adoptive families; adoption
        reunions; birth mothers
adoption practitioners, 210
adoption reunions, 31, 207, 208–209
    desired information, 32, 209
    effect, 208
    international, 209
    rituals, 209
adoptive families, 3, 205–212
    adoptee self-concept, 206
    and birth family, 122, 206: *see also*
        adoption reunions
    discourse dependence, 119, 205
    entrance narratives, 205–206, 208,
        210, 211–212
    parenthood, 179

research findings, 209–210
adult children, 10, 69, 81, 229, 245–246
    adopted, 32, 209
    communication with parents, 79,
        110, 245–246
    distancing, 10, 69, 130, 132–133
    and helicopter parenting, 38, 81, 246
    and parental divorce, 198
    support for parents, 21, 246
advice, 146, 147–150, 181
    career, 39
    response to, 148–149
    sibling, 30, 263
    as turning point, 181
advice response theory (ART), 148–149, 154
    research findings, 149–150
affection communication, 19–23, 266–267
    benefits, 21
    exchange process *see* affection
        exchange theory (AET)
    individual variations, 21
    in-laws, 217, 218
    and loneliness, 23
    by men, 22
    nature/nurture, 22
    nonverbal expressions, 22, 94, 114–115
    reciprocity, 23
    siblings, 266
    and socialization, 22
    as survival strategy, 20

Communication in Family Contexts: Theories and Processes, First Edition.
Elizabeth Dorrance Hall and Kristina M. Scharp.
© 2020 John Wiley & Sons, Inc. Published 2020 by John Wiley & Sons, Inc.
Companion website: www.wiley.com/go/dorrance_hall/communication-in-family-contexts

affection exchange theory (AET),
    19–25, 243
  case study, 24–25
  propositions, 20–21
  research findings, 21–22
African American communities, 273
alcoholism, 279–280
Alzheimer's dementia, 83
assisted reproduction, 177
attachment styles, 87
attachment theory, 81–82, 241–242
autism, 122
autoethnography, 11
autonomy, 68, 113, 131, 246
avoiding behaviors, 90, 139

B

behavioral modeling, 57
Belgium, 39, 60
bias, implicit, 231
birth mothers, 207
  and adoption process, 207, 210
  cultural resistance, 207
  disclosure preferences, 32
  reunions with, 31, 32, 208–209
bisexuality, 237, 238
"Bringing the Baby Home"
    workshop, 181

C

caregiving, in families, 79–84
  of adults, 82–83
  of children, 80–81
  cultural differences, 83
  of the elderly, 82
  and gender, 79–80, 81
  hands-on, 82
  long-distance, 82
  negative attitudes, 83
  research findings, 83–84
case studies
  adoption, 211–212
  affection exchange, 24–25
  conflict, 97–98

discourse dependence, 123–124
family privacy, 306–307
information management, 142–143
in-law relationships, 220
mental health issues, 282–283
parent–child relationships, 248–250
sibling relationships, 267–268
social support, 153–154
work–life balance, 294–295
catalyst criteria, 30
centrifugal discourse, 65
centripetal discourse, 64
child custody decisions, 187
childfree couples, 179–180, *180*, 283
  discourse dependence, 180
Chinese culture, 39, 208
cognitive construal, 160
cohabitation, 167–170, 172
  as divorce predictor, 186
  and engagement, 169
  and marriage, 168, 186
  negative outcomes, 168–169
  research findings, 172
  stepfamily, 169–170
  transition to, 168
  see also partner relationships
cohabitation effect, the, 168
collectivist cultures, 216, 224
communicated narrative sense-making
    (CNSM) theory, 50–52, 53
  goals, 50
  heuristics, 50–51
  propositions, 50–51
communicated perspective-
    taking (CPT), 53
communication, definitions of, 3
  dyadic, 4
  as process, 3
  small group, 4
  triadic, 4
communication accommodation
    theory, 227–228
communication engagement, 159
communication privacy management
    (CPM) theory, 27–33, 138, 304
  origins, 27–28

ethnography, 11
extended families, 2, 188, 218
  as householod units, 272
  long-distance, 79, 301
  and voluntary kin, 273

F

Facebook, 301
  parental involvement, 31
  privacy management, 31, 304
face needs, 113, 146
family, definitions of, 1–4
  functional, 1, 2
  as in-group, 227
  modern, 2
  North American ideology, 1–2
  structural, 1, 2
  sub-systems, 43
  transactional, 1, 2
family communication patterns (FCP)
    theory, 8, 35–41, 242–243
  communication
    environments, 242–243
  origins, 35–36
  research findings, 38–39
  survey, 39–41
family communication processes, 3–4,
    44, 201–310
  cultural differences, 38–39
  everyday talk, 197–198
  foundational, 77–163
  harmful, 281
  major family transitions, 165–199
  multiple levels, 3–4, *4*, 44
  openness, 44, 87, 111, 171, 210
  patterns, 38, 60, 176: *see also* family
    communication patterns (FCP) theory
  reinforcement, 58–59
  sharing beliefs, 60, 61, 87
  and technology, 299–308
  in work contexts, 289–290
  see also messages; parent–child
    relationships
family communication scholarship, 1,
    2, 4, 7–15

consensus approach, 8, 9
dissensus approach, 8
field of *see* Communication Studies
methodology, 44: *see also* research
  methodology
research paradigms, 8–10, *9*
see also individual perspectives
family communication types, 36–38, 243
  see also theories of family
    communication
family conflict *see* conflict
family conversations, difficult, 109–116
  definition, 109
  problem-solving strategies, 112–114
  theories, 112–114
  topics, 109, 110–112: *see also*
    taboo topics
  see also conversation orientation
family coping, 101–102, 178
  natural disasters, 105
  transgender issues, 105–106
Family Determinant of Clinical
  Decisions Typology, 280
family distancing, 127–134
  alienation, 129, 131
  estrangement *see* family estrangement
  marginalization, 128–129, 131, *131*, 132
  process, 131, 132
  research findings, 132
  and uncertainty, 132–133
family estrangement, 120, 127–131, *131*
  chaotic dissociation, 130
  continuous, 130
  cultural beliefs, 130
  parent–child *see* parent–child
    estrangement
  reconciliation, 130
  research methodology, 10–11
family health problems, 277–283
  and communication, 110,
    279, 280–281
  effect on work, 289
  foster children, 208
  genetic inheritance, 280–281
  mental *see* mental health issues
  treatment decisions, 161, 236, 280

family hierarchies, 44–45
family identification, 227
family identity, shared, 226–227
   and boundary management, 120, 122
   creation, 119, 120, 121, 122
   and disability diagnosis, 121–122
   and discourse dependence, 119–124
   and grandparents, 225, 226–227
   narratives *see* family narratives
family narratives, 80
   entrance, 205–206, 208, 210, 211–212
   and family identity, 49–50, 225
family privacy, 30, 138–139, 304, 308
   case study, 306–307
   management, 28, 138, 304: *see also* communication privacy management (CPM) theory
   orientation types, 30
family roles, 3, 45
   changing, 44
   gender, 61, 79–80, 81, 226, 255, 256
   grandparents, 223–224, 226
family secrets, 30, 139–140
family storytelling *see* family narratives
family systems, 44–46, 81
   and conflict, 87
   dynamism, 44, 45
   goals, 45
   hierarchy, 44–45
   joint, 217
   mediation, 219
   openness, 44, 111
   self-reflectivity, 45
   wholeness, 44
   see also family systems theory
family systems theory, 43–47, 210
   concepts, 43, 44–45
   origins, 43
   research findings, 46, 105
family taboos *see* taboo topics
family–work conflict, 289, 290
feedback, 44, 104, 189
feminist theories, 291–292
Fetal Alcohol Syndrome, 70
fictive kin *see* voluntary kinship
financial education, 111

focus groups, 12, 14
forgiveness, 93–95
   see also reconciliation
foster care, children in, 208
   and adoption, 208
   cultural stigmatization, 208
   entrance narratives, 206
   health issues, 208
   identity narratives, 49–50
   teenage pregnancy, 71
fundamental attribution error, 89

G

gender dysphoria, 236
gender issues, 177, 292
   family roles, 61, 81, 226, 255, 256
   kinkeeping, 79–80
   parenthood, 177
   see also feminist theories
genograms, 305
grandchildren, 81, 223, 224–229
   adult, 227
   as carers, 229
   communication accommodation, 227
   co-residence with grandparents *see* grandfamilies
   and storytelling, 83, 225–226
grandfamilies, 83, 228–229
   discourse dependence, 229
grandparents, 180–181, 223, 229
   affection communication, 19
   as caregivers, 81, 83, 228–229, 294–295
   and family identity, 225, 226–227
   gender, 229
   receiving care, 82–83, 229
   roles, 223–224
   sexual orientation, 229
   types, 224–225
   see also intergenerational relationships

H

Haitian earthquake, 105
helicopter parenting, 38, 81
heurism, 9, 10

HIV/AIDS, 111, 281
holism, 43
 see also wholeness, concept of

I

identity gaps, 228, 230
independent variables, 13
individualism, 70
infertility, 160, 177
infidelity, 186, 187, 259
information management, 137–143, 161
 case study, 142–143
 sharing, 161–162
 taboo topics, 138, 139, 140, 281
 theories, 137–138, 160
information ownership, 29
 disclosure criteria, 29–30, 32
 and privacy rules, 32
 see also information management;
  privacy regulation
in-law relationships, 46, 215–221
 case study, 220–221
 cultural differences, 216
 parents, 217–218
 research findings, 218
 role ambiguity, 216
 siblings, 216–217
 socialization, 215–216
 uncertainty, 218
institutional review boards, 14
integrative conflict, 89, 91
interactional sense-making, 51
 storytelling, 51
 see also family narratives
interdependence, of family members,
  45, 159, 227
 couple, 256
 and divorce, 187
 in emerging adulthood, 245
 and interference *see* interference, by
  family members
 see also actor–partner
  interdependence model
interference, by family members,
  89, 159, 160

and conflict, 87
 generational, 82–83
 partner, 159, 160
intergenerational relationships, 223–231
 communication, 225–226
 diversity, 229
 geographical distance, 223, 225
 identity gaps, 228, 230
 living arrangements *see*
  multigenerational living
 maintenance, 230
 parent–child *see* parent–child relationships
 research findings, 229–230
 satisfaction of, 223, 224
 see also grandchildren; grandfamilies;
  grandparents
intergenerational stake hypothesis, 229
intergroup contact theory, 227
international adoption, 207–208
 adoptee experiences, 207–208
 from China, 208
 from Korea, 207, 209
internet technology, 245, 302, 303
 email, 304
interpersonal communication motives
  model, 266
interpretive narrative approach, 9, 49–50
interpretive perspective, 8–10
 methodology, 9, 10
intersectionality, 291–292
intimate partner violence, 92, 93
 cultural differences, 93
 cycle of abuse, 93
 narratives, 93

J

jealousy, 216, 258, 259
 types of communication, 259

K

kinkeeping, 83–84, 226
 digital, 83
 gendered, 79–80, 226
Korea, adoption from, 207, 209

L

laissez-faire families, 37–38, *40*, 41
latent variables, 13
lesbian motherhood, 68, 177, 229, 237
  see also LGBTQ parenting
LGBTQ community, 171, 172, 235
  and bisexuals, 238
  and foster care, 236
  and homophobia, 236
  legislation, 235, 237–238
  marriage, 171–172, 237, 239
  population, 235
  transgender *see* transgender people
  self-image, 239
  voluntary kin, 273
  see also LGTBQ families
LGBTQ families, 3, 177, 235–239
  discourse dependence, 235, 238, 239
  parenting *see* LGTBQ parenting
LGBTQ parenting, 22, 235–236, 237
logical-empirical perspective *see*
    post-positivism
longitudinal studies, 13
lying *see* deception

M

marital communication
  conflict, 185, 255–257
  destructive, 258–259
  maintenance, 253–254, 256
marriage, 46, 167, 170–172
  age, 167, 185
  and commitment, 170–171, 255
  communication behaviors *see* marital
    communication
  couple identity, 170
  delaying, 185
  dissolution *see* divorce
  dominant discourses, 65
  expectations, 170
  openness, 171, 253
  reasons for, 172–173
  rituals, 171
  same-sex, 171–172, 237, 239
  satisfaction predictors, 257–258

  tensions, 170
  transition to, 170, 171
  see also couples; partner relationships
meaning making, 63
  competing ideologies, 63–64
  discourses, 64–65
  and uncertainty, 162
  utterance chain, 65–66: *see also*
    interactional sense-making;
    utterance chain links
Meet the Parents (dir. Roach), 219
memorable messages, 247
men, 22
  affection exchange, 22, 243
  sexual orientation, 22
mental health issues, 81, 277–288
  and affection, 20, 21
  case study, 282–283
  eating disorders, 279, 281
  end of life, 110
  prevalence, 277
  and sexual coercion, 259
  social support, 145, 278
  stepfamilies, 195, 196
  stigma, 277–278
  see also depression; substance abuse
messages
  creation, 112–115
  and confirmation theory, 113
  memorable, 247
  nonverbal, 115
  relational, 115
  see also advice; dual-process models
    of persuasion
meta-analysis, 13
miscarriage, 53
Modern Family, 2, 41, 70
monologic discourses, 66–67
motherhood
  discourses of, 64, 67, 68, 207,
    278
  lesbian *see* lesbian motherhood
  and post-partum depression, 279
  responsibility, 70, 71
  and work, 292–293: *see also*
    work–life balance
  see also parenting

motivated information management
see theory of motivated
information management (TMIM)
multigenerational living, 83, 224
cultural differences, 224
multi-level modeling, 44

N

narrative performance theory (NPT),
10, 52–53
narratives
divorce, 188–189
identity, 49–50
partner violence, 93
family see family narratives
narrative theories, 49–54
assumptions, 50
and coherence, 50–51
research findings, 53–54
narrative therapy, 54
National Campaign to Prevent Teen and
Unplanned Pregnancy, 111
National Coalition Against Domestic
Violence, 92
National Health and Aging Trends
Study (2011), 82
nonverbal communication, 22, 94,
114–115
nonvoluntary relationships, 2, 134, 215,
216, 218, 219
North American culture, 1–2,
19, 140
compared with Belgian, 39
nuclear families, 1–2, 305

O

observational learning, 58
observed variables, 13

P

parent–child alienation, 129, 131, 141
parent–child estrangement, 10, 68–69,
128–130, 133, 134

legal implications, 131
process, 132–133
parent–child relationships, 241–250
alienation, 129, 131
attachment, 241–242: see also
attachment theory
breakdown, 129–130
case study, 248–250
development, 243–246
estrangement see parent–child
estrangement
hurtful interactions, 246–247
interdependence, 245
research findings, 246–247
parenthood, 175–182
adoptive, 179
and communication, 175, 176–177
coping strategies, 178, 181–182
delaying, 179–180
financial implications, 179
in-law, 217–218
interventions, 181
LGBTQ, 177
and marital satisfaction, 176, 177
premarital, 186
research findings, 180–181
role expectations, 176, 177
single, 178: see also single-parent
families
supportive, 175, 176, 178, 179, 181, 246
transition to, 176–177
undergraduate, 179
see also parenting
parenting, 177, 178
abuse, 130, 131, 132
and attachment see attachment theory
caregiving, 79–82
cultural differences, 39
inconsistent, 110
in-law criticism of, 217
LGBTQ see LGBTQ parenting
programs, 176
and sex communication, 111–112, 244
styles, 243, 247
see also co-parenting;family
distancing; helicopter parenting;
parent–child relationships

participant observation, 11–12
partner facilitation, 159, 170
partner interference, 159, 160, 170
partner relationships, 253–261
   asymmetrical commitment, 255
   communication, 253–254, 255–256,
      258–259: *see also* marital
      communication
   conflict management, 255–257
   cyber-affairs, 302
   dissolution, 186: *see also* divorce
   emotion regulation, 257
   interventions, 260
   investment, 254–255, 259, 260
   maintenance, 253–254, 256
   negative behaviors, 21–22,
      254, 258–259
   phubbing, 302
   research findings, 259–260
   sexual coercion, 259
   violent *see* intimate partner
      violence (IPV)
   see also couples; marriage
Pew Research Center, 172–173
pluralistic families, 37, *40*, 41
politeness strategies, 112–113, 148
postmodern families, 2
post-partum depression, 64, 67, 278
   and meaning of motherhood,
      67, 278–279
   stigma, 64, 279
   and suicide, 279
post-positivism, 8, *9*, 50
   methodology, 8, 10, 50
post-structural perspective *see* dialogic
   perspective
power structures, 10, 64, 291
   parental, 36
pregnancy
   moral dilemmas, 70, 71–72
   unintended, 71–72
   see also motherhood
privacy, 27–28
   collective boundaries, 28, 190
   family *see* family privacy
   personal boundaries, 28

   management *see* privacy regulation
   see also information ownership
privacy regulation, 28–29, 32, 33
   deception, 138, 140–141
   recalibration, 30, 32
   turbulence, 29, 30
   see also communication privacy
      management (CPM) theory
protective families, 37, *40*, 41

Q

qualitative research, 11–12
   methods, 9, 11–12: *see also* research
      interviews
   terms, 11
quantitative research, 8, 12–13, 122
   methods, 13
   terms, 12–13, 14
queer motherhood, 68
   see also lesbian motherhood

R

race, 292
rape *see* sexual coercion
reciprocity, 23, 141, 145, 151
reconciliation, 95, 130, 131, 133
reflexivity, 10, 45, 291
reinforcement, 58–59, 110, 242
relational dialectics theory (RDT),
   10, 63–72
   importance, 69–70
   key concepts, 64–66
   methodology, 66
   research findings, 68–69, 70
relational messages, 115
relational moral hazard, 69
relational transgression, 21–22
   see also partner relationships
relational turbulence theory (RTT), 8,
   158–160, 173
   key concepts, 158–159
   research findings, 160
relationship maintenance behaviors,
   254–255, 260

intergenerational, 230
using technology, 305
remarriage, 193–194
and children *see* stepfamilies
and divorce, 193–194
and parenting *see* stepparents
rituals, 194
remarriage market hypothesis, 194
research interviews, 12, 50
focus groups, 12, 14
protocols, 12
research methodology
key terms, 14
interviews *see* research interviews
qualitative, 9, 11–12
quantitative, 8, 12–13, 122
resilience, 101, 103–105
family, 103, 105–106, 120, 197, 236
individual, 104
and marginalization, 128
processes, 104
relationship, 104–105
strategies, 105–106, 128
theories, 103, 104, 260
resource dilution hypothesis, 267
resources, within the family,
88–89, 103, 289
and conflict, 87, 88–89, 93, 197
couples, 254
parents as, 150, 267
and resilience, 104
retirement, 292, 294–295
retrospective storytelling,
50–51
revelation risk model (RRM), 138

S

same-sex couples, 2, 254
marriage, 171–172, 237, 238
as parents *see* LGBTQ parenting
sampling techniques, 14
secrecy, 138–139
family, 139–140
reasons for, 140
and taboo topics, 140

self, authentic, 228, 230
see also identity gaps
self-disclosure, 138, 141, 253
self-efficacy, 59, 161
self-presentation, 139
self-reflexivity, 45
semi-structured interviews, 12
sexual coercion, 259
sexually transmitted infections (STIs), 111
siblings, 263–269
adult, 264
case study, 268–269
communication, 19, 260–261, 266–267
envy, 216–217
in-law relationships, 216–217
parenting of, 89
relationships, 59–60, 263–266, 267, 268
research findings, 266–267
and substance abuse, 110
typology, 264–265
single-parent families, 178, 293
challenges, 178
discourse dependence, 178
small group communication, 4
social cognitive theory (SCT), 57–62
key concepts, 57–59
and gender roles, 61
mimicking behaviors, 61
research findings, 59–60
social competence, 281
social constructionism, 121
social identity theory, 226–227
socialization
and affection exchange, 22
in-law relationships, 215–216
as parental responsibility, 241
social learning theory, 57, 60
see also social cognitive theory
social media
co-viewing, 301
and family communication, 299, 300–303
friendship, 31, 306
miscommunication, 302
privacy management, 31, 304, 306–307
romantic relationships, 259
support, 151

turning points, relational, 180–181
    positive, 181
    negative, 181
    sibling, 268
    study of, 194–195

U

uncertainty, 157–163
    and family distancing, 132–133
    key concepts, 157
    management *see* uncertainty
        management theory
    and polarization, 158
    relational, 158–159, 172–173, 218
    and stepfamilies, 198
    theories of, 158–161, 162–163
uncertainty management theory, 162–163
unstructured interviews, 12
U.S. Census, 1
utterance chain links, 65–66
    already-spoken, 65–66
    distal, 65
    not-yet-spoken, 66
    proximal, 65

V

variables, 13
    correlation of, 12–13
    definition, 13
verbal aggression, 92–93

violence, 92–93
    patterns, 92–93
    perpetrators, 93
    victims, 93
    see also intimate partner violence
voluntary kinship, 3, 271–274
    communication structures, 273
    discourse dependence, 271
    key concepts, 272
    research, 273
    typology, 272, 273

W

wholeness, concept of, 43, 44
willingness to leave marriage
        hypothesis, 194
work/family border theory, 291
work–family conflict, 288–290
work–life balance, 287, 288,
        288, 290–291
    case study, 294–295
    defensive communication, 293
    flexible working practices, 294
    and communication technology,
        302
    research findings, 292–293
    in retirement, 292
    for women, 288, 292–293
    see also family–work conflict;
        work–family conflict
worksheets, xi–xii, 106, 151–153